NEW ORDER OF THE AGES

NEW ORDER OF THE AGES

Time, the Constitution, and the
Making of Modern American
Political Thought

MICHAEL LIENESCH

PRINCETON UNIVERSITY PRESS
PRINCETON, NEW JERSEY
1988

Copyright © 1988 by Princeton University Press
Published by Princeton University Press,
41 William Street, Princeton, New Jersey 08540
In the United Kingdom:
Princeton University Press, Guildford, Surrey

Library of Congress Cataloging-in-Publication Data

Lienesch, Michael, 1948–
New order of the ages : time, the constitution, and the making of
modern American political thought / Michael Lienesch.
p. cm.   Bibliography: p.   Includes index.
ISBN 0–691–07779–7 (alk. paper)
1. Liberty—History—18th century. 2. Liberalism—United States—History—18th century.
3. United States—Constitutional history.
I. Title.
JC599.U5L48 1988   320.5′1′0973—dc 19   88–1503 CIP

This book has been composed in Linotron Monticello

Printed in the United States of America
by Princeton University Press,
Princeton, New Jersey

TO MY PARENTS

CONTENTS

CONTENTS

-6-
FOUNDING
Audacity, Ambition, Adaptability
138

ACKNOWLEDGMENTS

"WHAT THEN IS TIME?" asked St. Augustine somewhere around the beginning of the fifth century. "I know what it is if no one asks me what it is: but if I want to explain it to someone who has asked me, I find that I do not know."

In coming to the close of writing this book about time and politics, I find myself thinking often of Augustine's words. I think back especially to those many conversations that I began with the ingenuous intent of explaining some perfectly obvious point, only to realize somewhere in the middle that I did not know what I was talking about at all. Those discussions, though almost always embarrassing, made this a better book. In the process, I have accumulated some enormous debts to those patient and talented friends who have been willing not only to listen to me, but to criticize and suggest changes in my thinking and writing.

First among these are Norman Jacobson, Michael Paul Rogin, Hanna Pitkin, and Samuel Haber, all of the University of California, Berkeley, who not only encouraged me to write this book in the first place, but who spent many hours reading and rereading what must have seemed like an endless line of early drafts. Just as important are my colleagues at the University of North Carolina at Chapel Hill, especially in the Department of Political Science, who have provided one of those rare academic settings that is both supportive and stimulating. Particularly precious are those friends William Adams, Jack Donnelly, Bob Holsworth, Peter Onuf, Dick Richardson, and Joel Schwartz, each of whom read the manuscript in part or in full, and who offered, along with their suggestions, encouragement and enthusiasm. I also want to thank Russell Hanson and Wilson Carey McWilliams, who carefully and thoughtfully commented on the completed manuscript, and all those reviewers who read the articles and papers that were earlier versions of some of these chapters, and who inspired revisions that have improved it more than I could have imagined. Many of these reviewers were and will probably always be anonymous, and to these silent benefactors I give special thanks.

I also want to express my great gratitude to Gail Ullman for her kindness and extraordinary efficiency in acting as editor of this book, and to all of the people at Princeton University Press who helped bring it to publication.

ix

Because portions of several chapters were previously published, I gratefully acknowledge the editors of *The Review of Politics*, *American Politics Quarterly*, *History of Political Thought*, *The Journal of Politics*, and *The Western Political Quarterly* for permission to reprint them.

Not the least of my debts—thankfully not financial—are to the institutions that provided generous monetary support: the Research Council of the University of North Carolina, the National Endowment for the Humanities, and the Earhart Foundation, which made possible an exceedingly timely year of research and writing.

Most of all, I owe the people I love: my parents, to whom this book is dedicated; Ann, who has had faith in me; and now Nicholas and Elizabeth, who have taught me a lot about time—how much of it they take, how little of it there is, and how precious a moment with them can be.

Chapel Hill, North Carolina
June 1987

NEW ORDER OF THE AGES

INTRODUCTION

BETWEEN THE PEACE OF PARIS in 1783 and the election of Thomas Jefferson in 1800, America became a modern nation. The end of the War of Independence announced the first successful anticolonial rebellion by a major modern state. The creation of the federal Constitution, the ab novo formation of a self-constituting and self-sustaining republic, was an unparalleled event as well, a prototype for the postcolonial world. The process of nation building that began at this time was equally unprecedented, providing an example to be emulated by emerging nations throughout the world, and for hundreds of years to come.

In addition to these, however, another transformation was taking place at this time, an intellectual and theoretical realignment that would redefine not only the form and structure but also the very meaning and purpose of the new nation, inspiring in the process a modern version of American political thought. Among all these changes, this may have been most critical in shaping the modern world. For from 1783 to 1800 the American republic became the symbol of a new order, political and temporal alike, a modern nation for a modern age.

In late 1782, nearing the close of the war, the Confederation Congress officially announced that this new age had arrived, and that a new historical era was at hand. In fact, the announcement implied something even greater—not simply the coming of a modern age, but the creation of an entirely new way of thinking about time itself. The Congress summed up the change eloquently, and with symbolic simplicity, inscribing the Great Seal of the United States with the Latin phrase *novus ordo seclorum*, a "new order of the ages."

This book is about the creation of this new order. It describes at least some of the political changes that occurred during the turbulent days that ran from Revolution to Constitution and beyond. At the same time, and much more extensively, it details the transition taking place in political thinking as classical republican theory began to be challenged by what would come to be called modern liberalism. Beyond this, it analyzes an even more fundamental transformation, the change from classical to modern ways of viewing the world. And it tries to show how these political and temporal ways of thinking converged in the politics of the period, inspiring

3

Americans to transform the fundamental precepts of their politics, and to create in the process a new political order. In short, this book is about time and politics, or, to borrow a phrase from J.G.A. Pocock, about the "politics of time."[1]

Until recently, historians and political theorists have tended to overlook the role of time in American politics, in large part because scholars have tended to see America as a uniquely modern nation. According to Tocqueville, Americans were moderns almost by definition, a people notable for their innate independence, their natural predisposition to rationality and enlightened self-interest, and their unquestioning faith in progress. Born without a medieval past, they had never been required to throw off the bonds of ecclesiastical or feudal power. Liberal and Lockean in their thought, rational rather than traditional, they felt free to adopt or cast off, according to their usefulness, the customs and conventions that had been passed along to them by virtue of their English common law birthright. This freedom also allowed them to look forward confidently and optimistically to an endlessly progressive future. Writing in 1954 in his immensely influential *The Liberal Tradition in America*, Louis Hartz would raise this Tocquevillian theme to new and even more eloquent heights, presenting Americans as a people without a past: "Instead of recapturing our past," Hartz summed up with a flourish, "we have got to transcend it. As for a child who is leaving adolescence, there is no going home again for America."[2]

Only ten years later, however, growing numbers of thinkers had begun to question the notion that America was an exclusively modern experiment. Instrumental in this regard was what Donald Winch has called "the remarkable historiographical upheaval" that marked the rediscovery of the classical republican tradition.[3] Among American scholars, the historian Bernard Bailyn played a particularly significant part in this process, beginning in the mid-1960s to propose a dramatic reinterpretation of eighteenth-century Anglo-American political theory.[4] In *The Ideological Origins of the*

---

[1] J.G.A. Pocock, *Politics, Language, and Time* (New York: Atheneum, 1971), p. 39.

[2] Louis Hartz, *The Liberal Tradition in America* (New York: Harcourt, Brace & World, 1955), p. 32.

[3] Donald Winch, *Adam Smith's Politics* (Cambridge: Cambridge University Press, 1978), p. 29.

[4] It should be noted that Bailyn drew on significant earlier studies, including Caroline A. Robbins, *The Eighteenth-Century Commonwealthman* (Cambridge, Mass.: Harvard University Press, 1959). Also influential were Zera S. Fink, *The Classical Republicans* (Evanston, Ill.: Northwestern University Press, 1945); Clinton Rossiter, *Seedtime of the Republic* (New York: Harcourt, Brace, 1953); and H. Trevor Colbourn, "Thomas Jefferson's Use of the Past," *The William and Mary Quarterly*, 3rd ser., 15, 1 (January 1958): 56–70.

American Revolution, he told of his astonishment at finding that American Revolutionaries were motivated not by a modern liberal spirit of independence, rationality, and optimism, but by a premodern, or classical republican mentality, complete with an almost obsessive concern with power and its corruption, a conspiratorial and exceedingly irrational view of the world, and a millennial vision of the future.[5] Tracing these assumptions into the past, Bailyn uncovered an early eighteenth-century libertarian theory that he and others would come to label variously as "Commonwealth," "Country," "Whig," or "Opposition" thought.[6] Reaching back even further, he found this theory to be itself the product of the seventeenth-century Whig radicalism of writers like James Harrington, Henry Neville, and Algernon Sidney.[7] He went on to suggest, while leaving it to those such as Pocock to show, that the republican line could be followed back through the civic humanism of Machiavelli's Florentine Renaissance to its earliest origins in the classical republican thought of Aristotle, Cicero, and certain of the Greek and Roman historians.[8]

Bailyn's revelation evoked a dramatic effect on American scholarship. By 1972, historian Robert Shalhope could announce widespread agreement among American historians on the existence of what he would call a "republican synthesis," a diffuse but discernable theory that in its classic form held that liberty was fragile and power corrupt; that the truest check on tyranny was a vigilant citizenry; and that the only way for citizens to remain free was through the exercise of public virtue, requiring frugality, industry, simplicity, and, above all, a commitment to the public good.[9] Long accustomed to looking at early American politics as liberal and Lockean, reluctant scholars found themselves admitting, often grudgingly, the incontestable reality of America's republican roots. More disconcerting still, they were forced to concede that eighteenth-century political theory, modern as it may have seemed, was to some extent premodern, the product of ancient, mostly Greco-Roman, assumptions. In short, far from a nation without a past, eighteenth-century America began to seem more like a traditional society, the last of the classical republics.[10]

In Bailyn's wake, scholars faced the troublesome task of recovering this

[5] Bernard Bailyn, *The Ideological Origins of the American Revolution* (Cambridge, Mass.: Harvard University Press, 1967; reprint, 1973), p. ix.

[6] Ibid., pp. 55–93.

[7] Ibid., pp. 34–54.

[8] Ibid., pp. 23–26.

[9] Robert E. Shalhope, "Toward a Republican Synthesis: The Emergence of an Understanding of Republicanism in American Historiography," *The William and Mary Quarterly*, 3rd ser., 29, 1 (January 1972): 49–80.

[10] Ibid.

6 INTRODUCTION

premodern way of thinking, and charting its influence on what would eventually become modern political thought. Students of the early republic assumed that at some point classical republicanism must have been transformed into a more modern, more liberal theory, allowing for private as well as public virtue, self-interest in addition to self-sacrifice, and a commitment to individual advancement along with the pursuit of the public good. But they were unsure as to exactly when this transformation had taken place. In the *Ideological Origins*, Bailyn himself had depicted the transition happening with the American Revolution, speaking of the "transforming vision" of Revolutionary republicanism.[11] Gordon S. Wood, writing shortly thereafter in *The Creation of the American Republic*, concentrated on the American Constitution, which he saw as a distinctly modern document, the symbol, as he described it, of the "end of classical politics."[12] Lance Banning found these changes continuing several years later still, and his *The Jeffersonian Persuasion* pointed out the persistence of classical republican themes in the 1790s.[13] Since that time, Rowland Berthoff and John Murrin have suggested that traces of the ideology could be found well into the nineteenth century.[14]

In addition, and just as important, critics of the republican synthesis from liberal democrats like Jackson Turner Main and Joyce Appleby to libertarian conservatives like Gary Schmitt and Robert Webking have persisted in pointing to the early existence of liberal principles.[15] To picture the Revo-

[11] See Bailyn, *Ideological Origins*, p. 160; see also pp. 160–229.

[12] Gordon S. Wood, *The Creation of the American Republic, 1776–1787* (Chapel Hill, N.C.: University of North Carolina Press, 1969), p. 606.

[13] Lance Banning, *The Jeffersonian Persuasion* (Ithaca, N.Y.: Cornell University Press, 1978), pp. 13–18.

[14] See Rowland Berthoff, "Independence and Attachment, Virtue and Interest: From Republican Citizen to Free Enterpriser, 1787–1837," in *Uprooted Americans*, ed. Richard L. Bushman, Neil Harris, David Rothman, Barbara Miller Solomon, and Stephen Thernstrom (Boston: Little, Brown and Company, 1979), pp. 99–124; and John Murrin, "The Great Inversion, or Court versus Country: A Comparison of the Revolution Settlements in England (1688–1721) and America (1776–1816)," in *Three British Revolutions*, ed. J.G.A. Pocock (Princeton, N.J.: Princeton University Press, 1980), pp. 368–453. See also Rowland Berthoff and John Murrin, "Feudalism, Communalism, and the Yeoman Freeholder: The American Revolution Considered as a Social Accident," in *Essays on the American Revolution*, ed. Stephen G. Kurtz and James H. Hutson (Chapel Hill, N.C.: University of North Carolina Press, 1973), pp. 256–88.

[15] See Jackson Turner Main, review of *The Creation of the American Republic, 1776–1787*, by Gordon S. Wood, *The William and Mary Quarterly*, 3rd ser., 26, 4 (October 1969): 604–607; Joyce Appleby, "The Social Origins of American Revolutionary Ideology," *Journal of American History*, 64, 4 (March 1978): 935–58; and Gary J. Schmitt and Robert H. Webking, "Revolutionaries, Antifederalists, and Federalists: Comments on Gordon Wood's Understanding of the American Founding," *The Political Science Reviewer*, 9 (Fall 1979): 195–229. For a more sympathetic treatment, see Donald S. Lutz, "Bernard Bailyn, Gordon S. Wood, and Whig Political Theory," *The Political Science Reviewer*, 7 (Fall 1977): 111–44.

lution and Constitution as so pervasively republican, these writers have argued, is to overlook the sources of the individualism, the competitive capitalism, and the constantly changing pluralism that would eventually come to be so characteristic of American politics.[16] Among the critics of what he would call "republican revisionism," Isaac Kramnick has made a particularly compelling case, arguing that while eighteenth-century Anglo-Americans may indeed have turned to Aristotle's classical republicanism and Machiavelli's civic humanism, they relied much more often on Locke's liberalism, and, he concluded emphatically, "they knew their Locke."[17]

As a consequence of this criticism, the republican synthesis has come to be seriously reconsidered. Indeed, as early as 1982, Shalhope himself had been forced to admit that the synthesis had been shattered.[18] Moreover, since that time the criticism has continued, with liberal critics even more ardently attacking the republican thesis. Among the most articulate of these has been Appleby, who in her recent *Capitalism and a New Social Order* made the case for the crucial role of the marketplace in late eighteenth-century political thought, and for the egalitarian and libertarian implications of an expanding commercial economy.[19] The most ardent attack, however, has come from John P. Diggins, who in his *The Lost Soul of American Politics*, published in 1984, contended with uncompromising consistency that liberalism, not republicanism, has always been the touchstone, the very "soul" of American political thought.[20]

Thus, in recent historiography, the trend has been back to liberalism, to a rediscovery of the Hartzian "liberal tradition." Yet the case is not so clear. For while liberal scholars have provided a welcome antidote to rampant republicanism, they have gone too far: not only have they slighted the importance of republican themes, but they have also implied a liberal hegemony that never in fact existed.

The truth lies somewhere in between. That is, in the late eighteenth century, American political thought was in transition, moving from classical republicanism to modern liberalism. Yet the transition was inconclusive, neither clear nor complete, and the result was a hybrid mixture that combined republican and liberal themes in a creative but uneasy collaboration. More rational, more self-interested, and more progressive than its classical

[16] See especially Appleby, "Social Origins," p. 937.

[17] Isaac Kramnick, "Republican Revisionism Revisited," *American Historical Review*, 87, 3 (June 1982): 664.

[18] Robert E. Shalhope, "Republicanism and Early American Historiography," *The William and Mary Quarterly*, 3rd ser., 39, 2 (April 1982): 334–56.

[19] Joyce Appleby, *Capitalism and a New Social Order* (New York: New York University Press), esp. pp. 1–23.

[20] John P. Diggins, *The Lost Soul of American Politics* (New York: Basic Books, 1984).

republican predecessor, this mixture was still far removed from our own modern liberalism. Neither entirely republican nor exclusively liberal, but drawing from both, it was a complicated conglomeration, and it presided over the political thinking of the period. Shalhope himself had suggested something of this kind in his 1982 article, proposing that in the late eighteenth century, "liberal and classical ideas existed in constant tension. They shaped and influenced each other until the end result was a bastardized form of each."[21]

In a deeper sense, however, another transformation was taking place as well, a transformation in temporal thinking, in the way Americans thought about time. Americans of the 1780s and 1790s were in transition, on the road, as it were, between classical and modern ways of viewing the world. Yet here again, the change was inconclusive. Traditional people at the advent of the modern age, they found themselves clinging to the ideals of the classical past, while at the same time admitting the practical advantages of modern times. As a result, their temporal thinking was ambivalent, contradictory, and sometimes flatly paradoxical, marked by tensions that were the product of the stresses and strains placed on a people emerging into the modern age.

Ultimately, what makes this period so important is the way in which these changes in thinking converged and how this process inspired an extraordinary new phase in American political practice. For in reconciling the tensions between classical republicanism and modern liberalism, and in coming to terms with the deeper and more comprehensive change from classicism to modernity, Americans found themselves challenged to create a new kind of politics, one neither entirely republican nor exclusively liberal, neither classical nor modern, but a curious combination of both. As symbolized by the American Constitution, this unlikely mixture, compromising and self-contradictory though it may have been, has continued to characterize American politics for the last two hundred years. In this regard, this period can be seen, to borrow again from Pocock, as America's "Machiavellian moment," the time when citizens acting consciously and with intention created a new and enduring political order.[22]

This book describes this transformation and explores these tensions. It

---

[21] Shalhope, "Republicanism and Early American Historiography," p. 350. In a recent dialogue, Banning and Appleby have agreed on this point, albeit each with some significant reservations. See Lance Banning, "Jeffersonian Ideology Revisited: Liberal and Classical Ideas in the New American Republic," *The William and Mary Quarterly*, 3rd ser., 43, 1 (January 1986): 3–19, and Joyce Appleby, "Republicanism in Old and New Contexts," *The William and Mary Quarterly*, 3rd ser., 43, 1 (January 1986): 20–34.

[22] See J.G.A. Pocock, *The Machiavellian Moment* (Princeton, N.J.: Princeton University Press, 1975), pp. viii–ix.

attempts to document the continuous transition from classical republicanism to modern liberalism, and from classical to modern ways of thinking.
At the same time, it tries to show that the change was inconclusive, and it
details some of the inconsistencies and describes some of the tensions, the
stresses and strains that resulted from the attempt to reconcile classical ideals to modern realities. Throughout, it suggests that these tensions, there at
the beginning, were crucial to the making of American political thought,
and thus that they continue to be part of our politics today.

As a practical matter, such a study of the relation between time and politics would have been difficult if not impossible only a few years ago. With
few exceptions, ideas of time were consigned to intellectual historians and
ideas of politics to political theorists, with each tending to follow their separate paths. Both groups seemed content to rely on an accepted body of
thinkers—the historians on philosophers of history like Hume, Hegel,
Spencer, Bergson, and Collingwood; and the political theorists on philosophers of politics including Aristotle, Hobbes, Locke, Rousseau, and Marx.
Similarly, both schools tended to concentrate on "classic" or at least standard sources, on Hegel's *Philosophy of History*, for example, or Aristotle's
Politics. As a result, the study of ideas of time and ideas of politics, although
following parallel paths, had remained disparate and very distant disci-
plines.

Beginning in the late 1960s, however, a number of thinkers, including
Thomas Kuhn, Clifford Geertz, and Pocock, began to contend that history
and politics could be seen as elements of an undifferentiated whole. Working independently, these thinkers contended, each in somewhat different
ways, that political theorists, far from being detached philosophers producing perfect principles embodied in timeless and immortal texts, could better
be seen as active and politically involved participants offering realistic responses to the important issues of their times. Furthermore, and related,
they argued that political theories were not static systems of thought, but
rather dynamic processes in which thinking was subtly and continually
changing. Borrowing from ordinary-language theory, they suggested that
these changes could be charted best by following the transformations taking
place in public speech. Especially striking in this regard was the implication
that political vocabularies were shared widely within a population, and that
political ideas could hence be studied in the context of public discussion and
debate. Finally, they implied that political ideas were embedded in a matrix
of ongoing political activity. The study of political theory, it followed, was
inextricably intertwined with the study of political history.[23]

[23] See Thomas Kuhn, *The Structure of Scientific Revolutions*, 2nd. ed. (Chicago: University

This study continues this line of thought, applying these assumptions to America. In charting the connections between time and politics, it begins with a series of themes. For late eighteenth-century Americans, political time consisted of a complicated set of concepts, many of them the product of the classical republican temporality that had been handed down from Renaissance Florence to Commonwealth England to Revolutionary America.[24] This legacy included an astonishing assortment of conceptual categories, common but complex, that were used to distinguish the political past from the present and the present from the predicted future.[25] Among these, at the very least, were the eight themes that provide the titles for the eight chapters of this book: creation, change, reform, development, experience, founding, posterity, and destiny.[26]

These themes were common in public discourse. Originating in ordinary usage, they were staples of the late eighteenth-century vocabulary. As such, they were used with ease and great frequency, and can readily be recognized as important ingredients of American politics.[27] Moreover, they were terms common in public debate.[28] That is, themes such as change, reform, or experience can be seen as common concepts that at some point lost their consensual quality, so that latent differences became manifest and the terms quickly became controversial.[29] Above all, they were political terms, the product not only of philosophy but also of an age of extraordinary politics.[30]

---

of Chicago Press, 1970), pp. 10–34; Clifford Geertz, "Ideology as a Cultural System," in *Ideology and Discontent*, ed. David Apter (New York: Free Press of Glencoe, 1964), pp. 47–76; and J.G.A. Pocock, "The History of Political Thought: A Methodological Enquiry," in *Philosophy, Politics and Society*, 2nd. ser., ed. Peter Laslett and W. C. Runciman (Oxford: Basil Blackwell, 1962), pp. 183–202.

[24] See Pocock, *Machiavellian Moment*, p. 3.

[25] See ibid., pp. 5–9.

[26] The choice of these terms is to some extent subjective. As in any historical analysis, decisions have been made here about the significance and sequence of ideas and events. The result is one reader's reconstruction, and does not pretend to be an exhaustive study. But it does stay scrupulously close to the words of these early writers. See J.G.A. Pocock, "Reconstructing the Traditions: Quentin Skinner's Historian's History of Political Thought," *Canadian Journal of Political and Social Theory*, 3, 3 (Fall 1979): 97–98.

[27] On language, see J.G.A. Pocock, "Verbalizing as a Political Act: Towards a Politics of Speech," *Political Theory*, 1, 1 (February 1973): 27–45.

[28] On public speech (which he calls "rhetoric"), see Russell Hanson, *The Democratic Imagination in America* (Princeton, N.J.: Princeton University Press, 1985), pp. 22–53.

[29] On conceptual conflict, see W. B. Gallie, "Essentially Contested Concepts," *Proceedings of the Aristotelian Society*, 56 (1955–56): 167–98; John Gray, "On the Contestability of Social and Political Concepts," *Political Theory*, 5, 3 (August 1977): 331–48; and Hanson, *Democratic Imagination*, pp. 28–37. See also Forrest McDonald, *Novus Ordo Seclorum: The Intellectual Origins of the Constitution* (Lawrence, Kan.: University of Kansas Press, 1985), p. 4.

[30] See J.G.A. Pocock, "Political Ideas as Historical Events: Political Philosophers as Histor-

The focus here is on this discourse, on public speech and public writing, including debates, essays, and treatises, along with speeches, orations, and politically oriented sermons. Although private correspondence has been used to supplement and verify these public sources in some cases, most of the sources cited are popular, designed to address a popular audience. As such they can be seen as political primers, lexicons of the language of republican politics.

Crucial to this discourse were the speakers and writers. A few, including the Adamses, Madisons, and Hamiltons, were recognized members of the nation's intellectual elite. Others, such as the delegates to the federal and state ratifying conventions, were political notables who sometimes held positions of leadership in national or state politics. However, most were less often political philosophers or party leaders than they were local lawyers, ministers, and teachers. Respected in their communities, though sometimes not known very far beyond them, these small-town elites were educated enough to be aware of broader intellectual currents, but sensitive enough to their surroundings to reflect popular opinion as well. In this sense they can be seen as teachers and translators who brought cosmopolitan assumptions to local listeners, while at the same time communicating the concerns of their local communities.

Their audiences were important as well. In eighteenth-century America, the written word was a public commodity. As numerous studies have shown, most political writing was read not only privately but publicly, often out loud, in churches, taverns, and other public places.[31] Under these conditions, it was accessible to large numbers of people, lettered and unlettered alike.[32] In addition, much of this writing appeared first in the form of sermons and speeches. Many of these apparently won the approval of their audiences, for they were frequently printed at the request and the expense of the listeners.[33] These sources in particular can be seen, at least to some extent, as reflecting the sentiments of both speakers and listeners. Moreover, all of them offer an opportunity to see concepts in the process of change, with authors and orators altering ideas and images in order to influence the assumptions and actions of their audiences.

---

ical Actors," in *Political Theory and Political Education*, ed. Melvin Richter (Princeton, N.J.: Princeton University Press, 1980), pp. 139–58.

[31] See for example Nathan O. Hatch, *The Sacred Cause of Liberty* (New Haven, Conn.: Yale University Press, 1977), pp. 176–82.

[32] Ibid. Admittedly, this audience did not include everyone. For the truly disenfranchised, including servants and slaves, many laborers, and large numbers of women, these sources cannot be claimed as in any way representative. To consider this population, other methods, including the demographic techniques of social history, are essential.

[33] See ibid.

At every point, this public discourse existed within a political context. Intellectually, political language is created and changed through a process of debate, in which issues are joined and policies enacted. In the early republic in particular, at a time when political rhetoric was held in high esteem, debate was a profoundly important part of this policy-making process. In addition, political thinking was very much in flux. For example, while virtually all Americans of the time could consider themselves to be republicans, they often held startlingly dissimilar notions of the meaning of republicanism itself. Thus, when Federalists confronted Antifederalists, they fought not only over interests but over ideas, and their weapons were words. In short, conflict was conceptual as well as pragmatic and, as such, was part of the ongoing political process.

At the same time, conflict was also ideological. As the political thought of the time divided and redivided into divergent intellectual strains, so thinkers of the time could be found forming and reforming into contending ideological camps—evangelical and rationalist, country and court, Antifederalist and Federalist, to name only a few. These camps, far from conventional parties, were rather what Banning, following Marvin Meyers, has called "persuasions," ideologically identifiable clusters of thinkers who shared more or less coherent sets of assumptions, ideas, and values.[34] The members of these persuasions attended no annual conventions, used no secret handshakes, swore no common oaths. But their thinking, as revealed in their writing, showed startling similarities. Thus, although working separately, they can be considered as working together, creating the changing constellations of interests that were so prevalent throughout the period.

The concentration on "persuasion" offers an appealing alternative to more conventional studies of "party." It does not imply that the parties of the period were nonexistent or unimportant. On the contrary, in 1787 the first American party system was on the verge of being created, and by 1795 demarcations between Republican and Federalist had become quite clear.[35] Every bit as important as party, however, were the attachments to ideology. Especially in the context of the deep republican suspicion of factionalism, these less institutional, more ideological groupings tended to provide an often preferred means for practicing politics.[36] Thus even when partylike alignments such as those between Antifederalists and Federalists arose, they

34 Banning, *The Jeffersonian Persuasion*, p. 15. See also Marvin Meyers, *The Jacksonian Persuasion* (Stanford, Calif.: Stanford University Press, 1957).

35 See William N. Chambers, *Political Parties in a New Nation* (New York: Oxford University Press, 1963), esp. pp. 17–33.

36 See John R. Howe, Jr., "Republican Thought and the Political Violence of the 1790s," *American Quarterly*, 19, 2 (Summer 1967): 147–65.

tended to be informal and relatively unstructured.[37] In addition, these ideological groupings were imprecise and fairly porous, allowing not only for
internal inconsistencies and internecine conflicts, but also for rapid realignment, with thinkers moving from persuasion to persuasion with more ease
than they would later transfer their loyalties from party to party.

The fact that such realignments were so typical makes this perspective
all the more essential. In some cases, however rare, political thinkers could
be found aligning into predictable patterns. Samuel Adams, for example,
Boston's stolid Christian Spartan, remained true to classical republican precepts throughout the period, and hence at any given moment could be
found in alliance with the practitioners of classical republican politics.[38] Far
more commonly, however, thinkers followed inconsistent and unpredictable patterns. The movement of leading Antifederalists into the Federalist
party in the 1790s, for example, along with the equally unlikely conversion
of Federalists such as James Madison to the principles of Jeffersonian Republicanism, were typical of the surprising transitions taking place.[39]

Equally important, because of the porous and penetrable nature of these
persuasions, a thinker of the time could even be attracted simultaneously to
contradictory or even mutually exclusive concepts. Indeed, because the political thought of the 1790s was often inconsistent, and because reform was
to a great degree inspired by this inconsistency, those who found themselves in the uncomfortable position of attempting to hold two or more divergent persuasions at once were often those who took the lead in the process of reform. Prominent among these divided thinkers were no less than
Washington, Madison, and Jefferson. In general, Americans of the 1790s
practiced a sophisticated politics—in a few cases continuous and consistent,
in many others discontinuous and inconsistent, but in general a politics of
tension in which the classical and modern converged and diverged, sometimes even within the minds of these very thinkers themselves.

To paraphrase Michel Foucault, the present book is an archaeology of
this politics.[40] Taken as a whole, it is a "tunnel history," a remarkable cross-
section revealing the transition from classical to modern politics, a change
that in other parts of the world had taken centuries but in America was
carried out in a matter of some seventeen stressful years.[41]

[37] See James Sterling Young, *The Washington Community, 1800–1828* (New York: Columbia University Press, 1966).
[38] See Pauline Maier, *The Old Revolutionaries* (New York: Alfred A. Knopf, 1980), pp. 3–
50.
[39] The best review of these realignments is Banning, *The Jeffersonian Persuasion*, pp. 161–
78.
[40] Michel Foucault, *The Archaeology of Knowledge* (New York: Pantheon Books, 1972).
[41] Pocock, "Reconstructing the Traditions," p. 104.

Simultaneously, when viewed individually, the themes treated in the several chapters represent what have been called "thin sections," distinct strata, each discrete and recognizable.[42] Embedded in these strata are the faults and fissures, the contradictions and inconsistencies that from time to time have erupted in the tremors that have rattled the complacency of our modern liberalism. This study reminds us that no matter how contemporary we become in our thinking, Americans still cherish some ancient ways of looking at the world.

Considered more closely still, and focusing on the details of the sections themselves, the book is a study of what Peter Berger and Thomas Luckmann have called the "sedimentation" of society.[43] These astonishing artifacts—the ideas, institutions, and political initiatives of the time—provide the archaeological evidence that can be used to reconstruct eighteenth-century political experience in all its magnificent complexity. Indeed, like the very earth beneath our feet, this sedimentation provides the foundation for our modern American politics.

[42] See Iain Hampsher-Monk, "Political Languages in Time: The Work of J.G.A. Pocock," *British Journal of Political Science*, 14, 1 (January 1984): 104.

[43] Peter L. Berger and Thomas Luckmann, *The Social Construction of Reality* (Garden City, N.Y.: Doubleday, 1964), pp. 67–72.

PART ONE

The Paradoxical Past

-‹1›-

CREATION

Sacred and Secular History

IN 1783, twenty years of protest and war came suddenly to a close. With the signing of the Peace of Paris, the War of Independence was officially won. Americans greeted the news with celebration and thanksgiving. The army was demobilized swiftly and relatively surely, thanks largely to the firmness and generosity of General Washington, and enlisted men and officers alike set out for their farms and homes, many leading the horses that had pulled the cannon during the war. By April 1783, the army had been disbanded, in time for late spring planting.

Ending the war was easy, however, compared to beginning the peace. For having carried out the modern world's first anticolonial revolution, Americans turned with trepidation to the task of creating its first independent republic. Their situation was unique. But perhaps because it was so unprecedented, they seemed all the more determined to find precedents. Faced with the challenge of beginning anew, thinkers of the time could be found asking how their ancestors had begun this extraordinary experiment in the first place, how they had founded a new world, settled a new continent, and won independence for a new nation.[1] Simply said, in creating the American republic, they began by considering how their ancestors had created America itself.

Americans looked to their history in 1783. As to what they found, there is considerable disagreement, because historians have been at odds for some time over the character of eighteenth-century conceptions of history. On the one hand, inspired in part by Perry Miller, religious historians such as Alan Heimert, Edmund Morgan, and Nathan Hatch have described the enduring influence of Puritan history, with its providential interpretation of the past.[2] On the other hand, intellectual historians in the tradition of Trevor

[1] See Wesley Frank Craven, *The Legend of the Founding Fathers* (Ithaca, N.Y.: Cornell University Press, 1980), pp. 1–32.

[2] See Perry Miller, *The New England Mind: The Seventeenth Century* (New York: Macmillan, 1939); idem, *The New England Mind: From Colony to Province* (Boston: Beacon Press, 1953); Alan Heimert, *Religion and the American Mind* (Cambridge, Mass.: Harvard University Press, 1966); Edmund S. Morgan, "The Puritan Ethic and the American Revolution," *The William and Mary Quarterly*, 3rd ser., 24, 1 (January 1967): 3–43, and Hatch, *Sacred Cause*, pp. 1–20. See also Henry May, *The Enlightenment in America* (New York: Oxford University Press, 1976), esp. pp. 153–76.

Colbourn have contended that eighteenth-century history was predominantly secular and legalistic, premised on Enlightenment principles and focusing on the English common law.[3] Among relatively recent writers,
John Berens has elaborated on the argument that providential history remained pervasive throughout the late eighteenth century, while Lester
Cohen has contended, very much to the contrary, that a rationalist reading
of the past became predominant in America at the time of the Revolution.[4]

In fact, both interpretations miss the most important point, that in their
reading of the past, many eighteenth-century Americans tended to combine
the sacred and the secular. It is true that certain evangelicals would remain
loyal to providential history, and that some secular thinkers would adhere
to an almost exclusively rationalistic interpretation. But an even larger
group, combining religion and rationality, would create a conception of
American history in which piety and pragmatism were inextricably bound
together. The result would be a paradoxical interpretation of the past, comprehensive but contradictory, inspiring feelings of enormous self-confidence
and enormous self-doubt.

New World Israel

In the late eighteenth century, American evangelicals preferred a strictly
sacred reading of the past. On the whole, their theory of history followed
from their reading of the Bible and, in particular, the Old Testament. These
early Protestants saw history commencing with the Creation of Genesis.
Yet for them the beginning of the world seemed somehow very close. Although all may not have agreed with Archbishop Ussher's calculation that
the world had come into being in 4004 B.C., they did see the creation of
the world as a literal and relatively recent event.[5]

The evangelical reading of history was cataclysmic, consisting of epochal

[3] See H. Trevor Colbourn, *The Lamp of Experience* (Chapel Hill, N.C.: University of North
Carolina Press, 1965).

[4] Compare John F. Berens, *Providence and Patriotism in Early America, 1640–1815* (Char-
lottesville, Va.: University Press of Virginia, 1978) with Lester H. Cohen, *The Revolutionary
Histories* (Ithaca, N.Y.: Cornell University Press, 1980). For slightly different perspectives on
the same problem, see James West Davidson, *The Logic of Millennial Thought* (New Haven,
Conn.: Yale University Press, 1977), pp. 12–36; Arthur H. Shaffer, *The Politics of History*
(Chicago: Precedent Publishing, 1975); and William Raymond Smith, *History as Argument*
(The Hague: Mouton, 1966).

[5] On early concepts of the past, see Arnaldo Momigliano, "Time in Ancient Historiography,"
in *History and the Concept of Time* (Middletown, Conn.: Wesleyan University Press, 1966), pp.
1–23; Elizabeth L. Eisenstein, "Clio and Chronos: Some Concepts of History Book Time," in
History and the Concept of Time, pp. 42–49; and M. I. Finley, "Myth, Memory, and History,"
History and Theory, 4 (1964): 231–302.

events: Creation, the flood of Noah, the birth of Jesus. History seemed to leap from one of these great moments to the next; between these events, time, for all practical purposes, did not exist. Thus evangelicals could talk of ancient acts as if they had only just happened, and of Biblical figures as if they had been almost contemporaries. After all, as late as 1625, Samuel Purchas had begun his history of Virginia with a sketch of the lives of Adam and Eve. Throughout the seventeenth century, works like *An Historical Treatise on the Travels of Noah in Europe* had circulated. Even in the early eighteenth century, American Protestants could continue to speak of ancient Jerusalem in the same way that they described contemporary London or Paris.[6]

Furthermore, evangelicals held a covenant theory of history, in which the past was seen as a process in which God periodically chose certain nations to play the role of his chosen people. According to the Bible, Abraham had passed this national covenant to his children, who comprised the nation of Israel. For centuries, Protestant theologians had argued that from Israel the covenant had been transferred to the first Christians, who in turn had passed it to the early modern Protestants of Europe and England.[7] With the American Puritans, it had been carried to the New World. Thus eighteenth-century evangelicals tended to see themselves as descendants, literal or metaphorical, of the ancient Israelites.[8] In 1783 it was still quite common to hear American Protestants describing themselves as the chosen people of God, what the Reverend Rozel Cook, pastor of a New London, Connecticut, church, would call the "American Israel."[9]

By the eighteenth century, however, certain rationalists had begun to discover an alternative reading of history. To these less self-consciously religious writers, the past seemed to be primarily the product of secular events. Specifically, their reading of history consisted of the story of the rise and fall of the classical civilizations. In a 1783 oration, the Boston lawyer John Gardiner described the outlines of the theory. Ironically, he began with ancient Israel, which he described as the earliest example of a civilized nation. With their emphasis on education, along with their respect for the individual, the Israelites had begun the process that would culminate in modern secular society. From Israel the germ of civilization had been passed

[6] See Stephen Toulmin and June Goodfield, *The Discovery of Time* (London: Hutchinson of London, 1965), p. 76.

[7] On covenant history, see William Haller, *The Elect Nation* (New York: Harper & Row, 1963), pp. 224–50.

[8] See J. F. Maclear, "The Republic and the Millennium," in *The Religion of the Republic*, ed. Elwyn A. Smith (Philadelphia: Fortress Press, 1971), p. 188.

[9] Rozel Cook, A.M., *A Sermon, Delivered at New-London* . . . (New London, Conn.: Timothy Green, 1784), p. 25.

to Greece, where, as the classically educated Gardiner put it, "the human
mind expanded freely, and reached the sublimest heights of elevation."[10]
With the Greeks, civilization had come into its full glory, with labor and
learning combining to create an almost perfect civilized state, a model for
ages to come, providing, in Gardiner's words, "infinite satisfaction, enter-
tainment, and instruction to the *modern* world."[11]

Nevertheless, this secular history was neither continuous nor cumulative.
Instead, it remained cataclysmic, with reason leaping from one civilization
to the next, the light of learning suddenly blazing forth from darkness. Between these sudden bursts of illumination, ignorance continued to cast its
pall over a benighted world. Gardiner described the passage of civilization
from Greece to Rome, where, following the fall of the Alexandrian empire,
the spirit of the liberal arts and sciences had risen again. Over time, however, the love of learning was lost, and Roman republicans grew slothful
and profligate. A series of despots proceeded further to sap the spirit of the
Roman people, and eventually, as Gardiner observed, "cast a deep gloom
upon everything liberal, great, and noble."[12] By the fourth century, Roman
civilization had grown too corrupt to defend itself from the barbarian invad-
ers who struck the final blow to classical civilization. "Dark thick clouds of
Gothick night soon obscured the face of science," Gardiner described this
cataclysmic age, "and enveloped every trace of the polite arts, and the European world sunk gradually into ignorance, stupidity, and superstition."[13]

Yet rationalist historians made it clear that ultimately reason always
triumphed over ignorance. For though cataclysmic and discontinuous, their
history was cumulative and at least implicitly progressive. Eighteenth-century republicans of all kinds showed a peculiar fascination with the Dark
Ages, which they viewed as a long night of ecclesiastical and feudal tyranny
that had followed the fall of Rome. At the same time, they were equally
fascinated with the coming of modern times. Evangelicals saw the catalyst
as the Reformation, which put a violent end to spiritual ignorance and
church tyranny. Rationalist writers, by contrast, attributed the coming of
modern times more to the Renaissance. Thus, starting about the eleventh
century, as Gardiner saw it, "gleams of scientific light began to beam
through the Gothick clouds."[14] The progress of knowledge was slow until
the fourteenth century. Then, "in this remarkable century, literature suddenly diffused itself through most parts of Europe, *gun-powder, the art of*

[10] John Gardiner, Esq., *An Oration, Delivered July 4, 1785, at . . . Boston* (Boston: Peter
Edes, 1785), p. 10.
[11] Ibid.
[12] Ibid.
[13] Ibid., pp. 11–12.
[14] Ibid., p. 13.

printing, and the *mariner's compass* were invented."[15] These advances in the liberal arts and sciences, however, were only preparatory to the most significant development of early modern times, the discovery of the New World. America had been discovered and explored through the aid of scientific inventions. It had been colonized and settled by educated, rational people. In other words, to these secular historians, America symbolized the rebirth of civilization: "For times of greater freedom," Gardiner concluded, "of nobler improvement, and of more perfect knowledge was reserved the particular discovery of *this happy land*, the place of our nativity."[16]

For all their differences, these competing versions of sacred and secular history were surprisingly complementary. After all, for centuries modern scholars had been combining Biblical description with secular chronology, showing how the prophet Jeremiah had taught the philosopher Plato, or how Moses had predated Bacchus, or that Egypt was not as old as Israel. This attempt to reconcile theology with science had created a half-skeptical, half-credulous form of early modern history in which the fantastic combined spectacularly with the mundane. The English scientist William Whiston had dedicated himself to showing how the flood of Noah had been caused by a comet passing near the earth; Sir Isaac Newton had apparently believed that Chiron the Centaur was responsible for the first astronomical calculations; Sir Edward Coke had thought that Aeneas's grandson had discovered the British Isles.[17] In the eighteenth century, this reconciliation of the mythic and the mundane past continued, so that by the end of the century an elaborate synthesis had been developed.[18] Brought to the New World, this synthetic history allowed Americans to assume that their nation was descended from both ancient Israel and the classical civilizations: In effect, America had both a sacred and a secular heritage. Dr. Benjamin Rush, appropriately enough a founder of both the American Bible Society and the American Philosophical Society, may have put it best when he referred to the new United States as "the Kingdom of Christ and the empire of reason and science."[19]

[15] Ibid.
[16] Ibid., p. 16. On the rationalist reading of history, see R. V. Sampson, *Progress in the Age of Reason* (Cambridge, Mass.: Harvard University Press, 1956), p. 31; R. N. Stromberg, "History in the Eighteenth Century," *Journal of the History of Ideas*, 12, 2 (April 1951): 300–301; and R. G. Collingwood, *The Idea of History* (London: Clarendon Press, 1946), p. 81.
[17] On Whiston, see Perry Miller, "The End of the World," in *Errand Into the Wilderness* (1956; reprint, New York: Harper & Row, 1964), pp. 230–33; on Newton, see Frank Manuel, *Isaac Newton* (Cambridge, Mass.: Harvard University Press, 1963), pp. 139–65; and on Coke, see Eisenstadt, "Clio and Chronos," p. 51.
[18] See Frank Manuel, *The Eighteenth Century Confronts the Gods* (Cambridge, Mass.: Harvard University Press, 1959), pp. 85–125.
[19] Benjamin Rush to Charles Nisbit, 27 April 1784, in *Letters of Benjamin Rush*, ed. L. H. Butterfield (Princeton, N.J.: Princeton University Press, 1951), 1: 339.

Following the Revolution, preachers and popular speakers in large numbers began to draw on both evangelical and rationalist legacies to interpret Independence. In their sermons and orations celebrating the peace, they emphasized the theme of American uniqueness. Many recalled the circumstances surrounding the discovery and first founding of America: its miraculous appearance on the stage of history, its unique New World character, its primordial innocence. These same features, the ministers and orators argued, were also characteristic of their own times. Independence, like founding, was described as an act of providential creation, an American Genesis. In their thanksgiving sermons of 1783 and 1784, the ministers spoke often on this theme of creation, turning frequently for their sermon topic to the passage from Isaiah, "Shall the earth be made to bring forth in a day? Shall a nation be brought forth at once?"[20]

Yet the creation of the American nation, like the discovery of the New World, was an unprecedented human event as well, one of those moments, according to no less a figure than General George Washington, that "have seldom, if ever, taken place on the stage of human action; nor can they ever happen again."[21] As such, the significance of American Independence was both sacred and secular, a turning point in both providential and human history. When combined, as they often were, these interpretations rendered Independence an event of unique significance, "unexampled," suggested Philadelphia's Reverend George Duffield, a leader of the patriot clergy, "in the records of time."[22] As to the post-Revolutionary period, the ministers and orators described it as the beginning of a new historical era. America was the first postcolonial power, the first truly "new" nation. With its birth, a new age had begun: "a new world has started in existence," the Reverend Thomas Brockaway told his Lebanon, Connecticut, congregation, "the day is new—the circumstances are new."[23]

In the same manner, the celebrants suggested that America was specially favored by its peculiar place as the prototypical modern nation. For centuries, thinkers had argued that the discovery of the New World had announced the symbolic end of the Middle Ages. In the seventeenth century, for example, Puritans had described America as a Reformation land, spared

[20] George Duffield, A.M., *A Sermon Preached in the Third Presbyterian Church . . . December 11, 1783 . . .* (Philadelphia: F. Bailey, 1784), p. 3.

[21] George Washington, "Farewell Address to the Armies of the United States," in *The Writings of George Washington*, ed. Worthington Chauncey Ford (New York: G. P. Putnam's Sons, 1889–93), 10: 331.

[22] Duffield, *A Sermon*, p. 24.

[23] Thomas Brockaway, A.M., *America Saved . . . A Thanksgiving Sermon* (Hartford, Conn.: Hudson & Goodwin, 1784), p. 14. See also R.W.B. Lewis, *The American Adam* (Chicago: University of Chicago Press, 1955), esp. pp. 4–10.

from ecclesiastical and feudal tyranny to create a religious republic. As late as 1765, in his *Dissertation on the Canon and Feudal Law*, John Adams could continue to recite this Reformation theme.[24] Yet to postwar thinkers, America was the New World embodiment of both the Reformation and the European Enlightenment. "The foundation of our empire," Washington wrote at the end of the war in his famous Circular Letter to the state governors, "was not laid in the gloomy age of ignorance and superstition."[25] Instead, it had been placed aside to be founded in an age of enlightened reason. As a result, its citizens could call upon the "treasures of knowledge, acquired by the labors of philosophers, sages, and legislators."[26] With this store of learning laid open for their use, Washington concluded, Americans had a "fairer opportunity for political happiness, than any other nation has ever been favoured with."[27]

In the sermons and popular orations of the early postwar period, Washington's letter was cited repeatedly, as ministers and orators described America as an empire of both religion and rationality. In essence, God and reason had combined to bring forth America at this most propitious modern moment. "Empire, learning and religion have in past ages, been travelling from east to west, and this continent is their last western state," announced the Reverend Brockaway. "Here then is God erecting a stage on which to exhibit the great things of his kingdom."[28]

Above all, the new nation was an example for the rest of the world. From the time of the first founding, American Puritans had seen themselves as having the divine responsibility to make themselves a model for others to follow. As John Winthrop had said so eloquently in *A Model of Christian Charity*—his famous shipboard sermon delivered in 1630, shortly before he and his fellow Congregationalists landed at Massachusetts Bay—"For we must consider that we shall be as a city upon a hill, the eyes of all people are upon us."[29] With the Revolution, the mission had been extended from Protestant religion to republican politics, and America became, in the eyes of Revolutionary republicans, a beacon of liberty. In 1783, however, the successful break with the colonial past allowed Americans to consider themselves also a model of modern civilization. The new republic, by allowing

[24] On early interpretations of the first founding, see Craven, *Legend of the Founding Fathers*, pp. 1–32.

[25] George Washington, "Circular Letter Addressed to the Governors of All the States on Disbanding the Army," 8 June 1783, *Writings*, 10: 256.

[26] Ibid.

[27] Ibid.

[28] Brockaway, *America Saved*, p. 23. See Cushing Strout, *The American Image of the Old World* (New York: Harper & Row, 1963), pp. 18–38.

[29] John Winthrop, *A Model of Christian Charity*, in *The American Puritans*, ed. Perry Miller (Garden City, N.Y.: Anchor Books, 1956), p. 83.

free thought and open expression, had already become a leader in the arts and sciences. Its example would surely provide inspiration to the world. The cumulative lessons of the past, Yale's President Ezra Stiles stated, had been "brought home and treasured up in America, and being there digested and carried to the highest perfection, may reblaze back from America to Europe, Asia, and Africa, and illuminate the world with truth and liberty."[30] For better or worse, post-Revolutionary Americans were eager to offer their religion, politics, and culture to the rest of the world. Typical was the Presbyterian clergyman John Rodgers, who, returning from the war to find his New York City church in ruins, could still confidently predict that the Revolution would prove nothing less than "a new era in the history of mankind."[31]

Nevertheless, as a chosen people, Americans felt a peculiar obligation to live up to their special status. As John Winthrop had explained in his early sermon, God demanded that his people retain their faith, whatever the temptations. Postwar ministers echoed Winthrop in their own restatement of the demands of the covenant. Their duty, as Duffield told the congregation of Philadelphia's Third Presbyterian Church, was "to walk in his ways, and keep his commandments, to observe his statements and judgments."[32] The ministers called on their congregations not to lose sight of their religious responsibilities, reminding them repeatedly that "Righteousness exalteth a nation."[33] In the course of the century, however, religious duties had been supplemented by a new set of secular obligations. Some tried to argue that the twin roles of maintaining religion and extending rationality were complementary. Others were not so sure, for in secularity they saw pride, and in pride, a loss of piety. Indeed, throughout the period, even liberal-leaning ministers and orators could be found citing the dangers and evils that surrounded them, the risks they ran, the possibilities of failure. Above all, they referred to the fragility of their experiment. Should America fall into "impiety and irreligion," the Portsmouth, New Hampshire, Congregationalist Joseph Buckminster summed up nicely, "the fair foundation which has been laid for our future greatness must remain without the su-

[30] Ezra Stiles, D.D., *The United States elevated to Glory and Honor; A Sermon, Preached . . . May 8th, 1783* (New Haven, Conn.: Thomas & Samuel Green, 1783), p. 7.

[31] John Rodgers, D.D., *The Divine Goodness Displayed in the American Revolution: A Sermon, Delivered in New-York, December 11, 1784 . . .* (New York: Samuel London, 1784), p. 11. See also Seymour Martin Lipset, *The First New Nation* (New York: Basic Books, 1963), pp. 1–13.

[32] Duffield, *A Sermon*, p. 28.

[33] Benjamin Trumbull, A.M., *God is to be praised for the Glory of his Majesty and for his Mighty Works: A Sermon Delivered at North-Haven, November 11, 1783* (New Haven, Conn.: Thomas and Samuel Green, 1784), p. 36.

perstructure, and we become as much an object of derision, as we at present are of admiration to the nations of the earth."[34]

All told, post-Revolutionary rhetoric combined extreme self-confidence with equally extreme self-doubt. America held a special place in the history of the world; it was a "highly favored community."[35] At the same time, this special status implied special responsibilities. Even amid the first flush of Independence, many Americans were willing to admit that they were not living up to these obligations. There was, a cautious Reverend David Tappan lamented in a sermon to his Newbury, Massachusetts, congregation, no "peculiar excellence in our national character. Alas, Sirs, the moral face of our country effectively confutes such a vain-glorious sentiment."[36] Hence, their sermons and orations, even those celebrating the peace, seemed anxious and equivocal: "The present occasion then loudly calls us to mingle the most humble penitence and contrition with our joyful gratitude and praise," Tappan concluded. "These considerations call upon us to rejoice with trembling, with humility, with a sober, cautious, serious air."[37]

Errand into the Wilderness

For eighteenth-century evangelicals, sacred history included the providential story of the colonization and settlement of the continent. From the time of the first founding, American Puritans had contended that the colonial experience could best be understood as a mission of salvation. Initially, they saw themselves as preserving a saving remnant of the true church in the world. As Perry Miller has shown, these early Puritans had a profound sense of their role in rescuing the universal church from its corruption. However, as Miller also pointed out, their "errand into the wilderness" had a second meaning, for they considered themselves to be engaged in two missions, one to save the Old World by maintaining a remnant of the true church, and one to save themselves, building their own Christian commonwealth in the new land.[38] In the course of the seventeenth century, as the events of the English Civil War led Europe to look away from America, they tended more to the second errand, creating an independent identity for the American colonies. So it was that American Protestants became aware

---

[34] Joseph Buckminster, A.M., *A Discourse Delivered in the First Church of Christ . . .* (Portsmouth, N.H.: Robert Gerrish, 1784), p. 25.

[35] David Tappan, *A Discourse Delivered in the Third Parish in Newbury, on the First of May, 1783 . . .* (Salem, Mass.: Samuel Hall, 1783), p. 16.

[36] Ibid.

[37] Ibid.

[38] See Miller, "Errand Into the Wilderness," in *Errand*, pp. 1–15.

of the role of the wilderness in creating the national character.[39] Even after the Revolution, evangelicals continued to cite its importance. The process of colonization and settlement, according to the Reverend Joseph Huntington, was an essential element of God's plan for America: "he was there," Huntington told a Hartford, Connecticut, congregation, "laying the foundation for what we now see; rolling us into future empire."[40]

For evangelicals, the errand into the wilderness was a profoundly religious mission. From biblical times, the wilderness had provided the chosen people with a setting of temptation and purification. By meeting and overcoming the trials of the wilds, they could convince themselves that God was watching over them, confirming their special status. Even in the late eighteenth century, evangelical ministers were emphasizing this sacred meaning of the wilderness. God had sent the first founders on a mission into the wilds: "He found them in a desert land," as Huntington said in his 1784 Hartford sermon, "in a waste howling wilderness."[41] There he had guided them through trials and temptations, leading them about, instructing them, keeping them "as the apple of his eye."[42] In the wilderness, Americans had learned that God was watching over them, relieving them in distress, protecting them in danger, delivering them from destruction at the hands of wild beasts and wild men. "The God whom they served forsook them not," Huntington observed; "he commanded the deep in their favour, and guarded them from the powers of numerous heathen savages: they made him the glory in the midst of them, and he was a wall of fire about them."[43] The wilderness, in other words, provided just one more proof of America's providential selection. As Eliphalet Porter reminded his Roxbury, Massachusetts, parishioners, "if the Lord had not been on their side, then they would have been swallowed up quick."[44]

To others, however, the history of American settlement was better told in social and economic terms. From earliest times there had been thinkers who put less emphasis on salvation and more on settlement. By the early eighteenth century, some of these had begun to suggest that the process of opening the wilderness was really more economic than religious in intent. But with Independence, peace and the prospects of prosperity led rationalists like the Boston lawyer Gardiner to tell the story of American settlement

[39] See ibid.

[40] Joseph Huntington, D.D., *God ruling the Nations for the most glorious end. A Sermon . . . at Hartford, May 13th, 1784* (Hartford, Conn.: Hudson and Goodwin, 1784), p. 29.

[41] Ibid.

[42] Ibid.

[43] Ibid.

[44] Eliphalet Porter, A.M., *A Sermon Delivered to the First Religious Society in Roxbury, December 11, 1783 . . .* (Boston: Adams and Morse, 1984), p. 11.

as an almost exclusively materialistic mission. Theological values notwithstanding, the early settlers had come to America with a commitment to
commerce. The earliest founders, Gardiner recalled, were solid, sensible
people, "strong to labor and impatient of fatigue."[45] These industrious immigrants knew well both the necessity of survival and the desirability of
success. In this spirit, they set themselves against the wilds, and, in Gardiner's words, "the tall, thick woods of the ancient forest fell before them."[46]
Within a few years, the early settlers had begun to transform the new land.
Out of the wilds, American colonials created a civilized society. As Gardiner put it, "the country around them soon began to blossom like the Garden
of Eden."[47]

More commonly, at the end of the eighteenth century many Americans
could be found combining these sacred and secular readings of the colonial
past, apparently with some ease. As the literary historian Sacvan Bercovitch
has shown, American Protestants had long managed to link religious zeal
to commercial enterprise.[48] With the Protestant ethic, they had developed
a practical theology in which faith seemed to reap the rewards of both redemption in heaven and riches on earth. The result had been a conception
of America as a place where, in the words of one early Puritan, "religion
and profit jump together."[49] Eighteenth-century ministers continued to
combine these themes. It was, said the Reverend Henry Cumings, one of
the deans of American Congregationalism, through the "wonders of divine
goodness" that American Puritans had been led "into the inhospitable wilds
of America."[50] At the same time, Cumings was eager to point out that they
had emigrated for more mundane reasons as well, not the least of which was
the "iron rod of civil and ecclesiastical tyranny."[51] Moreover, as colonization
continued, social and economic interests intervened, as "under the smiles of
a propitious providence" the American colonies "prospered and flourished."[52] Over the ensuing generations, Cumings observed from his Biller-
ica, Massachusetts, pulpit, religion and prosperity had gone hand in hand,
for "under the continual unremitted care of Heaven," Americans "spread
themselves over the face of the land and grew up to a great people."[53] In the

[45] Gardiner, *An Oration*, p. 18.
[46] Ibid.
[47] Ibid.
[48] See Sacvan Bercovitch, *The American Jeremiad* (Madison, Wis.: University of Wisconsin
Press, 1978), pp. 3–30.
[49] Edward Winslow cited in ibid., p. 46.
[50] Henry Cumings, A.M., *A Sermon Preached in Bellerica, December 11, 1783* . . . (Boston:
T. and J. Fleet, 1784), p. 9.
[51] Ibid.
[52] Ibid.
[53] Ibid.

sermons of the time, New England's ministers in particular proved adept at using religious images to depict commercial gains. Connecticut's Brockaway was only one of many who made use of Isaiah's vision: "And when we consider almost three thousand miles of western territory, yet uninhabited: can we suppose, this is *the wilderness and solitary place* that *shall be glad, and the desert that shall blossom as the rose.*"[54]

After the Revolution, these thinkers relied heavily on the theme of the errand in their search for a sense of national character. With the peace, thousands of acres of western land had been opened to unrestricted settlement. The sermons and orations of the time described this vast continent in almost compulsive detail, listing the climates, soils, and myriad natural resources of the West. Washington's Circular Letter set the tone, announcing that Americans were from that moment "sole lords and proprietors of a vast tract of continent, comprehending all the various soils and climates of the world, and abounding with all the necessaries and conveniences of life."[55] Frequent reference was made to the physical security that the continent afforded. America, Philadelphia's Duffield noted with evident satisfaction, was "far removed from the noise and tumult of contending kingdoms and empires; from the wars of Europe and Asia, and the barbarous African coast."[56] This geographical isolation offered economic independence, an opportunity, as Duffield went on, for the husbandman to "enjoy the fruits of his labour; the merchant trade, secure of his gain; the mechanic indulge his inventive genius; and the sons of science pursue their delightful employment."[57] To the east lay the forbidding barrier of an immense ocean; to the west, the beckoning frontiers of a virgin land. It was both providential and practical for Americans to think of themselves as a continental people. Tappan's Newbury sermon was only one of many calling on Americans to take up the cause of civilizing the wilderness, "extending their benign influence to the utmost bounds of this vast continent."[58]

The continent was proof that the American mission was expansion and economic development. Postwar ministers and orators relied heavily on the theme of the errand in making the case for economic expansionism. In the process, they all but transformed the image of the continent, referring to the West not as a dark and howling wilderness, but as a "great, healthful, well-watered and fertile country."[59] In fact, as Benjamin Trumbull told his North Hartford, Connecticut, congregation, this beneficent continent, far

[54] Brockaway, *America Saved*, p. 23.
[55] Washington, "Circular Letter," in *Writings*, 10: 255.
[56] Duffield, *A Sermon*, p. 16.
[57] Ibid.
[58] Tappan, *A Discourse*, p. 18.
[59] Trumbull, *God is to be praised*, pp. 12–13.

from wilderness, was a veritable garden, "abounding with everything necessary to make a nation great and happy."[60] For Trumbull and those like
him, the continent offered the prospect of economic progress, "our wilderness turned into fields, gardens, and pleasant habitations."[61] The speakers
made clear that civilization required expansion. Many referred to America's
constantly increasing population, to the immigrants who would soon cover
vast tracts of cultivated lands. ("What innumerable multitudes!" exclaimed
a near-ecstatic Reverend Buckminster. "What inconceivable numbers!"[62])
In the same manner, they sang the praises of economic expansion, showing
how business was opening every avenue of commerce. Invariably, they described the potential for continental development as almost limitless. As
Brockaway predicted, Americans would surely proceed with their expansion westward, bounded only by "the great Pacific Ocean."[63] Most important, the orators described continental expansion in the same terms that
they had told the story of the original settlement, as a religious pilgrimage
for commercial profit. As Tappan summed up enthusiastically, Americans
had a "fair opportunity, for converting this immense northern continent
into a seat of knowledge and freedom, of agriculture and commerce, of the
useful arts and manufactures, of Christian piety and virtue, . . . the delight
of God and good men, the joy and praise of the whole earth."[64]

Yet in the post-Revolutionary period, the American errand was not limited to the continent alone. In fact, some orators seemed unwilling to set
any limits whatsoever on national expansion. Among the singular advantages of the New World, the Reverend David Osgood pointed out in a Med-
ford, Massachusetts, sermon entitled *Reflections on the goodness of God*,
were "many hundred leagues of seacoast for the advantage of trade."[65] The
extensive network of lakes and rivers leading to the sea invited a maritime
economy, opening the way to international trade. Indeed, as Osgood argued
in his 1784 sermon, with Independence, commerce would grow unchecked: "The ports of all nations are open for the welcome reception of our
flag; and the various treasures of the earth present themselves as the object
of our traffic."[66]

Expansion was both economic and evangelistic. Predictably enough,

[60] Ibid., p. 20.
[61] Ibid.
[62] Buckminster, *A Discourse*, p. 19.
[63] Brockaway, *America Saved*, p. 21. See Albert Weinberg, *Manifest Destiny* (Baltimore:
Johns Hopkins University Press, 1935), p. 3.
[64] Tappan, *A Discourse*, p. 11.
[65] David Osgood, A.M., *Reflections on the goodness of God in supporting the People of the
United States through the late war, and giving them so advantageous and honorable a peace. A
Sermon* . . . (Boston: T. and J. Fleet, 1784), p. 25.
[66] Ibid.

Portsmouth's Reverend Buckminster was heartened by the potential profits that lay in a flourishing international trade. Yet to Buckminster, these economic advantages, so important to his seaport congregation, would "not only be a source of wealth" but would also "expand and humanize the heart, soften the spirit of bigotry and superstition, and eradicate those rooted prejudices that are the jaundice of the mind."[67] According to this view, the pursuit of commerce, whether at home or abroad, was also the pursuit of righteousness. As Buckminster concluded, international trade was a capitalistic crusade, allowing Americans to bring the rest of the world both goods and gospel learning, "that grace of the gospel which maketh wisdom and eternal life."[68]

Still, the reconciliation of faith with commerce could never be complete. As Bercovitch has shown, American Puritans of an earlier era could be both devout and comfortable; they did not have to sacrifice religious principle to making money. But these same Puritans were not able to be both moral and rich, because excess wealth, like excess pride, was sinful. As Winthrop had warned in his *Model*, if they fell to worshiping their "pleasures and profits," God would break out in wrath against them, and they would be "consumed out of the good land whither we are going."[69] Amid the prosperity of the postwar period, Americans once more faced this old dilemma of distinguishing honest industry and decent profit from avarice and greed. The chosen people had the responsibility to increase and improve their God-given economic gifts. At the same time, however, it was their duty to avoid the evils that had been committed in the name of economics—what Tappan went so far as to call the "multitudes of abominations."[70] In effect, eighteenth-century Americans were faced with the fact that there was an inherent contradiction in their attempt to be pious capitalists. How easy it would be, Tappan speculated from his Newbury pulpit, to "abuse the blessings of returning peace" by indulging in "a spirit of pride, luxury, dissipation, venality, infidelity, and other concommitant vices."[71] To Tappan, the implications seemed clear: "our very prosperity," he warned, "will finally destroy us in the most aggravated manner."[72]

Thus the postwar celebrations of economic success were often tempered with Calvinist caution. Should Americans fall into vice, Tappan warned, echoing the old Puritan prophecy, "God will pronounce the designs of his

[67] Buckminster, *A Discourse*, pp. 21–22.

[68] Ibid., p. 22. See also David M. Potter, *People of Plenty* (Chicago: University of Chicago Press, 1954), pp. 134–41.

[69] Winthrop, *Model*, in *American Puritans*, pp. 84; 83.

[70] Tappan, *A Discourse*, p. 16.

[71] Ibid., p. 17.

[72] Ibid.

glory in our examplary ruin, as he has now been doing in our surprising salvation.—These ideas," he cautioned, "may well give a solemnity to our joy."[73]

American Exodus

For eighteenth-century evangelicals, Independence was the culmination of years of wandering in the wilderness, a passage, as they liked to describe it, from the House of Bondage into the Promised Land.[74] Throughout their history, American Protestants had relied on the Exodus theme to depict periods of hardship and perseverance that were also times of heavenly intervention. But in recalling the Revolution, evangelicals found the idea of God's guiding hand to be particularly powerful. A tiny colonial nation of three million persons, without substantial finances or industry, defended by an ill-equipped, poorly supplied, untrained citizen militia, had defeated the most experienced armies of the greatest imperial power of the day. The outcome was extraordinary enough to suggest heavenly intervention. "Surely," remarked Duffield, who as chaplain of the Continental Congress had witnessed at first hand the confused desperation of wartime, "the hand of God was in it."[75]

Many of the sermons and orations celebrating the peace took as their theme a verse from Psalm 126, celebrating the liberation of the Israelites from the Babylonian captivity, "The Lord hath done great things for us, whereof we are glad."[76] This idea of a partisan God provided an explanation for almost any extraordinary event. The orators cited his role in instilling a revolutionary spirit in the American colonies, in inciting British parliamentary resistance to the war, and in confounding English diplomats and war planners. They saw his hand in battles won, in garrisons captured, in ships seized. Some told how, "by means unexpected," the Lord had furnished the continental army with clothing and ammunition.[77] Others described how God had intervened to uncover the plot of Benedict Arnold, and how, for that matter, he had been "especially conspicuous in seasonably detecting dangerous plots and conspirators."[78] None of the orators even suggested that God might have helped the British. After all, the Revolution was God's

[73] Ibid.

[74] For an illuminating introduction to the concept of Exodus, see Michael Walzer, *Exodus and Revolution* (New York: Basic Books, 1985).

[75] Duffield, *A Sermon*, p. 53.

[76] Tappan, *A Discourse*, p. 5.

[77] John Marsh, A.M., *A Discourse Delivered at Weathersfield, December 11th 1783* . . . (Hartford, Conn.: Hudson and Goodwin, 1784), p. 10.

[78] Osgood, *Reflections*, p. 19.

doing: "it is abundantly evident," the Reverend Cook advised, "that the Lord hath been on our side."[79]

In some of the Independence orations, however, heaven had begun to disappear as the motive force of political life. On the whole, in comparison to earlier discourse, post-Revolutionary writers frequently described their God as remarkably bloodless. Even the most pious of ministers talked of him in impersonal terms, as "the Deity," "universal Providence," or "the great Disposer of all things." Speaking to an Ipswich, Massachusetts, audience, the Reverend Levi Frisbie could refer rather distantly to the "Lord of nature" and "Governor of the World."[80] At one point, he went so far as to recast the personal Puritan God as an abstract rationalistic principle, the "infinite summary of perfections."[81] Many seemed to use Providence only as an explanation of last resort, to account for otherwise unexplainable events. "The greater the disproportion between the means and the effect," reasoned New Hampshire's Reverend Samuel McClintock, "the more evident is divine power."[82] In general, these speakers assumed that Providence intervened only through secondary causes, by relying on human agents. Sometimes they suggested that human action alone was enough to explain human events; their speeches were filled with references to "human institutions," "human happiness," "human greatness." It followed that these more rationalistic Protestants could see politics as primarily the responsibility of enlightened citizens. Providence had set the "stage of human affairs," as General Washington described it.[83] The real actors were now Americans themselves, "actors on a most conspicuous theatre," designed, he ventured in the Circular Letter, "for the display of human greatness and felicity."[84]

In fact, in most of the sermons and speeches of 1783 and 1784, both of these explanations were present. Usually, the speakers described the Revolution as a rough collaboration between heaven and earth. In a Charleston, South Carolina, oration, Dr. Joseph Ladd captured this spirit with enviable elegance by referring to "the sword of the Lord, and of Washington."[85] More often they talked of the armies and generals, the heroes and statesmen

---

[79] Cook, A Sermon, p. 54.

[80] Levi Frisbie, An Oration, Delivered at Ipswich, . . . April, 1783 . . . (Boston: E. Russell, 1783), p. 54.

[81] Ibid., p. 18.

[82] Samuel McClintock, A.M., A Sermon Preached Before the Honorable the Council . . . of the State of New-Hampshire, June 3, 1784 . . . (Portsmouth, N.H.: Robert Gerrish, 1784), p. 17.

[83] Washington, "General Orders," in Principles and Acts of the Revolution in Ameria, ed. Hezekiah Niles (New York: A. S. Barnes & Co., 1876), p. 466.

[84] Washington, "Circular Letter," in Writings, 10: 255.

[85] Joseph Ladd, "An Oration Delivered . . . the fourth of July, 1785," in Principles and Acts, p. 384.

whom God had raised up to lead them out of bondage. Here they seemed
to consider God a kind of heavenly recruiting agent. In effect, the speakers
suggested that Americans themselves had won the war, with heaven providing much needed moral support. Many expressed this view, apparently
unselfconsciously, in referring to the fact that the Lord had been "on our
side."[86] Moreover, with victory God had seemed to retire as an active agent
in the affairs of the world. Although he retained an interest in American
politics, his role had been transformed from ally to spectator. As the Reverend Rodgers explained in his New York sermon on the peace, the Lord
and all his angels were now "looking on with eager expectation," watching
the American people closely, "to see what use they make of the great things
God has done for us."[87]

Thus, these ministers and orators can be seen as beginning to construct
a post-Revolutionary conception of politics. With the Revolution, Providence had signaled its approval of liberty. Heaven had been instrumental as
well in forming a constitutional form of government. For example, as Rodgers explained, God had played a role in bringing together the several states
under the Articles of Confederation. It followed, according to Rodgers, that
citizens had the "sacred responsibility" to "support and strengthen this federal bond."[88] God had taken great pains to lead his chosen people into the
promised land of Independence. His Revolutionary heroes had purchased
their liberty "at the price of their blood."[89] Under the circumstances, post-
Revolutionary citizens had a profound responsibility to maintain this newfound freedom. Their duty, as Reverend Frisbie put it, was to "preserve and
perpetuate."[90]

The ministers and orators expanded on the meaning of citizenship in the
post-Revolutionary period, citing the need for citizens to perform contracts,
obey laws, and respect rulers. They mentioned the need for debts to be paid
and credit established. A surprisingly large number insisted on a stronger
national union. Above all, they reminded their listeners that there could be
no factionalism, no treason, and, ironically enough, no revolution in the
Revolutionary republic. In short, as early as 1783, many Americans were
already concerned with the creation of constitutional order, along with the
enhancement of constitutional government: "And may every one be roused
to the most vigorous exertions for the support of the civil constitution,"

[86] Cook, *A Sermon*, p. 25.

[87] Rodgers, *Divine Goodness*, p. 37.

[88] Ibid., p. 28.

[89] John Murray, A.M., *Jerubbaal, or Tyranny's Grove Destroyed, and the Altar of Liberty Finished. A Discourse, on America's Duty and Danger* ... (Newbury-Port, Mass.: John Mycall,
1784), p. 55.

[90] Frisbie, *An Oration*, p. 22.

concluded the Reverend John Marsh, himself a power in Connecticut politics, "that a new energy may be given to government."[91]

In addition to political preservation, however, post-Revolutionary citizens had socioeconomic obligations as well. Independence, according to Tappan, had a great "intrinsic value."[92] But beyond the Revolution's political advantages were social and economic prospects that seemed nothing less than "extensive and glorious."[93] Virtually all of the orations followed the example of Washington's Circular Letter in celebrating the blessings of peacetime. They also followed Washington's lead in concluding their long lists of blessings with equally long lists of obligations. During the Revolution, American Independence had required heroism and protest. With peace, it demanded a new form of public virtue, less heroic and rebellious, more industrious and orderly. The role of republicans, the orations suggested, was to secure liberty without licentiousness, and independence without anarchy or confusion. Thus, they called on citizens to commit themselves to the pursuit of what one called the "milder arts":[94] science and the technical arts, industry and manufacturing, commerce and trade. Above all, citizens had the responsibility to keep order, to "lead a quiet and peaceable life, in all goodliness as well as honesty."[95]

These private virtues were to peacetime every bit as important as public service had been to war. In fact, they were more important, for while the patriots of the Revolution had laid the foundations of the republic, it remained for the citizens of the post-Revolutionary period to "rear the superstructure."[96] The orators apparently saw nothing contradictory in the demand that citizens combine private innovation with political stability. Indeed, only by preserving their political order could Americans develop their economic system to the highest degree. "Wise and just political institutions," argued Osgood, relying on the well-worn verse from Isaiah to tie economics to politics, "a free and happy government will encourage industry which turns *the wilderness into a fruitful field*, and causes *the desert to blossom as the rose*."[97]

Above all, Americans had the responsibility to pursue progress. With Independence, few orators missed the chance to wax eloquent on the future. From that time, America could be expected to advance steadily, "soaring," in Tappan's words, "to a greater height of perfection and glory than the

[91] Marsh, *A Discourse*, p. 20.
[92] Tappan, *A Discourse*, p. 9.
[93] Ibid.
[94] Frisbie, *An Oration*, p. 13.
[95] Marsh, *A Discourse*, p. 21.
[96] Osgood, *Reflections*, p. 36.
[97] Ibid., pp. 24–25.

world has ever yet seen."⁹⁸ Yet for eighteenth-century thinkers such as these, progress was by no means assured. Far from inevitable, it depended exclusively on human initiative, what Buckminster called "manly, vigorous efforts."⁹⁹ In essence, progress was an obligation, a burden to be borne in the name of civilization. As Reverend Rodgers said, "we have nothing to do now, but *wisely* improve this event, to render it a fruitful source of happiness to ourselves, and millions yet unborn."¹⁰⁰ Whether they approved or not, Americans had been chosen to carry out a progressive mission. Apparently they approved, for the ministers and orators spoke proudly of their role in bringing free government ("our boast and our glory"¹⁰¹) to others: "The eyes of the world are now turned upon us," Rodgers proclaimed, "to see in what manner we rear the superstructure, and what use we make of the liberty we have been so earnest to obtain . . . *with us* it lies to give an example, whether mankind is capable of freedom."¹⁰²

Yet progress was at best problematic. At the first founding, Winthrop had told his band of immigrants that the choice was their own—to live up to the covenant and be rewarded, or to falter and be destroyed. In his shipboard sermon, he had counseled solemnly, "let us choose life."¹⁰³ Post-Revolutionary orators repeated his admonition. Frequently they reminded their audiences of the distinct possibility of political decline. A surprisingly large number worried that the republic might be failing already, as factionalism and party spirit replaced patriotism and concern for the common good. Bonds were not being discharged, taxes not levied, and public credit not maintained. Worst of all, citizens seemed unconcerned. The orators made it clear that political failure would be a matter of public responsibility. Pervasive in their language was a profound sense of obligation: "our option," "our choice," "our conduct," "our folly," "our guilt." As always, God was watching his chosen people. Should they fail, warned the dour Presbyterian John Murray, Americans would surely become a "monument to his tremendous judgments."¹⁰⁴ In the same manner, to fail would bring disgrace on "the ancestors from whose loins we spring."¹⁰⁵ Finally, as if these burdens were not enough, all the world would be affected. A number of the orations cited the admiring Englishman Richard Price: "The consequences will be," Price had declared ominously, "that the fairest experiment, ever

⁹⁸ Tappan, *A Discourse*, p. 11.
⁹⁹ Buckminster, *A Discourse*, p. 24.
¹⁰⁰ Rodgers, *Divine Goodness*, p. 11.
¹⁰¹ Osgood, *Reflections*, p. 25.
¹⁰² Rodgers, *Divine Goodness*, p. 31.
¹⁰³ Winthrop, *Model*, in *American Puritans*, p. 84.
¹⁰⁴ Murray, *Jerubbaal*, p. 56.
¹⁰⁵ Ibid., p. 62.

tried in human affairs will miscarry; and that a revolution that had revived the hopes of good men, and promised an opening to better times, will become a discouragement to all future efforts in favor of liberty, and prove only an opening to new scenes of human degeneracy and misery."[106]

The result was anxiety and ambivalence. Never before had a people been so blessed. "Perhaps there never was a nation," observed Rodgers, "that had the fair opportunity of becoming the happiest people on earth, that we now have."[107] By the same token, never before had a people borne such a burden. "But *misery*," Rodgers went on, "as well as *happiness*, lies before us, (and both in the extreme) unless the present state of things is wisely improved by us. They are both at our option."[108] Perhaps most troubling of all, never before had the rest of the world seemed so interested: "And heaven and earth are looking with eager expectation to see which we shall choose."[109]

At stake was the nation's very survival. In his Circular Letter, Washington captured the momentous significance of the situation. The events of the postwar period would prove, he predicted, "whether the revolution must be considered a blessing or a curse."[110] At the same time, he pointed to the situation's unpredictability, for, as he admitted, it remained to be seen whether the new nation would "stand or fall."[111] The practical result was a sense of uncertainty, along with an urgency that made the period seem portentous from the start. It was, Washington summed up with his usual solemnity, "the moment to establish or ruin their character forever."[112]

With the winning of the war, American thinkers confronted the issue of their independence, turning back to the past in search of themselves, their purpose as a people. On the whole, history gave them little help. Instead, they found conflict, or at least they found themselves to be at odds, for where evangelicals saw their ancestors as a chosen people dedicated to the cause of religious revival, rationalists described them as a society of rugged individualists pursuing property and profit. More often, in turning to the past they found contradiction and uncertainty, in that most tended to consider themselves inheritors of both of these traditions. Hence, their political thought was from the start fragile and unsettled, a contradictory combination of the sacred and secular that drew them in two directions at once.

Yet the important point is that in reconsidering their history, they had

---

[106] Richard Price, D.D., *Observations on the Importance of the American Revolution, and the Means of Making it a Benefit to the World* (Boston: Powars and Willis, 1784), p. 7.

[107] Rodgers, *Divine Goodness*, p. 37.

[108] Ibid.

[109] Ibid.

[110] Washington, "Circular Letter," in *Writings*, 10: 256.

[111] Ibid., 257.

[112] Ibid., 256.

begun to reformulate their politics. The transition to a new way of political thinking had barely begun. Having looked to those incomparable moments of creation, and found little in the way of inspiration or instruction, they began to turn more to the times that followed them, attempting to arrive at some sense of the changing character of their history. Here, in considering their conceptions of change, they would for the first time come into real conflict.

◄2►

CHANGE

Themes of Decline and Progress

FOR A PAST-CONSCIOUS PEOPLE, the early 1780s was a disconcerting time. Independence had announced a break with the past. Whatever the continuity, and there was considerable, the transition to peacetime brought with it unprecedented problems. Old social patterns were everywhere giving way to new ones, as a Tory society was replaced by a Whig one. New businesses were being formed, new lands opened, new fortunes founded. Political affairs were chaotic, because government had all but disappeared during the last days of the war, and was only now reviving. In response, concerned citizens sought a sense of continuity. Having looked to the past and found few precedents, they began to revise their reading of history, searching not so much for customs or conventions as for connections, charting the course that events had followed from the beginning down to their own day. In essence, they can be seen as attempting to forge a concept of historicity, through which they could connect the past to the present. In the midst of remarkably rapid changes, they found themselves searching for the meaning of change.

Over the last few years, there has been much debate concerning the concept of change in the late eighteenth century. At issue has been the relative importance of the themes of corruption and decay on the one hand, and progress on the other. Crucial in making the case for corruption has been Gordon Wood, who in his *Creation of the American Republic* argued that eighteenth-century republicanism, far from being premised on progress, was grounded instead in an historical theory of moral and political decline. As Wood described it, republican theory held that states tended to decay over time, following an inexorable course from freedom to tyranny. In effect, according to this interpretation, early republicans believed that time ran downhill, and that corruption was the way of the world.[1] Very much in contrast, Joyce Appleby has asserted that progress was not only present but prominent in eighteenth-century thinking. Indeed, Appleby has argued that, although certain Federalists tended to maintain a belief in corruption,

---

[1] Wood, *Creation*, pp. 3–46. See also Gordon S. Wood, "Conspiracy and the Paranoid Style: Causality and Deceit in the Eighteenth Century," *The William and Mary Quarterly*, 3rd ser., 39, 3 (July 1982); 401–41; J. R. Pole, *Political Representation in England and the Origins of the American Republic* (London: Macmillan, 1966); and Bailyn, *Ideological Origins*, pp. 55–93.

most Republicans—and, by implication, most Americans at the end of the century—had faith in an improved and ever-improving future, what she called "the principle of hope."[2]

To a great extent, the debate has been framed in Pocock's terms. In an early essay, Pocock suggested that eighteenth-century republican thought could be understood as a continuing conflict between an identifiable party of corruption and historical decline, practitioners of what he called "country" philosophy, and a party of commercial and historical progress, consisting of "court" thinkers.[3] Elaborating on the suggestion, and applying it to America, James Hutson, Lance Banning, and John Murrin have all demonstrated the existence of this country–court division in early American politics, and have traced out the relative influence of these parties over a period of several decades.[4] Recently, in reviewing his earlier treatment of eighteenth-century England, Pocock has come to admit that the country–court dichotomy may well have been overstated, and that the division between parties of corruption and progress may not have been as clear or as extreme as he earlier had suggested.[5] In the case of America, however, he has remained firm, insisting that the centerpiece of early American political thought was the clash between country and court, the continuing conflict between the parties of corruption and progress.[6]

In truth, America was hardly so exceptional. Country and court did indeed do battle in the late eighteenth century. In the early 1780s especially, responding to postwar prosperity, country and court contingents would clash repeatedly. But the battle lines were not always clear. That is, in the process of adapting their classical republican principles to the realities of a modern liberal economy, at least some Americans could be found combining themes of corruption and progress with surprising alacrity.[7] Fearful of decline but hopeful about the possibilities for human betterment, these tran-

---

[2] See Appleby, *Capitalism and a New Social Order*, pp. 79–105. See also her "What Is Still American in the Political Philosophy of Thomas Jefferson?" *The William and Mary Quarterly*, 3rd ser., 39, 2 (April 1982): 294–97.

[3] J.G.A. Pocock, "Virtue and Commerce in the Eighteenth Century," *Journal of Interdisciplinary History*, 3, 2 (Summer 1972): 119–34.

[4] See James H. Hutson, "Country, Court, and Constitution: Antifederalism and the Constitution," *The William and Mary Quarterly*, 3rd ser., 38, 2 (July 1981): 337–68; Banning, *The Jeffersonian Persuasion*, pp. 51–69; and Murrin, "The Great Inversion," pp. 404–30.

[5] See J.G.A. Pocock, "Cambridge Paradigms and Scotch Philosophers: A Study of the Relations Between the Civic Humanist and the Civil Jurisprudential Interpretation of Eighteenth-Century Social Thought," in *Wealth and Virtue*, ed. Istvan Hont and Michael Ignatieff (Cambridge: Cambridge University Press, 1983), pp. 235–52.

[6] Ibid., p. 252.

[7] Drew R. McCoy has made a similar suggestion in *The Elusive Republic* (Chapel Hill, N.C.: University of North Carolina Press, 1980), p. 10.

sitional thinkers, including leaders such as Washington and Madison, can
be seen as attempting to create a more comprehensive concept of change
and, with it, a politics more appropriate to their changing times. Yet at least
in this early postwar period, their attempt was not entirely successful, leaving them fearful and hopeful at the same time and, as a result, confused and
frustrated.

Historical Decline

Although today it seems hard to conceive, eighteenth-century Americans
did not all believe in progress. Indeed, by education and inclination, they
were predisposed to hold that history, far from progressing upward, followed a downhill course of degeneration and decay. In ancient philosophy,
they found perfect states existing in the past: in the ancient myth of the
Golden Age; in philosophical utopias like that of Plato, set some nine thousand years before the birth of Solon; or in historical precedents like Periclean Athens or the Roman republic. By the same token, in reading late
medieval and early modern theory, they saw the world depicted as in decline: the soils growing barren and the seas foul, people becoming shorter
in stature and less intelligent, the sun itself growing cold.[8] Much of their
popular literature suggested that corruption was the universal characteristic
of civilization, and that progress was in fact synonymous with decline.[9] But
in republican theory in particular, and notably in the work of Montesquieu,
Americans of this early era found history described as a process of decay in
which states tended to follow a well-worn course from freedom to tyranny.[10]

Applied to politics, the theory suggested that things got worse before
they got better. Pocock described how English country Whigs had relied
on the classical republican principle of corruption to explain the disillusioning decline from the enlightened monarchy of the Glorious Revolution to
the autocratic kings of their own time.[11] Bailyn showed how American republicans had taken up the idea, describing the Revolution of 1776 as a last
desperate attempt to halt the decline of the Hanoverian Court.[12] Yet as Hutson, Banning, and Murrin have all suggested, after Independence the as-

[8] J. Huizinga, *The Waning of the Middle Ages* (1924; reprint, Garden City, N.Y.: Doubleday,
1954), pp. 31–54.

[9] Lois Whitney, *Primitivism and the Idea of Progress in English Popular Literature of the Eight-
eenth Century* (Baltimore: Johns Hopkins Press, 1934), pp. 42–44. See also Victor Harris, *All
Coherence Gone* (Chicago: University of Chicago Press, 1949), pp. 1–46; and Randolph Starn,
"Meaning-Levels in the Theme of Historical Decline," *History and Theory*, 14 (1975): 1–31.

[10] See Montesquieu, *The Spirit of Laws*, ed. David Wallace Carrithers (Berkeley, Calif.: University of California Press, 1977), pp. 170–79.

[11] Pocock, *Machiavellian Moment*, pp. 506–52.

[12] Bailyn, *Ideological Origins*, pp. 55–93.

sumption did not disappear, for Americans could commonly be found contending that their infant republic was as capable of degeneration as any
other state. The highly respected Reverend McClintock, one of the leaders
of New Hampshire's Congregationalists, made the point most eloquently in
his 1784 address to the legislature: "All empires have had their period, and
without doubt ours, like them, will also be lost in the lapse of time."[13]

Theologically, evangelicals were predisposed to think in terms of degeneration. From its beginnings in the early seventeenth century, Protestant
theology had been based on the concept of original sin, the idea that with
the fall from grace humanity had been condemned to eternal damnation.
Nor was there anything mortals could do to return to the state of paradise,
for no good works, good thoughts, or good intentions could win the sinner
a place in heaven. Salvation was God's free gift alone; the Puritan deity was
an unpredictable despot who handed out salvation according to his own
unfathomable purposes, offering immortality equally to the unbelieving, the
degenerate, and sometimes even the unrepentant. Conversely, this capricious God seemed just as likely to consign the best people to the fires of
eternal damnation.[14] Later Protestants, relying on their ingenious work
ethic, would propose that clean living and hard work would ease the way
along the road to eternity. But even in the 1780s, evangelicals were holding
out against such heresy. The Reverend Charles Turner, minister of a Dux-
bury, Massachusetts, church, was typical of those who used their pulpits to
denounce the decline of true religion. Americans were, he advised in 1783,
"on the whole, as sinful, or more sinful, than they were, when the war com-
menced." Although no Calvinist, Turner was nonetheless uncompromising
when it came to corruption, for he saw apostasy all around him, as Puritan
faith declined into Yankee secularity. He denounced this spirtual degeneracy, the "disregard to the Lords-Days, and Christian institutions, pro-
phaneness, and deism." In the election sermons of the times, those such as
Turner commonly could be found making the case that corruption was,
sadly enough, more pronounced than ever. The sins of all Americans, he
warned his Boston audience, were "so great and aggravated" that they
ought "to be deeply humbled, in the sight of God, confessing our merit of
utter destruction."[15]

In the same manner, evangelicals found corruption in their reading of
Biblical history. Protestant historiography had been based largely on the
principle of generational decay, the idea that extraordinary parents were
succeeded by undistinguished children. In earliest times Adam had been

[13] McClintock, *A Sermon*, p. 42.
[14] See Perry Miller, *The Seventeenth Century*, pp. 365–97.
[15] Charles Turner, V.D.M., *Due Glory to be given to God. A Discoure . . . May 15, 1783 . . .*
(Boston: T. and J. Fleet, 1783), pp. 13; 17–18.

followed by Cain, Abraham by Ishmael, Isaac by Esau. The strongest kings of Israel had given way all too often to its weakest leaders. According to this reading of the Bible, its history suggested that times of upbuilding would be followed by periods of breakdown. Moreover, as Robert Middlekauff has shown, because seventeenth-century and early eighteenth-century historians interpreted the past by using the method of typology, contending that certain events prefigured or "typified" others, they could describe Israel as an ancient archetype of their modern chosen nation.[16] Hence they read their own colonial history as a similar story of decline, with heroic founders having been succeeded by backsliding children, and pious Puritans followed by later generations of doubters and deists.

With the Revolution, American patriots contended that they had recaptured some of the heroism of their original mission. In their wartime sermons, patriotic preachers had described American Revolutionaries as Israelites being led out of Egyptian enslavement or breaking free from Babylonian captivity, conquering their enemies under the heroic leadership of Moses, Nehemiah, and Joshua. With peacetime, however, the references to religious history seemed to change, for in the election sermons of 1784 and 1785, the children of Israel were shown in the Promised Land, "soon after their happy settlement in the land of Canaan," "in the times of their Judges and Kings," or in "their highest state of wealth and power under the reign of Solomon."[17]

After 1783, evangelical ministers referred repeatedly in their sermons to these times of peace and prosperity that were also, paradoxically enough, periods in which piety had deteriorated and moral character declined. Applied to America, the message was unmistakable. Yale's Professor of Divinity Samuel Wales explained the thinking in a sermon preached before the Connecticut General Assembly: "Scarcely a prosperous period in their history can be pointed out," observed Wales of the Israelites, "which was not followed by a decay of piety, and a corruption of morals."[18]

The same perception of corruption was common in the way classical republican thinkers read civil history. Throughout the eighteenth century, classical republicans had been citing examples endlessly of the decline and fall of corrupt states. From ancient Babylon and Persia to modern Venice and the Dutch republics, they found the insidious effects of peace and prosperity. But as Bailyn has shown, those of the Revolutionary era were particularly fascinated with the history of republican Rome, which they read as a

[16] On typology, see Robert Middlekauff, *The Mathers* (New York: Oxford University Press, 1971), pp. 96–112.

[17] Samuel Wales, D.D., *The Dangers of our national Prosperity; and the Way to avoid them. A Sermon* . . . (Hartford, Conn.: Barlow and Babcock, 1785), p. 8.

[18] Ibid.

secular prototype for republican America.[19] During the Revolution, classical republicans had concentrated on the founding and early formation of the Roman republic, emulating the heroes and statesmen of these early days. Afterward, by contrast, they tended to look more often to the corruption and decline of the Roman state. As long as Rome was at war, its citizens remained committed and virtuous. As soon as it entered a period of peace, they became selfish and morally weak. With the final victory over Carthage, recalled Boston's Gardiner in his 1785 oration, piety had lapsed, "all veneration for religion, oaths, justice, modesty, and decency become annihilated." Moral character had declined, as Romans became "selfish, avaritious, factious, dissipated, rapacious, and effeminate." Eventually law and discipline had broken down, becoming, in Gardiner's words, "neglected and contemned."[20]

The Roman republic provided proof that with peace and prosperity, republics would tend to become tyrannies. Freedom required virtue, the commitment of citizens to check the power of their rulers by staying vigilant, keeping informed, and acting when necessary to protect their liberties. Peace, on the other hand, brought complacency, along with the invitation for rulers to become tyrants. To classical republicans emerging from the Revolution, the example of postwar Rome seemed all too applicable to their own situation: "unless we are properly apprized of, and duly armed against this evil," warned the patriot physician Dr. John Warren in the first of Boston's Fourth of July orations, "the *United States* will *one day* experience a similar fate."[21]

Taken together, these evangelicals and classical republicans can be seen as propounding a postwar version of American country philosophy. Human nature was flawed; faith was fragile; freedom was always threatened. Under these conditions, virtue and constant vigilance were essential. But because peace and prosperity brought ease and indulgence, they promised certain decline. "So nearly is the most prosperous condition of a people, allied to decay and ruin," Warren explained, "that even this flattering appearance conceals the seeds, that must finally produce her destruction."[22]

These care-worn republicans had little doubt that their own new nation would travel this same path. That commerce brought corruption was a universal truth, the "experience of mankind in every age," Wales concluded, "and in every part of the world."[23] The youth of the new republic mattered

[19] See Bailyn, *Ideological Origins*, p. 26. For background on classical republicanism, see Wood, *Creation*, pp. 46–90.

[20] Gardiner, *An Oration*, pp. 9; 8–9.

[21] John Warren, *An Oration, Delivered July 4th, 1783* . . . (Boston: John Gill, 1783), p. 20.

[22] Ibid.

[23] Wales, *Dangers*, p. 23.

little, for young states like young people could easily be lulled into complacency. In fact, as the Reverend Asa Burton suggested, young states were
even more susceptible, in that their immaturity left them heedless of the
dangers around them. Even their youthful energy worked against them, for
in rapidly creating new wealth, they would rapidly discover new vices, leading them swiftly and surely, in Burton's words, "to a shameful end."[24]
Thus, even at the moment of Independence, these country republicans were
resigned to the fact that before long their infant republic would become
corrupted from within. "Prevailing vice will assuredly sap our privileges
sooner or later," concluded the Reverend Rodgers in his 1784 sermon on
the peace; "nor is any great length of time necessary for this fatal purpose."[25]

To country republicans, historical theory required a politics premised on
corruption. Their sermons and speeches suggest a republican version of the
Protestant jeremiad. For more than a century, American Protestants had
relied on the jeremiad sermon, a ritual of contrition and commitment, to
turn their concern over corruption into a resolution to reform. As Perry
Miller showed, the late seventeenth-century jeremiad preachers denounced
their congregations repeatedly, admonishing them for their sins and reminding them of their weaknesses. In addition, they insisted on abasement,
requiring that their people apologize to God for their mistakes, atoning for
their sins through renewed dedication. Through this admission of weakness, these early congregations found strength, as in their desperation they
discovered the commitment to continue in their mission.[26] On the eve of the
Revolution, patriotic clergy had relied on a political version of the sermon
to implore Revolutionaries to repent their sins and throw off the corrupt
government that had brought them into iniquity.[27] After the war the jeremiad format remained surprisingly influential, for ministers persisted in decrying the loss of the old religion. More important, it retained its political
role, for country orators frequently adopted the incantation to denounce the
decline of republican virtue, the breakdown of "industry, economy, frugality" into "luxury, dissipation, extravagance."[28] Preachers and orators alike
joined in the ritual, warning of the perils of prosperity, the "pride, and avarice," "luxurious excesses, and superfluities," "extensive commerce, and
accumulated opulence."[29] Many of their sermons celebrating the peace,
while filled with enthusiasm and high hopes, were remarkably somber in

[24] Asa Burton, A.M., *A Sermon Preached at Windsor . . . on the Day of the Anniversary Election, October 13, 1785* (Windsor, Vt.: Hough and Spooner, 1786), p. 22.
[25] Rodgers, *Divine Goodness*, p. 41.
[26] See Miller, "Errand into the Wilderness," in *Errand*, pp. 1–15.
[27] See Morgan, "The Puritan Ethic and the American Revolution," pp. 6–7.
[28] McClintock, *A Sermon*, p. 35.
[29] Turner, *Due Glory*, p. 33.

their assessment of the future. For these republican Jeremiahs, corruption remained an ancient and insidious enemy. "Although it is possible that we may be a flourishing and happy people," Yale's gloomy Reverend Wales balefully declared to Connecticut's legislators, "it is equally possible we may be far otherwise. When we have reached the pinnacle of our hopes, it is often connected with evils far greater than the loss of that envied height would have been."[30]

Historical Progress

At the same time, nearing the close of the eighteenth century, others had begun to explore an early concept of progress. The idea was by no means novel, for although the fear of decline has been one of the oldest and most enduring of Western ideas, the faith in development has been persistent and undeniable. Arthur Lovejoy found that as early as the sixth century B.C. Presocratic philosophers were making the case for the cumulative character of human knowledge. Plato and Aristotle themselves at times seemed to describe a continuous course of improvement in philosophy and the arts. Hellenistic and Roman philosophers embraced the theme.[31] In more recent times, however, especially after the mid-seventeenth century, the idea of progress became infectious: early modern theologians like George Hakewill began to rebut the theory of cosmological corruption; scientists like Sir Francis Bacon showed that the soil was not growing barren or the seas foul; philosophers like Bodin and Le Roy contended that the Golden Age had been a myth and that ancient civilizations were in fact no match for modern times.[32] By the beginning of the eighteenth century, Enlightenment thinkers like Bernard Mandeville were advancing the proposition that the private pursuit of pleasure would lead, ironically but inevitably, to social progress, as society became cumulatively more productive and prosperous.[33]

In the course of the early eighteenth century, these assumptions, along with those of economic writers like Adam Smith, had come to be contained in a fairly consistent English court ideology, adopted by Tories as well as some Whigs, that held that the country concern with corruption was backward-looking and nostalgic, and that commercial development, along with the individualism, rationalism, and pragmatism it required, was the coming

[30] Wales, *Dangers*, p. 28.

[31] See Arthur O. Lovejoy and George Boas, *Primitivism and Related Ideas in Antiquity* (Baltimore: Johns Hopkins Press, 1935), pp. 194–259.

[32] See Toulmin and Goodfield, *The Discovery of Time*, pp. 106–10; Richard Foster Jones, *Ancients and Moderns* (St. Louis, Mo.: Washington University Studies, 1936), pp. 124–53; and Harris, *All Coherence Gone*, pp. 173–204.

[33] On Mandeville, see McCoy, *The Elusive Republic*, pp. 25–27.

way of the world.[34] By the end of the century, a significant and vocal number of American thinkers held a version of this commercial theory. Typical of them was the progressive Reverend William Symmes, minister of a North Andover, Massachusetts, church, who boasted in a 1785 election sermon that with the war behind them, the American people could now behold "a hopeful prospect of prosperity in times to come."[35]

At least in part, this idea of progress resulted from rational religion. From the mid-seventeenth century, liberal theologians had been speaking less about sin and more about salvation, softening their condemnation of depravity while stressing the potential for redemption. According to these theological reformers, Christians could impress heaven so much with their godly behavior that they might be admitted to immortality on the strength of their good works alone. In addition, they argued that godly behavior would be rewarded on earth as well as in heaven. By the end of the eighteenth century, liberal ministers could frequently be found contending that worldly success was all but synonymous with heavenly salvation. As Harvard's President Joseph Willard told a Boston congregation, God in his powers doled out prosperity as well as punishment. In the face of such largess, good Christians had a duty to be grateful, for a "grateful mind" was always "acceptable to God."[36]

In addition, because prosperity was a gift from heaven, it was their responsibility not only to accept but also positively to enjoy economic benefits. As the Reverend Samuel West informed his Needham, Massachusetts, parishioners, "to enjoy the blessings of Heaven is one mark of gratitude to him who bestowes them."[37] In fact, according to William Patten, one of the boldest of the rationalists, not only did Christians have an obligation to enjoy these advantages but also to increase them, it being "the duty of all, whom Providence succeeds, to improve their prosperity." God did not grant wealth to be wasted, to "shine in our coffers, or be lavishly squandered." Rather he required its constant investment, and was pleased, suggested the Reverend Patten, "when his blessings are suitably improved." For his part, God demonstrated his pleasure by increasing his bounty, for favors improved were favors multiplied. "We have," Patten concluded,

[34] See Pocock, "Virtue and Commerce," p. 128; Isaac Kramnick, *Bolingbroke and His Circle* (Cambridge, Mass.: Harvard University Press, 1968), pp. 70–76; and Appleby, "Social Origins," pp. 935–58.

[35] William Symmes, A.M., *A Sermon, Preached Before His Honor Thomas Cushing, Esq. . . . May 25, 1785 . . .* (Boston: Adams and Nourse, 1785), p. 22.

[36] Joseph Willard, A.M., *A Thanksgiving Sermon Delivered at Boston December 11, 1783 . . .* (Boston: T. and J. Fleet, 1784), p. 17.

[37] Samuel West, A.M., *Two Discourses Delivered at Needham, First Parish: On the Occasion of the Public Feast, April 7, 1785* (Boston: Benjamin Edes and Sons, 1785), p. 31.

"more reason to expect his blessings, if we suitably improve his gifts, than if we neglect the use of them."[38]

At the same time, these same rationalists began to reinterpret religious history, finding innovation and improvement where others had seen corruption and decline. Like other Protestants of the time, they emphasized the theme of deliverance, the redemption of the Jews from the persecution of their enemies. Similarly, they pictured Israel in the Promised Land, "their tents . . . spread along the banks of Jordan."[39] Yet unlike their evangelical colleagues, who considered peace and prosperity to be cause for great concern, these rationalists saw them as calling for celebration and thanksgiving. In a New Hampshire election sermon of 1785, the clergyman-historian Jeremy Belknap pointed approvingly to the example of King David, who, having delivered his people from the wrath of the Philistines, committed his reign to preserving an unprecedented period of peace. To the retiring and scholarly Belknap, who had observed the Revolution from the relative safety of his Dover, New Hampshire, pulpit, war was the worst of evils, tending "to deprave the morals of the people, as well as to take off the strength and flower of our youth from the labours of the field, to reduce our numbers, and invoke breaches in our families." Peacetime, on the other hand, allowed for the expansion of human energies into religion, education, and politics. "A time of peace," Belknap went on to tell New Hampshire's leaders, "is the proper season to make use of national advantages, and put things into a way of improvement." Above all, peace implied prosperity, the advancement of agriculture, the creation of manufactures, and the extension of trade. Belknap was explicit in calling for the establishment of a sound economic system, which he referred to as "the future means of national prosperity."[40]

In their reading of history, these revisionists said little about the course of corruption, picturing the era of the judges and kings as a happy and prosperous period. In the same way, they described their New World saga as a story of advancement rather than decline. It followed that they would look on the postwar period with little fear of corruption. Americans should "take care," insisted Harvard's redoubtable Willard, scion of one of Boston's oldest Puritan families, not to "run into . . . extravagance, luxury, and excess." Nevertheless, as long as they followed the "rules of reason and reli-

[38] William Patten, A.M., *Directions with Regard to the improvement of temporal blessings. A Thanksgiving Sermon* . . . (New London, Conn.: T. Green, 1784), pp. 12; 13.

[39] William White, D.D., *A Sermon, On the Due Celebration of the Festival, appointed as a Thanksgiving for the Fruits of the Earth* . . . (Philadelphia: Hall and Sellars, 1786), p. 4.

[40] Jeremy Belknap, *An Election Sermon, Preached Before the General Court, of New-Hampshire, at Portsmouth, June 2, 1785* (Portsmouth, N.H.: Melcher and Osbourne, 1785), pp. 29; 28–29; 11.

gion," they could be certain that their expanding economy would be a blessing instead of a curse. For those like Willard, there was no mistaking the advantages of prosperity: "The wise man says," he wrote, citing Ecclesiastes, "In a day of prosperity be joyful."[41]

In the same manner, rationalist thinkers offered a revised reading of republican history. None explicitly dismissed the course of corruption that had followed Rome from virtuous republic to decadent empire. Most, however, chose to avoid the theme, looking more to the rise of the republic than to its decline and fall. In an oration on *The Causes of National Prosperity*, the Harvard-educated Enos Hitchcock, himself a Congregational minister, followed the rise of Rome from its "most contemptible beginnings" to the point where "her glory filled that part of the world."[42] More often, rationalists chose to question the applicability of the Roman example altogether. "I have not, indeed yet thought of a Remedy for Luxury," Benjamin Franklin wrote to his friend Benajmin Vaughan. "I am not sure, that in a great State it is capable of Remedy." In fact, Franklin went on to confess that he for one was not certain "that the Evil is in itself always so great as it is represented."[43] The possibility of corruption still worried Franklin, who admitted his fears that excess earnings might be "dissipated in vain and needless Expences." However, in the modern world such wastefulness was unusual, he wrote in "The Internal State of America," "for there seems to be in every Nation a greater Proportion of Industry and Frugality, which tend to enrich, than of Idleness and Prodigality, which occasion Poverty; so that upon the whole there is a continual Accumulation."[44] Besides, there might well be nations in which corruption might never occur. "It has been asserted as an undeniable position," said the rapidly rising Boston lawyer Benjamin Hichborn, referring to the old theme of Roman corruption in a 1783 oration, "that luxury is the offspring of commerce and parent of vice; but we may say from experience, which is the best source of knowledge we possess, that there must be some exceptions to the rule."[45]

By the mid-1780s there was a sizable and growing number of Americans eager to argue that the new nation had little to fear from corruption. In

[41] Willard, *Thanksgiving Sermon*, p. 35.

[42] Enos Hitchcock, A.M., *A Discourse on the Causes of National Prosperity . . . Addressed to the Society of the Cincinnati . . . July 4, 1786* (Providence, R.I.: Bennett Wheeler, 1786), p. 12.

[43] Benjamin Franklin to Benjamin Vaughan, 26 July 1784, in *The Writings of Benjamin Franklin*, ed. Albert Henry Smyth (New York: Macmillan, 1905–1907), 9: 243. On Franklin's changing view of luxury, see Drew R. McCoy, "Benjamin Franklin's Vision of a Republican Political Economy for America," *The William and Mary Quarterly*, 3rd ser., 35, 4 (October 1978): 625.

[44] Franklin, "The Internal State of America," 1786, in *Writings*, 10: 121.

[45] Benjamin Hichborn, Esq., *An Oration, Delivered July 5th, 1783 . . .* (Boston: John Gill, 1784), p. 18.

essence, these rationalist reformers can be seen as creating an American court party. Practitioners of the Protestant ethic, the liberal Christians among them, were pleased with the blessings of prosperity: *"eat thy bread with joy,"* Patten assured his New London, Connecticut, congregation, *"and drink thy wine with a merry heart."*[46] Unswerving in their patriotism, the more explicitly political thinkers like Hichborn believed that their new-model republic was inherently more virtuous than previous examples: "in a country like this, which knows no distinction but that which arises from merit," he counseled, "where honors are not to be purchased or the people won by the false splendor of prodigality, we have nothing to fear from the profusion of wealth which is tendered to us by the generous hand of commerce."[47] Sure in their commitment to the marketplace, the commercial capitalists in the ranks pointed out that in America shippers had always imported luxuries, merchants sold fine wares, and consumers bought expensive goods, but the people had maintained both moral character and economic comfort: "we bought and consum'd them," Franklin declared, "and yet we flourish'd and grew rich."[48] These reformers were well aware of the dangers of degeneration. Sonner or later, Hichborn admitted, Americans might well "become depraved in principle and dissolute in manners, till the pulse of republican virtue shall cease to beat." For the present, however, they assumed that the process of corruption would be extremely slow. Americans, Hichborn assured his Boston audience, held their "prosperity at command."[49]

After 1783, these court reformers began to formulate a more modern version of republican theory, based effectively on this early idea of progress. While these writers did not assume that improvement was inevitable, they did maintain that constant initiative would lead to a steadily improving state. As for the jeremiad, they had little use for its sour pessimism. Indeed, Bercovitch has argued convincingly that the Puritan ritual of confession had always contained an element of affirmation and exultation. In confessing their weaknesses, he contends, early Protestants also managed to celebrate their strengths, affirming their place as God's chosen people, confirming heaven's interest in their mission, and at times even calling attention to their own extraordinary accomplishments. Bercovitch showed that throughout the eighteenth century this element of celebration remained implicit in the jeremiad sermon.[50] By the end of the century, however, some had begun to emphasize this theme almost exclusively. Benjamin Franklin, for example,

[46] Patten, *Directions*, p. 5.
[47] Hichborn, *An Oration*, p. 19.
[48] Franklin, "The Internal State," in *Writings*, 10: 122.
[49] Hichborn, *An Oration*, p. 19.
[50] Bercovitch, *The American Jeremiad*, pp. 3–30.

expressed the change in story form. In the earliest days, he wrote in "The Internal State," church members had come together with ritual regularity to confess their weaknesses and recite their sins, praying for relief from their afflictions. On one typical day the congregation had gathered for its scheduled fast, "their Minds gloomy and discontented." In the course of the service, however, a simple farmer arose to say that although he had nothing against prayer and fasting, he thought it strange that they had never praised God for his blessings, while having "so often weary'd Heaven with their Complaints." How much better it would be, the farmer suggested, "if, instead of a Fast, they should proclaim a Thanksgiving."[51]

To Franklin, the story was symbolic of the decline of the jeremiad. In point of fact, by the mid-1780s thanksgivings were becoming as common as fasts in American Protestant churches. Furthermore, the same celebratory form had been adapted to republican politics, as warnings of prosperity dissolved into visions of ripening fields, populous towns, and busy harbors. For court republicans of the postwar period, the certainty of corruption had given way to the possibility of progress. In the foreseeable future, the ambitious Hichborn confidently predicted, we "must be independent, rich and happy."[52]

Country Perceptions

Throughout this period, country republicans could be found warning of economic corruption. Even during the war, concerned patriots had held out against the reckless expansion of the economy. The Christian Spartan Sam Adams had led the attack on what he called "Pomp & Parade," scornfully rebuking those who turned to "Superfluity of Dress & Ornament" rather than "support the Expense of cloathing a naked Army."[53] Long before the end of the war, Revolutionaries could commonly be found denouncing speculators, calling for sacrifice, and predicting economic catastrophe. The wartime jeremiads were few and insignificant, however, compared with the absolute deluge of condemnation that occurred afterward. Some writers contented themselves with criticizing British bankers and European financiers, whereas others denounced their own home-grown investors and speculators, "that smooth-speaking class of people, who mean to get their living out of others."[54] Only a few condemned the merchants, many of whom were in precarious economic positions. But, for the most part country thinkers

51 Franklin, "The Internal State," in *Writings*, 9: 116; 117.

52 Hichborn, *An Oration*, p. 19.

53 Samuel Adams to John Scollay, 30 December 1780, in *The Writings of Samuel Adams*, ed. Harry Alonzo Cushing (New York: G. P. Putnam's Sons, 1904–1908), 4: 236.

54 Wales, *Dangers*, p. 18.

placed the blame on consumers for their reckless overconsumption, pointing to what Adams called the "Equipage, the Furniture & expensive Living," the "Pride & Vanity of Dress," the "idle Amusement & expensive
Foppery."[55] Americans had been seduced by the charms of rapid commercial expansion. Even the most cautious of these republicans warned that
economic calamity would follow unless draconian measures were taken to
stem the rising tide of excess. To such thinkers, true to their belief in corruption, easy money promised speedy ruin: "our very prosperity," declared
the Reverend David Tappan in a 1783 sermon, "will finally destroy us."[56]

Furthermore, country thinkers saw economic prosperity as the cause of
most of their political problems. Their republicanism was premised on the
principle of civic virtue—the assumption that public action would always
come at private cost, that freedom required sacrifice. Understandably, they
felt uncomfortable with the liberal philosophy of enlightened self-interest.
As early as 1779 in the celebrated Lee–Deane affair, Virginia's republican
patrician Richard Henry Lee was warning that civic virtue was in decline,
that "there are Mandevilles among you who laugh at virtue, and with vain
ostentatious display of words will deduce from vice, public good."[57] Even
assuming that patriotism had not been pure at the beginning of the war, the
change from the golden days of 1774–1775 was disturbing. Returning to
America from Europe in 1780, William Bingham, the agent and diplomatic
representative of the Continental Congress, was struck by what he saw as
the transformation from patriotic self-sacrifice into speculating self-interest.
The sentiments of the people, he observed, were "no longer governed by
that pure, disinterested patriotism, which distinguished the Infancy of the
contest."[58] By 1781 John Jay was complaining that public good had been
overwhelmed by private interest, and that political life, as he confided to
General Philip Schuyler, consisted of nothing more than the "partial politics of self-interested and unfeeling land jobbers."[59]

In the postwar period, however, country republicans seemed nothing less
than astonished by the changes taking place around them. Veterans of the
Revolution had apparently assumed that the idea of civic virtue would be as

[55] Samuel Adams to John Adams, 2 July 1785, in *Writings*, 4: 315.

[56] Tappan, *A Discourse*, p. 17.

[57] Richard Henry Lee to Henry Laurens, 6 June 1779, in *The Letters of Richard Henry Lee*,
ed. James Curtis Ballagh (New York: Macmillan, 1911–14), 2: 62–63. On the Lee–Deane
conflict, see Wood, *Creation*, pp. 419–21. For the idea of civic virtue, see Hannah Arendt, *The
Human Condition* (Chicago: University of Chicago Press, 1958), pp. 22–78; Pocock, "Civic
Humanism and Its Role in Anglo-American Thought," in *Politics, Language, and Time*, pp.
80–103; and Pocock, *The Machiavellian Moment*, pp. 49–79.

[58] William Bingham to John Jay, 1 July 1780, in *The Correspondence and Public Papers of
John Jay*, ed. Henry P. Johnston (New York: G. P. Putnam's Sons, 1890–93), 1: 364.

[59] Jay to General Philip Schuyler, April 1781, in *Correspondence*, 2: 14.

prevalent in peace as in war. After 1783, it was clear to them that this assumption had been not only false but foolish. By the mid-1780s, they could be found lamenting the fact that public spirit had all but disappeared. "Private rage for property suppresses public considerations," Jay wrote to Washington in 1786, "and personal rather than national interests have become the great objects of attention."[60] Virtue, Washington observed sadly from his Mount Vernon retreat, had apparently "taken its departure from our land."[61]

One immensely important group of thinkers, which included leading Revolutionary figures such as Jay and Washington, seemed particularly disillusioned. In this group were transitional republicans—country thinkers who had also begun to embrace certain court tenets. In contrast to committed traditionalists like Sam Adams, these cautious modernizers could make the case that freedom and prosperity were, if not complementary, at least not totally inimical. In fact, they assumed that liberty could even be reconciled to moderate doses of luxury. Thus they envisioned a political economy that allowed for both the necessities ("necessaries") and the luxuries ("conveniencies") of life.[62]

In truth, these republicans-in-transition had given little thought to the inconsistencies involved in maintaining patriotism while at the same time seeking personal profit. Indeed, in the heady days following the peace, they assumed that liberty and property would both flourish in the free and expanding republican economy of the postwar period. Writing in his 1783 Circular Letter, Washington had cited the enormous potential of the period. The American people, he asserted, were from that time "surrounded with every thing, which can contribute to the completion of private and domestic enjoyment."[63] From that time, he counseled, citizens had the absolute duty to pursue private ends, attending, as he put it, "to the cheerful performance of their proper business."[64] At the same time, public life would apparently benefit, for economic enterprise, he advised, would "strengthen the hands of government."[65]

As early as 1783, however, certain of these thinkers, citing the disappearance of self-sacrifice and the rising tide of self-indulgence, had begun to

[60] Jay to George Washington, 27 June 1786, in *Correspondence*, 3: 204. For background, see Maier, *The Old Revolutionaries*, pp. xvii–xviii, 268–94.

[61] Washington to Jay, 18 May 1786, *Correspondence*, 3: 196.

[62] McCoy describes these transitional thinkers in his *The Elusive Republic*, p. 23. The reference to "necessaries" and "conveniences" is frequent enough that one can roughly categorize republican writers by their reliance on one, the other, or both. For background, see McCoy's discussion of Montesquieu (p. 77).

[63] Washington, "Circular Letter," in *Writings*, 10: 255.

[64] Ibid., 260.

[65] Ibid.

realize that patriotism and prosperity were not so easily reconciled. It was painful to see, the disillusioned General Schuyler admitted to Jay, that the American people gave "melancholy evidence, that however capable we were of bearing human adversity with magnanimity, we are too weak to support, with propriety, the prosperity we have so happily experienced."[66]

The disillusionment was exacerbated by changes they saw taking place in postwar politics. Revolutionary republicanism was a theory that antedated the marketplace, being based on a political economy of independent and self-sufficient freeholders. The self-selected republican aristocrats who had dominated Revolutionary politics considered themselves to represent all landholders, large and small alike, holding no private interest and speaking for no special class, but acting for the good of their fellow property-owning citizens as a whole. Yet in the postwar period, a new breed of politician had come into office, nonaristocrats whose major concerns seemed to be getting elected, along with helping themselves and padding the pockets of their political allies. Patricians like Jay and Washington seemed at first startled by the appearance of these marketplace politicians who "love their money better than their liberty."[67] By 1785, however, as veteran officials had begun to be defeated at the polls by upstart challengers, they were angrily attacking these newcomers as "not only the lowest but the most unworthy characters," "wretches that would disgrace the most despicable of all governments," and a faction "whose sole aim is to rise into importance on the ruins of others."[68]

Throughout the period, retired Revolutionaries could be found exhorting their fellow patriots, many of whom had retreated from public life in disgust or defeat, to maintain their places in government. "If the field is to be abandoned by men of Virtue," warned the South Carolinian Edward Rutledge, a signer of the Declaration of Independence who had continued on as a representative in the South Carolina legislature, "either from the clamour of the worthless, or the ingratitude of the foolish part of the faction, the condition of humanity would be wretched indeed."[69] Himself still deeply involved in Pennsylvania politics, Dr. Rush described his former colleagues as skillful mariners who, having steered the ship through the storm, had turned over the helm to their inexperienced crew. Jay also, writing from his office as Secretary of Foreign Affairs under the Confederation, could be found earnestly entreating his wartime comrades to stay active. Yet even in

[66] Schuyler to Jay, 18 February 1784, in *Correspondence*, 3: 113. See also Wood, *Creation*, pp. 413–25.

[67] William Livingston to Jay, 21 May 1783, *Correspondence*, 3: 47.

[68] Schuyler to Jay, 30 May 1785, in *Correspondence*, 3: 151.

[69] Edward Rutledge to Jay, 12 November 1785, in *Correspondence*, 3: 217. See also Wood, *Creation*, pp. 475–99.

1786, some among this group had come to the conclusion that the republic in its present form was already almost lost. "*We have probably*," Washington privately admitted, "*had too good an opinion of human nature in forming our confederation.*"[70]

Court Views

In contrast to these country thinkers, their court-style republican counterparts saw the postwar period in far more favorable terms. In general, while admitting problems, they pointed to the soundness of the new state, the fact that the nation's debt was small, its resources vast, and its people eager and industrious. Inflation was a major concern, but land values were up, crops were plentiful, and goods sold briskly in the towns and cities. There was local unemployment, but less than before the war, and labor received high wages everywhere. Politically there were some protests, but on the whole the people showed few manifestations of deep dissatisfaction. Especially after 1785, as postwar buying began to come under control, and the economy started to stabilize, references to better times were frequently heard. Correspondents writing to their friends abroad spoke in glowing terms of the expansion of agriculture and industry. Most prominent of these was Benjamin Franklin, who in a series of letters written in 1786 dismissed reports of economic troubles as English propaganda, and contended with all apparent confidence that Americans had never been more satisfied with their government, never more peaceful, and never more prosperous. Even considering the biases inherent in his unabashed boosterism, Franklin seemed honestly impressed with the progress of the new nation: "I never saw greater and more indubitable Marks of public Prosperity," he boasted in a letter to the Parisian banker Ferdinand Grand, "in any Country."[71]

These court thinkers commonly practiced an updated version of republican theory. Unlike their country counterparts, they did not assume that public virtue and private interest were inimical. Instead, they held that citizens could pursue personal concerns while doing no harm whatsoever to the polity as a whole. Proceeding on the theory developed by Mandeville, they argued that it was only when individual citizens pursued their own best interests, and those interests were combined with the interests of others, that the good of the general public could be served. The concept of civic virtue, it followed, while laudable, was inappropriate in a peacetime

[70] Washington to Jay, 15 August 1785, *Correspondence*, 3: 208. See also Rush, "On the Defects of the Confederation," 1787, in *The Selected Writings of Benjamin Rush*, ed. Dagobert D. Runes (New York: Philosophical Library, 1947), pp. 30–31.

[71] Franklin to Ferdinand Grand, 5 March 1786, in *Writings*, 9: 493. See also Merrill Jensen, *The New Nation* (New York: Vintage Books, 1950), pp. 245–57.

republic. The essayist-lexicographer Noah Webster took the position to its logical extreme, going so far as to suggest that such virtue was impossible. "Several writers on government and particularly the great Montesquieu," he observed, "maintain that virtue is the foundation of republics. If, by virtue is meant patriotism or disinterested public spirit, and love of one's country, . . . I must deny that such a principle ever did or ever can exist in human society." In republics above all, where political life was widely shared among the population, it was unreasonable to expect constant commitment to public service. Instead, Webster preferred to rely on self-interest, "the real principle that is predominant in every individual and directs his actions."[72]

Court republicans took up the theme, refusing to admit any distinction between public and private interest, speaking of "our happiness as individuals, as citizens," describing politics as an exercise in "public welfare and private bliss," and contending that the best government was one that combined "the principles of private and public justice and utility."[73] By creating profit, the industrious farmer or merchant grew rich. Nevertheless, his wealth also worked for the good of others, for, as America's leading political economist Peletiah Webster (no relation to the more famous Noah) explained, his product would "promote the wealth of the state." Far from fearing prosperity, the businessman-writer Webster saw it as the best insurance of freedom. A flourishing economy, he concluded in his *Essay on Credit*, was "the most valuable thing in society, it gives ease, it gives wealth, 'Tis a means of every social virtue, it makes a soil suitable for growth of public spirit and every public virtue."[74]

Some of these court thinkers, however, held at least a residual respect for the country idea of corruption. In fact, ironic as it seems, some of the most ardent attacks on postwar consumers were leveled by committed capitalists. In 1783, the American states had begun the transition from mercantilism to economic independence. It followed that American capitalists could in all innocence, and with complete consistency, denounce foreign mercantile corruption while praising domestic economic development. Among these was none other than Tench Coxe, the Philadelphia businessman and

[72] Noah Webster, Jun'r., Esq., *Sketches of American Policy* . . . (Hartford, Conn.: Hudson and Goodwin, 1785), p. 24n.

[73] Hitchcock, *National Prosperity*, p. 28; Enoch Huntington, A.M., *Political Wisdom, or, Honesty is the Best Policy, Illustrated in a Sermon* . . . (Middletown, Conn.: Woodward and Green, 1786), p. 18; Levi Hart, A.M., *The Description of a GOOD CHARACTER Attempted and Applied to the Subject of Jurisprudence and Civil Government. A Discourse* . . . (Hartford, Conn.: Hudson and Goodwin, 1786), p. 23.

[74] A Citizen of Philadelphia [Peletiah Webster], *An Essay on Credit* (Philadelphia: Eleazer Oswald, 1786), pp. 20; 12–13.

banker, organizer of the Pennsylvania Society for the Encouragement of
Manufactures, who could be found at this time castigating American buyers
for their "wanton consumption of imported luxuries."[75] Coxe made it clear
that his criticism was not of buying and selling, but of buying and selling
British luxury items. The artificial riches that were created by European
wage laborers benefited only conniving financiers, corrupt businessmen,
and improvident consumers. But the natural wealth that was the product of
virtuous American farmers and merchants could never lead to excess profit,
speculation, or waste. The result was perhaps the earliest example of American protectionism, a militant campaign to "buy American."[76]

For those like Coxe, transitional figures in their own right, virtue and
commerce were seen as complementary: frugality was called on in the cause
of prosperity; traditional religious values were put to use in creating the
infrastructure of the market; and the jeremiad became a servant of an emerging capitalism. The Reverend Belknap captured the inconsistencies inherent in this revised version of republicanism: "All attempts to introduce articles of luxury and needless expence should be carefully guarded against,"
he warned. "Every species of home-manufacture which can be carried to
advantage, ought to receive all possible encouragement; nor can we long
maintain the character of an independent people, unless we cultivate industry and economy."[77]

These transitional figures also seemed disillusioned with the course of
postwar politics. Very much like Jay and Washington, they had made the
assumption that virtue and commerce were compatible. Once again, recent
experience suggested otherwise.[78] Generally younger, these more cynical
but more realistic observers, including those like the youthful James Madison, placed little trust in the old patrician statesmen, and argued instead
for newer, more professional leadership. Yet they found the rising politicians of the time to be both immoral and incompetent—"designing, dishon-
est men," in the words of one, "the pests of society."[79] In the same way, they
had long campaigned for a politics of interest, arguing that government
should take steps to encourage both private profit and public credit. But
they seemed appalled by the selfishness of the newer postwar politicians,
and were quick to dissociate themselves from the "race of stockjobbers and

[75] Tench Coxe, *A View of the United States of America* . . . , *1787* (Philadelphia: William Hall,
1794), p. 5.

[76] See Brooke Hindle, *The Pursuit of Science in Revolutionary America, 1735–1789* (Chapel
Hill, N.C.: University of North Carolina Press, 1956), pp. 367–68.

[77] Belknap, *Election Sermon*, p. 27.

[78] On the attempt of these republicans to reconcile classical and modern precepts, see McCoy,
The Elusive Republic, p. 134; for background, see also his treatment of Hume on p. 29.

[79] Huntington, *Political Wisdom*, pp. 17; 16.

speculators" who, in Peletiah Webster's words, tended to "swarm, like flies about a sore, or crows around a carcase."[80] Above all, while considering themselves good republicans, they were angered by the behavior of the public, which appeared to be exercising its democratic right to destroy the nation's economy. How easy it was, Webster remarked acidly, for "one scabby sheep" to "spoil the whole flock."[81]

Among those most concerned with the issue of economic stability were nationalists like Robert Morris, Alexander Hamilton, and James Wilson. Throughout the war, they and their followers had urged the creation of a centralized fiscal policy, including the establishment of a state bank, the levying of congressional taxes, and the funding of the public debt. For years, they had been making the case for a stronger central government to oversee economic policy. From 1781 to 1783, in the desperate last years of the war, centralizers represented by Morris as superintendent of finance had exerted considerable political power. At its end, however, with the resurgence of prewar localism, the nationalists found themselves out of office with little to show for their efforts.[82] Frustrated and far from power, these disillusioned nationalists, who in other circumstances might have been expected to be singing the praises of prosperity, could express only anxiety about the future. "I fear," Hamilton lamented to Washington at the end of the war, "we have been contending for a shadow."[83]

Decline and Progress in Confederation Politics

After 1783, Americans came face to face with the issue of economic prosperity. At the war's end, the state governments had followed policies of rapid economic expansion, encouraging unprecedented imports, generating large amounts of paper money, and postponing payments of debts. Business revived, with consumers demanding previously scarce goods and merchants rushing to stay a step ahead in replenishing their war-depleted stocks. European shippers hurried their cargoes into American ports, offering ready credit and easy terms. American shopkeepers in turn provided every available article of European finery to their luxury-starved customers,

[80] A Citizen of Philadelphia [Peletiah Webster], *A Seventh Essay on Free Trade, and Finance* . . . (Philadelphia: Eleazer Oswald, 1785), p. 24.

[81] Ibid., p. 36.

[82] On the nationalists, see E. James Ferguson, "The Nationalists of 1781–1783 and the Economic Interpretation of the Constitution," *Journal of American History*, 56, 2 (September 1969): 241–61; idem, "Political Economy, Public Liberty, and the Formation of the Constitution," *The William and Mary Quarterly*, 3rd ser., 40, 3 (July 1983): 389–412; and Jensen, *The New Nation*, pp. 54–84.

[83] Alexander Hamilton to George Washington, 17 March 1783, in *The Papers of Alexander Hamilton*, ed. Harold C. Syrett (New York: Columbia University Press, 1961–), 3: 292.

who bought freely, then recklessly. Credit buying became common, hard money disappeared, and inflation followed. At best, the economy was exceedingly erratic.[84]

Yet thinkers of the time were predisposed to perceive these events in dramatically different ways, for where country republicans saw corruption and decay, their court contemporaries found the potential for prosperity and progress. These competing historical theories led to conflicting political positions. Predictably, country thinkers tended to rely on a theory of sacrifice and self-sufficiency, resisting the course of corruption by levying tariffs on imported goods and taxes on luxury items. For their part, court thinkers practiced a philosophy of commercial expansion, favoring free trade and lower commercial taxes. In the wake of economic confusion, the persuasions continued to polarize.

Caught in between were those growing numbers who saw events proceeding along no predictable path at all, for whom corruption and progress were both possible, and for whom neither was clearly the tendency of the times. Within this growing group there existed a diffuse sense of disillusionment, an ill-defined feeling that the new republic was foundering. A perspicacious David Humphreys captured the feeling best: citizens appeared "to be uneasy and to prognosticate revolutions," he reported from Connecticut in a letter to Thomas Jefferson, "but they hardly know how or why."[85]

Politically, the response to these perceptions was surprising. On the one hand, many counseled patience. Incongruously enough, among these were both country and court thinkers. Although unlikely, the alliance was probably predictable given their respective historical theories. To those aging Revolutionaries who assumed that decline was inevitable, the dislocations of the day were all too understandable. Like it or not, republics became corrupt over time. For the present, they reasoned, all that citizens could do was watch and wait, resisting when possible but resigning themselves in the long run to the inevitability of decline. In the same way, among the young modernizers there were those who counseled caution. For these believers in progress, the republic required only experience and maturity to set itself straight. At least for the present, proposals for reform were premature; citizens would do better to commit themselves to improving their existing governments gradually. All argued alike that Americans had emerged from the war with unrealistic expectations. The so-called Federal Farmer spoke for this diverse group, many of whom would later be found

[84] On the postwar economy, see Jensen, *The New Nation*, pp. 179–93. See also Jay to Benjamin Vaughan, 20 November 1784, in *Correspondence*, 3: 135.

[85] David Humphreys to Thomas Jefferson, 5 June 1786, in Jefferson, *The Papers of Thomas Jefferson*, ed. Julian P. Boyd (Princeton, N.J.: Princeton University Press, 1950–), 9: 609. On Confederation historiography, see Morris, "The Confederation Period," pp. 139–56.

opposing the new Constitution. They had simply "expected too much from the return of peace," Federal Farmer would write, "and of course we have been disappointed."[86]

On the other hand, there were those making the case for reform. Prominent among these early reformers were the transitional thinkers like Jay and Washington, for whom the turn from colonial protest to national government had been surprising and disturbing. Believers in corruption, they were nevertheless predisposed to encourage prosperity and progress. The contradictions inherent in their thinking left them open to confusion and easy disenchantment. Incredulity and despair was a common feature of their correspondence: "From the high ground on which we stood, from the plain path which invited our footsteps," Washington lamented in a 1786 letter to Jay, "to be so fallen! so lost! is really mortifying."[87]

By the same token, younger republicans like Madison, along with nationalists of the Morris–Hamilton–Wilson persuasion expressed equal if not greater distress. None had higher expectations, none more faith in the future than these champions of development. For them, the end of the war should have been the beginning of an age of progress, with strong government established, the public credit restored, and an able system of finances secured. Instead, they found their initiatives blocked at every turn by the same narrow provincialism that had been characteristic of colonial politics. In their own way, they too despaired of the events of the day. "What high expectations were formed concerning us by others!" Pennsylvania's Wilson would observe. "What high expectations did we form concerning ourselves."[88]

Together these two groups of transitional thinkers—disillusioned country thinkers led by Jay and Washington and frustrated court thinkers like Madison, Morris, Hamilton, and Wilson—would begin to converge, their common concerns leading them into alliances that would become the core of constitutional reform. In the mid-1780s, their influence was already increasing dramatically. In large part, their success would be a tribute to their reputations and personal resources, as well as to their talents and the strength of their personalities. But equally important was the fact that by 1787 growing numbers of thinkers, court and country alike, had come to the conclusion that some dramatically revised system was required to secure the new republic. Without such a change, dissolution seemed inevitable.

---

[86] The Federal Farmer to the Republican, "Observations . . . ," 8 October 1787, in *Complete Anti-Federalist*, 2: 226.

[87] Washington to Jay, 18 May 1786, in *Correspondence*, 3: 196.

[88] James Wilson, address to the Pennsylvania convention, 26 November 1787, *The Debates in the Several State Conventions on the Adoption of the Federal Constitution*, 2nd ed., ed. Jonathan Elliot (Philadelphia: J. B. Lippincott, 1861–63), 2: 430.

Stephen Higginson, one of Massachusetts's wealthiest merchants and a power in that state's politics, described what he saw as the coming calamity: "we appear to be verging fast to a Crisis," he warned. "A change of Ideas and measures must soon happen, either from conviction or necessity."[89]

Amid the disillusionment and uncertainty of the postwar period, Americans had turned to ideas of decline and progress in an attempt to create some sense of direction. In doing so, they had begun to diverge into competing camps, old-style critics of corruption on the one hand, new-model proponents of progress on the other. In between, there arose a growing group of transitional thinkers, increasingly frustrated by its inability to determine the direction of events, and increasingly determined to do something about it.

For these transitional thinkers, this frustration would be a source of inspiration. Confused and uncertain as they were, they had no alternative but to act, transcending the historical patterns, moving from a preoccupation with the past to a bolder concern for the present, and in the process, making a place for themselves in their politics. But in order to act, they first had to take the next step in transforming their political thinking. So it was that they took up the issue of reform.

[89] Stephen Higginson to John Adams, July 1786, "Letters of Stephen Higginson, 1783–1804," ed. J. Franklin Jameson, Talcott Williams, Frederick Jackson Turner, and William P. Nent, *Annual Report of the American Historical Association*, 1896, 1: 74.

PART TWO

Perceptions of the Present

⤙3⤚

REFORM

Cyclical Theory and the Idea of Imbalance

BY THE MID-1780S, critics had begun to consider the possibilities for re-
structuring the republic. In truth, however, they knew neither how nor
when. That is to say, thinkers of the time had little conception of the course
being taken by contemporary events, and even less of their own ability to
shape those events. So it was that before they could begin thinking about
how to reform their politics, they had first to take up the more fundamental
and more proximate problem of how to go about thinking about the meaning of reform.

In attempting to perceive some pattern to contemporary events, they
faced a formidable task. Even among relatively recent observers, writing
with the benefit of more or less dispassionate hindsight, few topics have
provoked more controversy than the character of the Confederation period,
to say nothing of such wildly dissimilar views. On one side, those like Forrest McDonald have contended that the era from the end of the Revolutionary War to the creation of the federal Constitution was a time of economic
confusion and political chaos, a "critical period" in which popular protest
became violent enough to threaten civil war. On the other side, critics of
this view led by Merrill Jensen have argued that the period was in fact
prosperous and relatively stable, that political protests were few and mostly
well behaved, and that, in short, the "critical period" was really not very
critical at all.[1] In any case, the character of the Confederation period remains controversial, a cause of contention that shows few signs of subsid-
ing.[2]

One approach to the problem has been to consider the concept of reform.
Beginning in 1959 with Caroline Robbins's *The Eighteenth-Century Com-
monwealthman*, and continuing through the following decade with Z. S.
Fink's *The Classical Republicans*, and Isaac Kramnick's *Bolingbroke and His
Circle*, historians of political theory have described how eighteenth-century
English Whigs combined themes of cyclical renewal and constitutional

---

[1] Compare Forrest McDonald, *E Pluribus Unum* (Indianapolis, Ind.: Liberty Press, 1965),
with Jensen, *The New Nation*, pp. 245–57. For background on the debates, see Morris, "The
Confederation Period," pp. 139–56.

[2] One recent restatement of the debate is Robert A. Goldwin and William A. Schambra, ed.,
How Democratic Is the Constitution? (Washington, D.C.: American Enterprise Institute, 1980).

63

equilibrium to create a classical Whig conception of reform, a happy amalgamation of civic vigilance and institutional order.[3] In a recent series of
studies, however, Pocock has shown that Whig republicanism was hardly
so serene. Beginning with an analysis of James Harrington, he described
how early republicans were able to synthesize the cyclical concept of revolution and the balanced model of constitutionalism, allowing, it seemed, for
both periodic reform and long-term stability. Yet he also showed that there
was always a tension in this curious combination of ideas; over time, the
strains began to show, with country Whigs, fearful of corruption, thinking
more in terms of cyclical decay and renewal, and court Whigs, concerned
for stability, turning more to schemes of institutional equilibrium.
Throughout the century, these two sides of the republican coalition would
continue to diverge, with the eventual collapse of the Whig idea of reform
taking place in America, where in the 1790s, according to Pocock, Jeffersonians would meet Federalists in what would become the final battle for
the soul of republican theory.[4]

Applied to the American "critical period," the argument is sound but
sketchy. Already in the mid-1780s, Americans were debating the meaning
of reform. Their discussions were heated and lengthy. Moreover, by the
middle of the decade two remarkably clear conceptions of political reform
had begun to appear, one cyclical and radical, the other balanced and conservative. In response to such traumatic events as Shays's rebellion, these
perspectives would continue to diverge, and thinkers would find themselves
being driven deep into competing camps, where they prepared to do battle
for their respective versions of reform. Here, in this highly charged ideological atmosphere, there seemed to be little room for confusion or doubt, and
even less for compromise.

The Idea of Periodic Revolution

In republican political thought, the earliest and most enduring theme has
been the idea of revolution. Its origins lay in a theory of cyclical renewal. In
the late eighteenth century, English Whigs drew on a vast set of sources to
validate their view that events took place according to a pattern of decline
and redemption. Their reading of classical history suggested that the ancient republics had followed a continuous cycle of founding, corruption, and
reform. In Polybius they found this historical process presented as a universal principle. Because they believed that in all ages similar causes produced
similar effects, these Whigs could apply this classical theory to modern

---

[3] Robbins, *Eighteenth-Century Commonwealthman*, pp. 3–21; Fink, *The Classical Republicans*; and Kramnick, *Bolingbroke and His Circle*, pp. 70–76.

[4] Pocock, *Machiavellian Moment*, p. 3; also see pp. 3–9, 462–552.

events, describing their own English history as an epic saga in which Saxon liberties gave way to Norman oppression, only to be rescued by republican patriots reasserting their ancient prerogatives in the Magna Charta. As patriotism waned, the rights of Englishmen gave way again to the power of the Stuart kings, who themselves were overthrown by a new generation of republicans. With the Glorious Revolution, the cycle was repeated. Already in the 1740s, as Stow Persons has shown, this cyclical theory had become pervasive in the thought of the American Enlightenment.[5] By the end of the century, American republicans would be taking the cyclical principle on faith: "To revert to first principles is so essentially requisite to public happiness and safety," explained an authoritative Dr. Warren to his Boston Fourth of July audience, "that Polybius has laid it down as an incontrovertible axiom, that every State must decline more or less rapidly, in proportion as she recedes from the principles on which she was founded."[6]

Cyclical theory assumed both corruption and renewal. Applying the Polybian scheme to the history of modern republics, Machiavelli had suggested in his *Discourses* that only the concerted action of virtuous citizens could pull states back from the final stages of decline, returning them to their original excellence. This theme, so crucial to creating the revolutionary strain in republicanism, was repeated by the radical Whig reformers, such as Harrington, Henry Neville, and Algernon Sidney, and, as Bailyn has shown, gained wide influence through the eighteenth-century libertarian tracts of John Trenchard and Thomas Gordon, who in the decades after 1688 called on their fellow republicans to rise up and recapture the liberties lost to scheming court politicians. Indeed, in the 1720s and 1730s, even Tory conservatives like Lord Bolingbroke would adopt the theory, arguing that a corrupted monarchy could be redeemed only by the introduction of a patriot prince. In effect, the popular idea of revolution implied restoration, the reversion to original principles. Before 1776 American radicals had made this cyclical reform the basic tenet of their own republican protest, arguing not for a radical break from their colonial oppressors, but a conservative return to their original constitutional rights—what Sam Adams liked to call the "true old English liberty." Even following Independence, some continued to make the case: The most effective means to the prevention of tyranny was "frequently [to] recur to *first principles*," the Reverend Buckminster observed in his 1784 sermon at Portsmouth, "as the only way of securing those rights, and of discovering the first encroachments of him who is *at heart* a tyrant."[7]

[5] See Stow Persons, "The Cyclical Theory of History in Eighteenth Century America," *American Quarterly*, 6, 2 (Summer 1954), 147–63.

[6] Warren, *An Oration*, p. 6.

[7] Buckminster, *A Discourse*, p. 31. See Bailyn, *Ideological Origins*, pp. 94–143. Perhaps the

This cyclical theory implied a politics of resignation and rebellion. Radical republicanism, assuming both declension and revision, combined long periods of watching and waiting with short bursts of protest. At best it was a psychologically demanding philosophy, for it required that citizens be constantly on guard against those ambitious leaders who would sacrifice public good for personal interest. The theory held that every ruler would sooner or later be corrupted by the prerogatives of power. As a result, republican radicals looked on their leaders as potential enemies. Buckminster cautioned his New Hampshire congregation: "Let us keep, not a *captious*, but, a *watchful* eye, over those in whose hands we place the reins of government." Americans had a duty to "support, encourage, and assist" rulers only so long as they "keep within the limits prescribed them by the Constitution." But as soon as leaders began to encroach on the rights of their subjects—and cyclical theory required that sooner or later they would "leap that impassible barrier"—citizens would need to act swiftly and surely to remove them, restoring their positions to more virtuous replacements. As to their fallen leaders, they had little sympathy: "let them return to the walks of private life," Buckminster suggested, almost smugly, "and recover the feelings of the *subject*, which they may have almost lost in those of the *ruler*."[8]

Radical republicans did rely on some constitutional antidotes to corruption. Early Whigs like James Burgh had argued that the surest invitation to tyranny was to allow politicians to hold power for long periods. Accordingly they had devised a series of constitutional checks radically limiting the length of public service.[9] Gordon Wood has shown how Americans of the Revolution made use of these limits in making their state constitutions. In all of the states, the tenure of office was severely restricted. The constitutions themselves varied widely, but most of them decreed that elections were held annually, offices were rotated (delegates being limited often to three years service in six, or four out of seven), and reelection was restricted.[10] In addition, in keeping with the principle of regular revision, most of them included statutes of limitation for laws, and sometimes even for offices. The determinedly democratic Pennsylvania charter, for example, provided that the state constitution itself be reviewed every seven years.[11] All told, the Revolutionary constitutions can be seen as institutionalizing

---

best account of this Copernican concept of revolution is Hannah Arendt, *On Revolution* (New York: The Viking Press, 1963), p. 35.

[8] Buckminster, *A Discourse*, p. 31.

[9] See Wood, *Creation*, pp. 127–32. Also helpful is Donald S. Lutz, *Popular Consent and Popular Control* (Baton Rouge, La.: Louisana State University Press, 1980), pp. 53–84.

[10] See Wood, *Creation*, pp. 132–61.

[11] See ibid., pp. 162–96.

the principle of periodic reform. In his 1784 Boston oration, Hichborn described the thinking: "But as the best of human systems may involve in them the seeds of future danger to people's rights, the constitution [he referred here to the Articles of Confederation] has wisely provided a periodical revision which must cure every possible defect."[12]

Yet periodic reform also required periodic protest. Constitutional checks went only so far. From time to time, power would have to revert to its original source in the people. Radical republicans considered government to be a painful sacrifice made mostly to the sad realities of international conflict. They accepted the role of the state in providing certain essential domestic services. But beyond the basics, they thought of government as a usurper of popular power. Stanley Elkins and Eric McKitrick have shown how their backgrounds in colonial politics had predisposed many of these radical republicans to assume that citizens would play an active role in politics, not only at annual elections, but also in the petition drives, town meetings, and mass assemblies that had been so common in the pre-Revolutionary period.[13] Even so seemingly conservative a republican as Hichborn, ironically one of Boston's justices of the peace, could refer back to the role of popular protest in the Revolution, recalling that the "right of meeting together uncontrouled" was "among the first privileges, reserved to the individual." Without these protests, suggested the plain-spoken jurist, the Revolution would have been "conquered without a struggle." Hence, the right of assembly had been repeatedly reaffirmed in the state constitutions, "expressly secured to the people." As to any fears of disorder, radical republicans maintained that popular participation would assure not only freedom, but stability, the "freedoms of a state of nature," as Hichborn put it, without "those inconveniences which so naturally and almost necessarily flow from such a situation."[14]

It followed that in cyclical theory the ultimate remedy to corruption was revolution. Petitions and protests could serve as palliatives, but the only antidote to tyranny was periodic rebellion. After all, many of these radical thinkers were themselves experienced revolutionaries. For some, their entire public lives had been given to the cause of resistance. Having survived and thrived through two decades of protest and war, they saw rebellion as a natural, even normal state of political affairs. In the final analysis, Jefferson would observe, the "irregular interpositions" of popular protests were the

[12] Hichborn, *An Oration*, p. 13.

[13] See Stanley Elkins and Eric McKitrick, "The Founding Fathers: Young Men of the Revolution," *Political Science Quarterly*, 76, 2 (June 1961): 200–206.

[14] Hichborn, *An Oration*, pp. 5; 6; 13. On popular protest in the Revolution, see Gordon S. Wood, "A Note on Mobs in the American Revolution," *The William and Mary Quarterly*, 3rd ser., 23, 4 (October 1966): 635–42.

"only safeguard of the public liberty."[15] Republics did well to foster a pre-disposition to rebellion: "The spirit of resistance to government is so valu-able on certain occasions," he wrote to Abigail Adams, "that I wish it to be always kept alive."[16] Rebellion was a periodic purge to cure the diseases of the corrupt state, "a medicine," as Jefferson told Madison, "necessary for the sound health of government."[17] In short, to these radical reformers a little revolution now and then was a good thing. As Jefferson concluded in the most eloquent statement of the cyclical theory, "The tree of liberty must be refreshed from time to time with the blood of patriots and tyrants."[18]

The Idea of Constitutional Balance

A second strain in republican theory was the concept of constitution. Its origins lay in the twin themes of balance and excess, ideas as important to conservative republicans as cyclical renewal was to their radical counter-parts. Conservative Whigs held that well-ordered states required the well-ordered interplay of their parts. In Aristotle, they found the constitution of a state described less as a document than as a set of assumptions about the rights and responsibilities of each member of society. In the well-consti-tuted regime, citizens would limit their own desires in order to secure the stability of the state. In the flawed system, however, they would throw off these limits, pursuing their own interests at the expense of social order. Eventually their excesses would create an imbalance between groups that would lead to conflict.[19] In a review of almost two hundred ancient revolu-tions, Aristotle had found repeated examples of this imbalance. Further-more, unlike Polybius, he saw no pattern of cyclical return. On the contrary, to Aristotle's thinking, the revolutions of the ancient republics seemed to end all too often in chaos and in that worst of horrors, civil war.

As Douglass Adair has shown, many eighteenth-century Americans em-braced this Aristotelian theory. Their reading of classical history pictured the ancient states beset by conflicts between kings and nobles, aristocrats and democrats, rich and poor.[20] In addition, they needed to look no further than the recent experience of states like Denmark and Holland to see ex-

---

[15] Jefferson to Edward Carrington, 16 January 1787, in *Papers*, 11: 49.

[16] Jefferson to Abigail Adams, 22 February 1787, in *Papers*, 11: 174.

[17] Jefferson to James Madison, 30 January 1787, in *Papers*, 11: 93.

[18] Jefferson to William Stephens Smith, 13 November 1787, in *Papers*, 12: 356.

[19] On constitutional theory, see Bailyn, *Ideological Origins*, pp. 67–77. Lutz prefers the term "traditional" to my "conservative"; see his *Popular Consent and Popular Control*, pp. 12–15.

[20] See Douglass Adair, "The Intellectual Origins of Jeffersonian Democracy" (Ph.D. diss., Yale University, 1943), pp. 96–121.

amples of excess and imbalance.[21] To these conservative thinkers, the threat of social breakdown apparently came perilously close to home, for in the aftermath of the Revolution, anxious observers could be found wondering whether social conflicts might not signal the continuation of revolutionary action. It was entirely possible, observed New Hampshire's uncompromisingly conservative Amicus Republicae, thought to be Benjamin Thurston, that American Revolutionaries, having struggled so valiantly against a common political enemy, might soon find themselves at war with one another. He warned of the terrible consequences of such social conflict: "Every man's sword would be turned against his fellow, and mutual jealousy, resentment, and malice, would operate in the acts of greatest cruelty. Our republics would become one general scene of plunder and slaughter."[22]

In this constitutional theory, the fear of excess was pervasive. Conservative Whigs, like all good republicans, assumed that an excess of power would create tyranny. But they also contended that an excess of liberty would lead to licentiousness. In the 1780s, certain American conservatives seemed determined to emphasize this trend towards lawlessness. Fundamentally, they believed that the abuse of power, although cause for concern, could never pose the threat to liberty that arose from an excess of license. According to the Reverend Moses Hemmenway, pastor of a church in Wells, Massachusetts, and a long-time friend of John Adams, the disorder that came from an excess of freedom was a form of debasement, as debilitating to free people as "the worst effects of slavery."[23] While republican citizens seemed all too aware of the abuses of excessive power, they tended to be lax in their fears of excessive freedom. Thus, license posed a more subtle, almost insidious threat to the republic. Above all, these conservative republicans could fear lawlessness because they saw it as a precondition to eventual tyranny. Their reading of classical history showed that once republics had declined into democratic disorder, demagogues and dictators would not be far behind. In particular, they read the history of the Roman republic as positive proof that popular discontent would lead to dictatorship. In 1783, they were predicting that the new nation would soon find itself traveling this same tragic path. Amicus Republicae made the case: "all these civil commotions, . . . would probably introduce a government that was abso-

[21] See Gerald J. Gruman, " 'Balance' and 'Excess' as Gibbon's Explanation for the Decline and Fall," *History and Theory*, 1 (1961): 75–86.

[22] Amicus Republicae [Benjamin Thurston], *An Address to the Public, Containing Some True Remarks on the Present Political State of the American Republicks, &c.* (Exeter, N.H.: Lamson and Ranlett, [1787]), pp. 13–14.

[23] Moses Hemmenway, A.M., *A Sermon Preached Before His Excellency John Hancock, Esq.; Governor . . . of . . . Massachusetts, May 26, 1784 . . .* (Boston: Benjamin Edes and Sons, 1784), p. 32.

lute; for if by experience it was evident, that our governments were over-
turned for want of energy, necessity would lead us to establish a government vested with more extensive power." In sum, he contended, "Anarchy
has a direct tendency to the introduction of tyranny. This is abundantly
evident from the experience of ages."[24]

Without balance, republican government was impossible. From Aristotle
on, constitutional thinkers had sought to control the excesses of one social
order by counterpoising the efforts of another. In Polybius, Montesquieu,
and the Commonwealth writers, the theme was elaborated into concepts of
mixed government, separation of powers, and checks and balances.[25] But
in America of the early 1780s, these ideas seemed somehow out of place.
The American states, after all, boasted neither feudal nobility nor hereditary
monarch. Their own republican version of balanced government would
come with the federal convention, still several years in the future. Before
that time, the ideal balanced government remained elusive.[26] At best, disparate thinkers could suggest such stopgaps as a stronger national government, more aristocratic influence, increased executive prerogatives. Most
conservative theorists, however, tended to see their own state as imbalanced
and dangerously instable.

In his multivolumed *Defence of the Constitutions of Government of the
United States*, John Adams made the classic indictment of this imbalance.
Relying on Thucydides, he described in detail the conflicts between demo-
cratic and oligarchic parties that had been endemic to Greece during the
Peloponnesian War: "The contagion spread through the whole extent of
Greece; factions raged in every city; the licentious many contending for the
Athenians, and the aspiring few for the Lacedemonians. The consequence
was, seditions in cities, with all their numerous and tragical incidents." In
the absence of balance, Adams contended, anarchy was succeeded by despotism. Nor did the despots put an end to conflict, for despotism evoked in
turn further rebellions, resulting, he wrote, in "perpetual alterations of rebellion and tyranny, and the butchery of thousands upon every revolution
from one to the other." The consequence was permanent warfare: without
balanced constitutions, Adams concluded of the Greek states, "the pendulum was forever on the swing."[27]

[24] Amicus, *Address*, p. 14.
[25] On the relation between mixed government, separation of powers, and balanced government, see W. B. Gwyn, *The Meaning of Separation of Powers* (New Orleans: Tulane University,
1965).
[26] On the problem of applying constitutional theory to American practice, see Wood, *Creation*, pp. 430–67.
[27] John Adams, *Defence of the Constitutions of Government of the United States*, 1787, in *The*

To constitutional conservatives such as Adams, the purpose of written constitutions was to limit popular excess. With this in mind, they argued that Revolutionary legislation had failed to check the trend from liberty to license. Indeed, the Revolutionary constitutions themselves had contributed to the instability of the new states. In his carefully constructed essay "The Vices of the Political System of the United States," the product of extensive reading and reflection during the early postwar years, Madison described the hopelessly transitory quality of recent state government. "We daily see laws repealed or superseded, before any trial can have been made of their merits; and even before a knowledge of them can have reached the remoter districts within which they were to operate." Statutes had been revised repeatedly, sometimes duplicated, sometimes contradicted, sometimes both. The result, according to Madison, was a "luxuriancy of legislation."[28] In an explicit challenge to the principle of periodic revision, Madison denounced the "repealing, explaining, and amending laws" as "but so many monuments of deficient wisdom; so many impeachments exhibited by each succeeding against every preceding session."[29]

Even more important to Madison was the fact that much of this legislation had been not only contradictory but also unwise. Ambitious legislators had pursued private interest at the expense of public good. These self-interested politicians, he contended, had become so adept at presenting themselves as self-sacrificing public servants that the traditional check of frequent elections had been made meaningless: "how easily," Madison observed, "are base and selfish measures, masked by pretexts of public good." In fact, he reported, the performance of the state legislatures had been disillusioning enough to lead many critics to "question the fundamental principle of republican Government, that the majority who rule in such Governments, are the safest Guardians both of public Good and of private rights."[30]

Thus these conservative republicans saw democracy as an inherently unstable system. As Elkins and McKitrick have shown, many had come of age in wartime, their political views being shaped by the national service in the army and congress, rather than the local experience of the militias or state legislatures.[31] Unlike their Revolutionary counterparts, they were not predisposed to look kindly on direct democracy. In keeping with Aristotelian

---

Works of John Adams, ed. Charles Francis Adams (Boston: Charles E. Little and James Brown, 1861–1865), 4: 285.

[28] James Madison, "Vices of the Political System of the United States," in *Papers*, 9:353.

[29] Madison, *Federalist* 62, in *The Federalist Papers*, ed. Clinton Rossiter (New York: Mentor Books, 1961), pp. 379–80.

[30] Madison, "Vices," in *Papers*, 9: 354.

[31] See Elkins and McKitrick, "Founding Fathers," p. 204.

theory, they assumed that democracy would tend to degenerate into disorder and then into anarchy. Popular participation, it followed, constituted an open invitation, in Hamilton's words, to "violence and turbulence."[32]

The purpose of a balanced polity was to prevent this breakdown into mob rule. Thus, conservative republicans argued that republican rulers, because they governed in the interest of the people, deserved confidence and support, rather than the traditional criticism and skepticism. The affairs of government were complicated and difficult; sometimes officials made mistakes. Their errors, however, "ought not to disaffect us to our governments."[33] Indeed, because citizens had the right to remove officials at the next election, they had no reason whatsoever to engage in public protest. As Amicus Republicae argued, it "can never be justifiable to throw the states into a civil war which perhaps would continue years to obtain redress of grievances, when it might be effected within one year constitutionally, and without any dangerous or injurious consequences."[34] To these American Aristotelians, protest could only lead to what one called "the horrours of anarchy."[35] "Our civil constitutions and administrators must be supported," Amicus warned, "or we can reasonably expect nothing but national ruin."[36]

Above all, they feared revolution. The ultimate consequence of such imbalance, after democracy had declined into anarchy, was despotism. Constitutional conservatives seemed unable to agree on whether future despots would come to power through foreign conquest or domestic insurrection, or whether the despot would be a military dictator or democratic demagogue. Above all, they speculated on the time it would take for popular protest to elicit some kind of authoritarian response. But few if any doubted the historical principle that disorder would lead back to a reinstitution of tyranny. Out of the chaos, some popular demagogue or military dictator would ride to power on the shoulders of the masses. "They will infallibly have a *Philip* or *Caesar*," the always cautious John Dickinson would write of the American people, "to bleed them into soberness of mind."[37] Yet in time, the mob would tire of its protector and revert again to revolution. On and on the conflict would continue, in what Hamilton would call the "perpetual vibration between the extremes of tyranny and anarchy."[38]

[32] Hamiton, address to the federal convention, 18 June 1787, in *Debates*, 5: 203.

[33] Amicus, *Address*, p. 17.

[34] Ibid., pp. 18–19.

[35] Cassius [James Sullivan], letter to the *Massachusetts Gazette*, 23 November 1787, in *Essays on the Constitution of the United States*, ed. Paul Leicester Ford (New York: Burt Franklin, 1892), p. 18.

[36] Amicus, *Address*, p. 16.

[37] John Dickinson, "Letters of Fabius, no. IV," 1788, in *The Political Writings of John Dickinson, Esquire . . .* (Wilmington, Del.: Bosnal and Niles, 1801), 2: 107.

[38] Hamilton, *Federalist 9*, in *Federalist Papers*, p. 71.

To these constitutional conservatives, rebellion was the ultimate threat to the republic. As Amicus said, it was "very impolitic to throw the public into convulsions, and attempt to overturn our government." Such subversion, he argued, commonly constituted "high treason." In fact, Amicus went on, it "is an offense that is capital, being an attempt upon the life of every subject in the community."[39] Revolution, far from assuring the health of the state, was a kind of political suicide. "Human nature," Adams submitted, "is as incapable now of going through revolutions with temper and sobriety, with patience and prudence, or without fury and madness, as it was among the Greeks so long ago."[40]

Confederation Politics: Radical Perspectives

In post-Revolutionary America, historical theory influenced not only the creation of political ideas, but also the perception of political events. In particular, radical republicans insisted on interpreting many public issues in terms of the time-honored premise that freedom would always be corrupted by power. Throughout the Revolutionary period, as Bailyn has shown, these radicals had been warning of the first signs of corruption: ministerial influence, unauthorized taxation, a standing army. Hence in 1783 they were startled by the suggestion of leading conservatives that Congress create a strong executive branch made up of single departments, each run by a single officer. They were equally surprised by the proposal that Congress be granted a taxing power, or impost. They seemed astonished at the plans of certain Continental Army officers to resist demobilization, combine forces with public creditors, and force prompt payment of war debts. Taken together, these measures suggested nothing short of conspiracy, a concerted plan to overthrow the republic, and "to erect on the Ruins, a proper Aristocracy."[41]

In radical Whiggism, the fear of a standing army had always run deep. The professional army of the eighteenth century, like the professional bureaucracy of the twentieth, seemed to answer to no popular source of power. In the hands of unscrupulous politicians, it could easily serve as a tool of tyranny. Among American radicals of the mid-1780s, this suspicion of mil-

---

[39] Amicus, *Address*, pp. 18–19; 28.

[40] Adams, *Defence*, in *Works*, 4: 287. See also David Humphreys, Joel Barlow, John Trumbull, and Lemuel Hopkins, *The Anarchiad*, ed. Luther G. Riggs (New Haven, Conn.: Thomas H. Pease, 1861), p. 61: "They see no object and perceive no cause; But feel, by turns, in one diastrous hour, Th' extremes of license, and th' extremes of power."

[41] Farrington [Connecticut] Revolutionary Records, 6 May 1783, cited in Jackson Turner Main, *The Antifederalists* (Chapel Hill, N.C.: University of North Carolina Press, 1961), p. 109.

itary power led to outrage over the creation of the Society of the Cincinnati,
the hereditary fraternal organization of former Revolutionary officers. Such
secret societies, the reasoning went, could only exist to conspire against
popular liberties. Before long, the new government would come under the
ministerial control of these influential military men. Furthermore, in the
absence of an indigenous aristocracy, such wealthy and well-bred leaders
seemed like likely candidates to establish themselves as a native nobility. In
turn, according to the radical republican reading of history, a corrupt nobility would always seek to introduce a corrupt monarchy. Societies such as
the Cincinnati, warned South Carolina's feisty Judge Aedanus Burke in a
detailed denunciation, could only "perpetuate family grandeur in an aristocratic Nobility, to terminate at last in monarchical tyranny."[42]

For radical thinkers, many of the issues of the postwar period pointed
toward increasing aristocratic influence. In republican theory, the fear of a
corrupt feudal nobility had always been a prominent theme, but in post-
Revolutionary America, the concern with aristocratic corruption was, according to Wood, nothing short of an obsession. Radical thinkers were able
to interpret proposals allowing the return of Tory loyalists to be part of a
plan to reintroduce an Anglophile aristocracy to America. More important,
they feared the establishment of their own indigenous aristocrats. In colonial America, popular discontent had been held in check by a sense of def-
erence to one's social superiors. During the war, any resentment against
persons of privilege was easily redirected to the absentee English oppressors; even the angriest petitioner could see that there could be no comparison between the heroic republican aristocrats whom they followed into battle and the simpering, sycophantic lords from whom they fought to be free.
After the War, however, resentment began to surface, as old Revolutionaries wondered whether certain new-style republicans were not positioning
themselves to take up the prerogatives of aristocratic nobility. In particular,
critics pictured financiers like Silas Deane and Robert Morris as potential
capitalist aristocrats. Behind many of the economic issues of the time—proposals like the impost, the funding of state debts, and the role of the national
bank—they saw what Sam Adams called the "Seeds of Aristocracy."[43]
Above all, radicals feared an alliance between the landed and commercial
classes. Plans were already being laid, the Reverend Belknap warned New
Hampshire's legislators in 1785, to create a "domineering aristocracy";

[42] Cassius [Aedanus Burke], *Considerations on the Society or Order of Cincinnati* . . . (Charleston, S.C.: A. Timothy, 1783), p. 29. See also Jensen, *The New Nation*, pp. 54–84, 261–81.
[43] Sam Adams to Richard Henry Lee, 3 December 1787, in *Anti-Federalist versus Federalist*,
ed. John D. Lewis (San Francisco, Calif.: Chandler Publishing Company, 1967), p. 160.

"and what that will degenerate into," he continued, "let the histories of fallen republics tell."[44]

Ultimately the events of the period seemed to be pointing toward a reintroduction of monarchy. America's recent experience with the unbridled power of a capricious king had led lawmakers to limit where possible the prerogatives of their own executives. In most of the state constitutions, governors were all but powerless, lacking the ability to initiate legislation, levy taxes, veto bills, or, for that matter, take almost any decisive action. Thus, when constitutional reformers in the mid-1780s began to call for more power to be allotted to these pitifully powerless officials, many radicals responded with alarm. After all, in the late eighteenth century, monarchy remained the political system most widespread in the Western world. Many European nations had managed to combine monarchical rule with a respect for constitutional liberties. At home, influential persons seemed to assume that Washington would soon be called on to play the role of republican king. Thus, radicals saw themselves as constantly on call to resist the reintroduction of monarchical rule. The memories of American patriots, they argued, were not so short; their own history showed that even well-intentioned monarchs like George III had ended as enemies of the people. As George Mason would later tell the federal convention, the distance from benevolent executive to cruel tyrant was but "an easy step."[45]

Given their perception of postwar events, it is understandable that these radicals found themselves speaking often of the need for protest. Annual elections, frequent turnover, and periodic revisions were all essential. But when necessary, republicans had to be ready to resist. It was in this context that they viewed the events surrounding Shays's rebellion. Throughout the 1780s, local leaders in western Massachusetts had been calling conventions and circulating petitions aimed at preventing presumed abuses of power, meaning in particular the abuses of high taxes and frequent foreclosures. Nor were the protests without cause; the historian Robert East has described how the Massachusetts legislature, controlled by creditor interests, had carried out fiscal and social policies that were harsh and unrealistic.[46] Throughout the 1780s, protests had won wide popular support, including

[44] Belknap, *An Election Sermon*, p. 19. On the fear of aristocracy, see Wood, *Creation*, pp. 75–90, 475–99. See also E. James Ferguson, *The Power of the Purse* (Chapel Hill, N.C.: University of North Carolina Press, 1961), pp. 146–76.

[45] George Mason, address to the federal convention, 17 July 1787, in *The Records of the Federal Convention of 1787*, ed. Max Farrand (New Haven, Conn.: Yale University Press, 1911), 2: 35. See also Wood, *Creation*, pp. 132–43, 430–38, 543–47.

[46] See Robert A. East, "The Massachusetts Conservatives in the Critical Period," in *The Era of the American Revolution*, ed. Richard B. Morris (New York: Columbia University Press, 1939), pp. 349–91.

that of many persons of status and wealth. Shays and his men, far from ragged rabble, were for the most part respectable property owners.[47] In addition, because of the time-honored role of crowds in presenting petitions, many interpreted this somewhat disorganized display of resentment as a fairly conventional form of protest.[48] As for Shays, his band of farmers seemed surprisingly well behaved. Even conservative critics like the Massachusetts jurist George Richards Minot had to admit that the recourse to violence was in large part the responsibility of an anxious militia. Not surprisingly, many citizens found themselves siding with these respectable rebels. (Judge Minot himself estimated that one-third of the population was sympathetic.[49]) Others found the protests to be cause for concern, though hardly for the ferocious response of the state and federal troops who routed the assembled farmers. In fact, observers like Jefferson could wonder from a distance how Shays and his men had managed to provoke such rage within the conservative ranks. After all, he wrote from Paris to his fellow diplomat William Carmichael, their protests were "not entirely without excuses."[50]

Confederation Politics: Conservative Concerns

Constitutional conservatives, relying on a different reading of history, viewed the same postwar events quite differently. Primarily, they saw popular excesses threatening the fragile balance that had maintained social order within the new republic. During the war, factional strife had been held in check by the common cause of rebellion. With peace, the disagreements of a decade had surfaced in continuing conflicts between creditors and debtors, merchants and farmers, easterners and westerners, "ins" and "outs." To conservatives, these contests suggested the breakdown of liberty into license, "unrestrained licentiousness," that threatened to "break through the laws of civil order, and destroy the peace of society."[51]

In response they began to call for a reassertion of the role of government in restoring the rough balance between power and liberty. The original

[47] See Main, *The Antifederalists*, pp. 59–71.

[48] On the role of popular assemblies and political protest, see Lloyd I. Rudolph, "The Eighteenth-Century Mob in America and Europe," *American Quarterly*, 11, 4 (Winter 1959): 447–69; Pauline Maier, "Popular Uprisings and Civil Authority in Eighteenth Century America," *The William and Mary Quarterly*, 3rd ser., 27, 1 (January 1970): 3–35; and Wood, "A Note on Mobs in the American Revolution," pp. 635–42.

[49] See George Richards Minot, *The History of the Insurrections, in Massachusetts . . .* (Worcester, Mass.: Isaiah Thomas, 1788), pp. 5–29, 89–91, 103–105, 110–12. The estimate of "a third part of the Commonwealth" is in Minot, *History*, p. 105.

[50] Jefferson to William Carmichael, 26 December 1786, in *Papers*, 10: 633.

[51] A Fellow Citizen, *The Political Establishments of the United States . . .* (Philadelphia: Robert Bell, 1784), p. 3.

object of government according to A Fellow Citizen, an anonymous Penn-
sylvanian, was to "restrain the turbulent passions of mankind, dispense justice, and support order and regulation in society." To these ends, the modern state required a strong national defense, an effective commercial system,
and internal police forces. According to the Citizen, these powerful institutions posed no threat to republican freedom. On the contrary, he argued
that republican citizens, realizing that these institutions promised to make
their liberty and property secure, would render their government "cheerful
obedience." As a result, such well-ordered republics would be strong
enough to "withstand the rage of many tempests."[52] Conservatives recognized that these and other suggestions of increased state power would be
greeted by howls of radical protest. But many contended that without a
stronger national state, factionalism could only lead to internal conflict. As
the Citizen reasoned, "where the people are under no supreme authority,
and are ultimately determined by individual and party opinions and reso-
lutions, anarchy, and confusion must necessarily be the fatal consequence."[53]

In the same manner, postwar conservatives saw the breakdown of constitutional balance in the rise of class conflict. Somewhat surprisingly, many
of them were quick to agree with their radical colleagues on the threat posed
to republican values by the rise of commercial wealth. In fact, wealthy conservatives often led the way in the denunciation of commercialism. Even
before the end of the war, representatives of the old agrarian elite had
warned of the rising power of the new capitalist upstarts. After 1783, as
landed patriots began to be defeated at the polls by merchant politicians,
their warnings became lamentations. By 1786, established figures seemed
ready to reassert themselves against those rising interlopers who, "by the
brass in their face, or the gold in their purse," had pushed themselves into
positions of power.[54] As the patrician John Adams explained, the role of
selfless, self-sacrificing aristocrats was to hold government out of the grasp
of the avaricious and ambitious rich.[55] The protestations of the landed class,
many of whom were themselves enormously wealthy, often seemed ironic.
"The Rich will strive to establish their dominion & enslave the rest," an
independently wealthy Gouverneur Morris would tell the federal convention. "They always did. They always will."[56] But their protests were hardly
hypocritical, for these agrarian aristocrats could fear oligarchy for the same

[52] Ibid., pp. 5; 4; 5.
[53] Ibid., p. 9. See Wood, *Creation*, pp. 543–47.
[54] Samuel Haven, D.D., *An Election Sermon, Preached Before the General Court of New-Hampshire, at Concord, June 8, 1786* (Portsmouth, N.H.: John Melcher, 1786), p. 12.
[55] On Adams, see Wood, *Creation*, pp. 574–87.
[56] Gouverneur Morris, address to the federal convention, 2 July 1787, in *Records*, 1: 512; 7 August 1787, in *Records*, 2: 209.

reasons they feared democracy. Indeed, to them, oligarchs were democrats in disguise. Above all others, Morris observed from the family estate at Morrisania, they feared those "opulent men whose business created numerous dependents to rule at all elections."[57] Squire Morris realized that much popular opinion was decidedly opposed to any reintroduction of aristocratic influence. But these democratic protests, he concluded with typical haughty candor, would never drown out the simple truth that "there never was, nor ever will be a civilized Society without an Aristocracy."[58]

To postwar conservatives, the trend of the times was to democratic despotism. Radical Whigs had always assumed that tyranny could exist only in the executive, that the popular branch could never be oppressive. After 1783, in a sweeping rejection of Whig principles, conservatives like Morris began to argue that the people were every bit as capable of oppression as any monarch. Conservative republicans needed to look no further than the reckless actions of the state legislatures—the paper money schemes, tender laws, suspensions of debts, seizures of property. These ill-advised, intemperate measures were certain proof, as an angry James Wilson suggested, that "*legislature* and *tyranny* . . . were most properly associated."[59]

Accordingly, many of these disillusioned republicans found themselves questioning the very principle of popular sovereignty. The woeful weakness of the state governors suggested that the time had come, as one wrote, to "give life and vigour to the executive authority."[60] Some minced no words in their call for a strong executive. Of all forms of government, said Fellow Citizen, that of "one man" was "best and most perfect."[61] Many apparently assumed that some form of monarchy was inevitable. There was, Franklin observed, "a natural Inclination in Mankind to kingly Government." Republican citizens, he wrote, would "rather have one Tyrant than 500. It gives them more of the Appearance of Equality among Citizens."[62] For the moment, political opinion made a reintroduction of monarchical rule impossible. In 1787, for example, a realistic Dickinson could admit that a king was "out of the question."[63] Nevertheless, there was wide agreement that democratic disorder would eventually elicit some version of monarchical rule. To Hamilton, the implication was clear: "if we incline too much to

[57] Ibid., 6 July 1787, in *Records*, 1: 545.
[58] Ibid.
[59] James Wilson, address to the federal convention, 15 August 1787, in *Records*, 2: 301.
[60] Fellow Citizen, *Political Establishments*, p. 4.
[61] Ibid., p. 9.
[62] Franklin, "Speech, in the Convention, on the Subject of Salaries," 2 June 1787, in *Writings*, 9: 593.
[63] Dickinson, address to the federal convention, 2 June 1787, in *Records*, 1: 87.

democracy," he would tell the federal convention, "we shall soon shoot into a monarchy."[64]

In the minds of these conservatives, postwar events pointed tragically toward anarchy. In constitutional theory, the return to first principles amounted to nothing more than the dissolution of government, the announcement that the constitution had come to an end. Popular protests would bring reversion to the state of war. As early as 1783, conservative writers had been warning that the masses were "growing turbulent and ungovernable," that laws are disregarded[,] civil officers insulted, and the constitution tottering to the foundation."[65] One year later they had found "internal broils" and "civil discord" that promised "horror and distress."[66] Well before any widespread protest, they had seen the "melancholy aspect" of "clamours and insurrections."[67] In short, these Aristotelians had long been preparing to view Shays's rebellion, or the next to come along, as the arrival of the predicted state of anarchy. As Douglass Adair suggested, their reading of history had prepared them to equate the respectable rebels of western Massachusetts with the blood-crazed citizens of ancient Corcyra, Syracuse, and Megara.[68] It was no wonder that frantic conservatives could see this band of worried farmers as an army of mad anarchists—"Ignorant, wrestless desperadoes," "mobish insurgents," the "deluded multitude."[69] Massachusetts Judge James Sullivan, who made a point of personally volunteering to march against the rebels, captured the extent of their fears: "Anarchy, with her haggard cheeks and extended jaws, stands ready," he wrote, himself half-enraged, half-terrified, "and all allow that unless some efficient form of government is adopted she will soon swallow us."[70]

The ultimate outcome of these events would be a return to tyranny. Aristotelian theory required that if anarchy went unchecked, it would end in dictatorship. All attempts at balance—stronger central government, more aristocratic influence, increased executive prerogatives—had met with determined popular resistance. Accordingly, conservative thinkers saw little hope for the present republican system. Through the waning days of the war, army officers led by Hamilton had spoken openly of establishing a military dictatorship. In 1783, as Merrill Jensen has shown, it was only the

[64] Hamilton, address to the federal convention, 26 June 1787, in *Records*, 1: 432.
[65] Honorius, "An Address to the Officers of the Connecticut Line," *The Vermont Gazette*, 18 September 1783.
[66] Fellow Citizen, *Political Establishments*, p. 11.
[67] Amicus, *Address*, p. 20.
[68] Adair, *Intellectual Origins*, p. 120.
[69] Abigail Adams to Thomas Jefferson, 29 January 1787, in *The Adams–Jefferson Letters*, ed. Lester J. Cappon (Chapel Hill, N.C.: University of North Carolina Press, 1959), 1: 169.
[70] Cassius [Sullivan], letter to the *Massachusetts Gazette*, 23 November 1787, in *Essays*, p. 15. See East, "Massachusetts Conservatives," p. 378.

determined opposition of General Washington that prevented a coup d'etat.[71] During the 1780s, Jensen reported, the talk of a dictator remained popular in conservative circles. By 1787, observers had become worried lest talk might soon become action: "the best citizens," a nervous Jay wrote to Adams, "naturally grow uneasy and look to other systems."[72]

Nor did their disillusionment with the republic seem likely to stop at limited reform. Those with property to protect, Jay observed, "prepare their minds for almost any change that may promise them quiet and security."[73] On the eve of the Philadelphia convention, observers could agree that the most serious danger to the new republic arose not from popular protest, but from authoritarian response. People in positions of power, Rush confided in a letter to Richard Price, "not only all the wealth but all the military men of our country . . . are in favor of a wise and efficient government." Most of them, he went on, were willing to allow "time, necessity, and the gradual operation of reason" to "carry it down." However, should incremental measures fail, he declared with some portent, "*force* will not be wanting to carry it into execution."[74]

Revolution, Counterrevolution, and Reform

By the mid-1780s, Americans had begun seriously to consider the possibility of some kind of constitutional reform. On the whole, while admitting the necessity of certain changes, radical republicans remained loyal to their time-honored cyclical theory, making the case for periodic renewal through a revitalization of the principles of the Confederation. At the extreme, there were at least a few who continued to maintain that the only antidote to corruption was another act of popular resistance.

In the course of the Confederation period, however, many reflective radicals seemed to lose their faith in periodic rebellion. At the very least, they admitted to lacking the stomach for another revolution. Instead, they began to consider the threat to order posed by periodic protest, and the danger of anarchy alternating with tyranny. "I know the people are too apt to vibrate from one extreme to another," New York's pragmatic George Clinton would finally come to confess. "The effects of this disposition are what I wish to warn against."[75]

By contrast, conservatives consistently drew attention to the evils of imbalance and excess. Shays's rebellion was proof that the new nation was

[71] See Jensen, *The New Nation*, pp. 46–54.
[72] Jay to John Adams, 1 November 1786, in *Correspondence*, 3: 214.
[73] Jay to George Washington, 27 June 1786, in *Correspondence*, 3: 205.
[74] Rush to Richard Price, 2 June 1787, in *Letters*, 1: 418.
[75] George Clinton, address to the New York ratifying convention, 28 June 1788, in *Debates*, 2: 359.

dissolving into civil war, and despotism could not be far behind. Thus they were predisposed to accept almost any alternative to anarchy and tyranny. Nevertheless, among these conservatives there was division as well, between moderate federalists who saw institutional innovation as the salvation of the states, and more authoritarian nationalists who seemed ready to rely on force to create a united nation. Throughout the period the concept of a counterrevolution would remain very much in the minds of some of these nationalists. For such persons, Jay had told Jefferson, nothing would suffice less than "systems in direct opposition to those which oppress and disquiet them."[76] Indeed, even the ardent Hamilton himself would in the end warn of the dangers of this counterrevolutionary sentiment: "That the human passions should flow from one extreme to another, I allow is natural," he would soon be telling the New York ratifying convention. "Hence the mad project of creating a *dictator*."[77]

In any case, in the mid-1780s American republicans saw themselves as facing simultaneous threats of revolution and counterrevolution, and neither prospect was appealing. More important, there seemed at this point no safe middle passage between the Scylla of another revolution and the Charybdis of a rightist counterrevolt. As a result, they felt lost, and very much in peril. For on at least one point, radicals and conservatives could agree: without some bold stroke, they seemed destined for conflict, "approaching a most interesting crisis," the Reverend Buckminster ominously predicted, by which "will be decided the fate of this empire."[78]

Yet even in 1787, constitutional reform remained elusive. For in responding to the issues of this uncertain interval, republicans continued to align themselves into clearly competing camps. By the mid-1780s, what remained of the Revolutionary consensus had been shattered, with radicals and conservatives diverging dramatically in their plans for political revision. In between, the fragile form of Whig republicanism, that anomalous amalgamation of periodic protest and balanced harmony, was irreparably torn asunder.

Still, the stage had begun to be set for constitutional reform. Although their differences seemed increasingly great, thinkers of all stripes could agree on the need for some kind of reform. Thus, they continued to search their political thought for ways to transform their political practice, turning for clues to the concept of development. In the meantime, they hesitated, continuing to drift, and to drift increasingly apart.

[76] Jay to Jefferson, 27 October 1786, in *Correspondence*, 3: 213.

[77] Hamilton, address to the New York ratifying convention, 28 June 1788, in *Debates*, 2: 360.

[78] Joseph Buckminster, A.M., *A Sermon, Preached Before his Excellency the President . . . of the State of New-Hampshire, June 7, 1787* (Portsmouth, N.H.: Robert Gerrish, 1787), p. 27.

⊸4⊸

DEVELOPMENT

The Economics of Expansionism

THROUGHOUT THE MID-1780S, political reformers continued to seek some realistic response to what seemed to be an increasingly intolerable situation. Certain as they were of coming calamity, but unsure of their ability to bring about any meaningful reform, they found themselves searching desperately for an appropriate course of action. In this effort, thinkers continued in these years to consider the course of recent events, trying somehow to locate themselves in time. Seizing on the science of social development, they thus attempted to chart their place on the scale of civilization, comparing the new American nation to older European societies. In the process, they discovered that America was in one major way unique. With the western frontier, the course of development, including economic development, would be directly and dramatically affected by the rate of geographical expansion. Movement through time would invariably be influenced by movement across space. In other words, time could be traded for space.[1]

Yet in America the relationship between time and space has been highly problematic. Some students of the American frontier, including Henry Nash Smith, R.W.B. Lewis, Charles Sanford, and Leo Marx, have argued that development and expansion were mutually exclusive. For these writers, concentrating on what they called respectively the "myth of the Garden," the "Adamic image," the "myth of Eden," and the "pastoral ideal," the West allowed Americans to avoid the problems of advanced civilization by returning to the original innocence of nature, transcending time, as it were, by traversing space.[2] Recently, Drew McCoy has elaborated on this theme, showing how those he called "Jeffersonian republicans" of the 1780s and 1790s, fearful of economic progress, found themselves in a race against time, moving rapidly westward in an attempt to forestall the corruption of a steadily advancing civilization.[3] At the same time, however, others have

[1] On this point, see Major L. Wilson, "The Concept of Time and the Political Dialogue in the United States, 1828–48," *American Quarterly*, 19, 4 (Winter 1967): 619–44. See also his *Space, Time and Freedom* (Westport, Conn.: Greenwood Press, 1974).

[2] See Henry Nash Smith, *Virgin Land* (New York: Vintage Books, 1957; reprint, 1970); Lewis, *American Adam*, pp. 1–10; Charles Sanford, *The Quest for Paradise* (Urbana, Ill.: University of Illinois Press, 1961); and Leo Marx, *The Machine in the Garden* (New York: Oxford University Press, 1964).

[3] McCoy, *The Elusive Republic*, esp. pp. 13–104.

contended that eastern development and western expansion were far from contradictory. Appleby for one has made the argument that they were in fact symbiotic and mutually reinforcing, answering McCoy's contentions by pointing out that Jefferson himself was able to favor development and expansion simultaneously, seeing both as essential ingredients of American progress.[4]

For examining the connections between development and expansion, the mid-1780s was a crucial time. The American economy, hurled headlong from mercantilist dependency into commercial free trade, was still in a state of transition, and clear differences were developing between agrarian, agricultural, and commercial thinkers. In this regard, McCoy's "Jeffersonians" were dividing themselves rapidly into competing intellectual camps, each with different definitions of development, including at the very least agrarians like Jefferson, proponents of the agricultural market like Madison, and more advanced commercial capitalists like William Barton. Furthermore, with Independence the frontier had been opened to settlement, and Americans were beginning to articulate competing conceptions of expansion, with thinkers led by none other than Jefferson, Madison, and Hamilton vying to define the future of the western lands. Above all, these thinkers found themselves searching for ways to link their concepts of development and expansion. In essence, they can be seen as seeking conceptual vocabularies—ways of thinking and talking—that would allow them to come to terms with the often overwhelming presence of the American West.

In addition, throughout the mid-1780s Americans were attempting to create policies to oversee the settlement of the West. The ties between theories and policies were sometimes tenuous, and the connections should not be overstated. But although they were often contingent and subject to change, connections were made. They show, or at least they suggest, that philosophical differences over the concept of development were present in political disagreements about policies for developing the West. The conflicts that ensued would reverberate on the larger issue of constitutional reform. Thus, the role of the West would become a polarizing factor, driving thinkers even further into competing camps, and setting the stage for the final contest over the Constitution.

Agrarianism

Eighteenth-century thinkers tended to describe social development in terms of a four-step evolutionary process. As Ronald Meek has shown in his *Social Science and the Ignoble Savage*, the specific characteristics of the stages sometimes varied, but the general pattern was consistent, with writ-

[4] See Appleby, "What Is Still American?" pp. 294–97.

ers from English liberals to French physiocrats to Scottish commonsense philosophers contending that all societies could be considered to be in transition through successive stages of hunting, pasturage, agriculture, and commerce.[5] Throughout the century, the Scottish philosophers in particular sought out examples of these respective stages and, as Meek described, created a voluminous literature in which the step-by-step transition from "rudeness" to "refinement" was set forth in detail.[6] For appropriate examples, these writers turned often and with endless fascination to the New World. Whatever their perspective on the four-stage theory, all seemed to agree with the Scottish historian William Robertson, who in his *History of America* argued that it was only with the discovery of America that the study of the human mind could be made complete. Only there, he wrote, could man finally be followed "in his progress through the different stages of society, as he gradually advances from the infant state of civil life towards its maturity and decline."[7]

Four-stage theory began with the earliest forms of society, the preproductive phase of fishing, gathering, and hunting. Lois Whitney has described how certain cultivated, cultured eighteenth-century thinkers eagerly embraced the simple, unspoiled life of this stage.[8] To these primitivists, this subsistence stage was the most perfect example of human existence, with people living in simple societies based on cooperation, mutual support, and peaceful good will.[9] As examples, they frequently cited the Indians of North America, picturing them as archetypes and idols, Adams and Eves in the Garden of Eden.[10] Others were not so sure; Meek has noted the strong strain of antiprimitivism that ran throughout eighteenth-century depictions of the New World.[11] Regardless, whether primitivist, antiprimitivist, or (much more often) some ambivalent mixture of each, all four-stage thinkers could agree that America was an archetype for the earliest form of human existence. The Scottish historian-philosopher Lord Kames, though himself among the ambivalent, may have described this earliest stage best: "In a

---

[5] Ronald L. Meek, *Social Science and the Ignoble Savage* (Cambridge: Cambridge University Press, 1976), pp. 5–36.

[6] Ibid., pp. 99–130.

[7] William Robertson, D.D., *The History of America* (London: W. Strahan, T. Cadell, and J. Balfour, 1777), 1, 281–82.

[8] Whitney, *Primitivism and the Idea of Progress*, pp. 91–136.

[9] For background, see Lovejoy and Boas, *Primitivism and Related Ideas in Antiquity*, pp. 103–16.

[10] See Hoxie Neale Fairchild, *The Noble Savage* (New York: Columbia University Press, 1928); Benjamin Bissell, *The American Indian in English Literature of the Eighteenth Century* (New Haven, Conn.: Yale University Press, 1925); and, for American sources, Roy Harvey Pearce, *Savagism and Civilization* (Baltimore: Johns Hopkins Press, 1953), pp. 76–104.

[11] Meek, *Social Science*, pp. 131–76.

nascent society, where men hunt and fish in common, where there is plenty of game, and where the sense of property is faint, mutual affection prevails, because there is no cause of discord; . . . Such is the condition of the North-American savages, who continue hunters and fishers to this day; and such is the condition of all brute animals that live in society."[12]

Nevertheless, by the end of the century it was far more common to find four-stage thinkers turning to the next level of social life, expanding on the advantages of the pastoral over the primitive existence. Theoretically, the second stage was dominated by pasturage, with the hunter making way for the herdsman and shepherd. Leo Marx has described this state as a "middle ground" or "middle landscape," rising above the rudeness of primitive life, while still far removed from the decadence of civilization.[13] In *The Machine in the Garden*, he traced its origins to Virgil's pastoral poems, and showed how the simple shepherd of the classical ode was transformed into the self-sufficient agrarian of eighteenth-century poetry.[14] By the end of the century this pastoral setting had come to be depicted as an agrarian society, with families living together on the land, raising crops and tending herds for their own consumption, and engaging in early forms of barter.[15] In this simple society, property was shared equally, possessions were secure, and public authority, what little existed, was just. Understandably, sympathetic observers viewed this updated pastoral setting as harmonious and happy, an Aristotelian golden mean. As Dr. Price put it, "The happiest state of man is the middle state between the *savage* and the *refined*, or between the wild and luxurious state."[16] According to Price, an urban Englishman much smitten by the charms of rural America, this perfect state existed not in the wild inland reaches among the native tribes, but along the agrarian frontier, where subsistence farmers lived together in pastoral harmony. "Where in these states do the purest manners prevail?" he asked rhetorically in his *Observations on the Importance of the American Revolution*. "Where do the inhabitants live most on an equality, and most at their ease? Is it not in those inland parts where agriculture gives health and plenty, and trade is scarcely known?"[17]

Among Americans of the time, this concept of agrarian pastoralism was common. In poetry and prose, the New World was pictured often as an agrarian utopia, with whitewashed barns, cattle grazing in the pastures,

[12] Henry Home, Lord Kames, *Sketches of the History of Man*, 2nd. ed. (Edinburgh: W. Creech, 1788/London: W. Strahan and T. Cadell, 1788), vol. 2, p. 204.

[13] Marx, *Machine in the Garden*, p. 71.

[14] Ibid., pp. 19–24.

[15] Ibid.

[16] Price, *Observations*, p. 59.

[17] Ibid., p. 64.

rows of barley ripe for cutting, and doves gleaning the fields. Presiding over this enormously pleasant landscape was the American version of the pastoral shepherd, the hardy, independent, self-sufficient yeoman farmer. The classic statement of this agrarian pastoralism was St. John de Crèvecoeur's *Letters From an American Farmer*, written mostly before the Revolution, published at the close of the war, and immensely popular in Europe and America in the mid-1780s. Looking back on the happy life he had led with his Anglo-American wife on their farm in rural Orange County, New York, Crèvecoeur described a scene of pastoral perfection, "an immense country filled with decent houses, good roads, orchards, meadows, and bridges, where an hundred years ago all was wild, woody, and uncultivated."[18]

To Crèvecoeur, this simple American setting was the antithesis of corrupt European civilization. Here he and his neighbors lived naturally in a state of perfect liberty and equality, existing independently on the production of their own lands, holding property essentially equal to one another. In fact, Americans were so naturally and unselfconsciously free that they had literally no words in their language for unearned dignities or undeserved honors. In this New World utopia, he concluded, there was none of the political and economic oppression of feudalism, no "aristocratical families, no courts, no kings, no bishops," no "hostile castle" or "haughty mansion" contrasted to the "clay-built hut and miserable cabbin."[19]

At the same time, Crèvecoeur's Americans were far from primitives, far from those wandering, half-wild frontiersmen who had opened the wilderness to settlement. For these Crèvecoeur expressed only scorn, considering them to be "no better than carnivorous animals."[20] Instead, his Americans were settled, sociable yeomen, simple without being base or vicious, civilized to a degree but not corrupted. In short, they were representatives of a perfect middle state, "the most perfect society," he boasted, "now existing in the world."[21]

Inherent in this agrarianism was an early American moral theory. To Crèvecoeur the cultivated land held a kind of spiritual purpose, in that the American farmer practiced agriculture as an exercise in piety, a baptism of the soil. "It is there," he wrote of life on the land, "that the salubrious effluvia of the earth animate our spirits and serve to inspire us."[22] In this sense, the land was a transformative force, offering a secularized and highly symbolic variation on salvation: "the simple cultivation of the earth," he wrote,

[18] J. Hector St. John [de Crèvecoeur], *Letters From an American Farmer* . . . (London: Thomas Davies and Lockyer Davis, 1782), p. 46.

[19] Ibid., pp. 46; 47.

[20] Ibid., p. 56.

[21] Ibid., p. 48.

[22] Ibid., p. 15.

"purifies them."[23] More directly, Crèvecoeur pictured settlement on the land as a process of rebirth, in which, through the regenerative power of the New World, Europeans were transformed into Americans. Here he adopted an organic metaphor, picturing Europeans as "so many useless plants, wanting vegitative mould, and refreshing showers."[24] Transplanted into the agrarian landscape, these useless plants became productive American organisms, having "taken root and flourished."[25]

By making this argument, however poetic, Crèvecoeur was propounding a primitive form of environmentalism. Unlike those of his eighteenth-century counterparts who saw human nature as universal and unchanging, he argued that people varied according to the circumstances of their surroundings. "We are nothing," he observed in a remarkably bold statement of this environmental theory, "but what we derive from the air we breathe, the climate we inhabit, the government we obey."[26] These new Americans were a totally new species, the sons and daughters not of every European fatherland, but of the bounteous American continent, "our great *Alma Mater*."[27] Through the transfiguring power of the land, the corruption of European urban culture had been replaced by the morality of American agrarian society, with its simplicity, frugality, and self-sacrificing civic virtue. Accordingly, the new American was *sui generis*, in moral terms a "new man."[28] "He begins to feel," as Crèvecoeur put it with a kind of pastoral piety, "the effects of a sort of resurrection."[29]

Equally important, this agrarianism implied a pastoral form of republican political theory. From the time of Aristotle, republican theorists had held that the self-sufficient farmer was the ablest guardian of liberty and source of civic virtue. Throughout the eighteenth century, leading republicans had cited Machiavelli, Montesquieu, and the English libertarians like Harrington and Sidney to the effect that independent landowners were the foundation on which all true republics would stand. American agrarians carried on the theme, with Jefferson putting the argument in its most elegant form: "Those who labour in the earth are the chosen people of God," he wrote glowingly in his *Notes on Virginia*. "Corruption of morals in the mass of cultivators is a phaenomenon of which no age nor nation has furnished an example."[30]

[23] Ibid., p. 54.
[24] Ibid., p. 50.
[25] Ibid.
[26] Ibid., pp. 53–54.
[27] Ibid., p. 52.
[28] Ibid., p. 53.
[29] Ibid., p. 73.
[30] Thomas Jefferson, *Notes on Virginia*, 1782, in *The Writings of Thomas Jefferson*, ed. Paul Leicester Ford (New York: The Knickerbocker Press, 1892–99), 3: 268–69.

According to Jefferson, there was a natural innocence in agricultural laborers that protected them from the specious reasoning of their educated
and urbane "superiors." "State a moral case to a ploughman and a professor," he told his nephew Peter Carr. "The former will decide it as well, and
often better than the latter, because he has not been led astray by artificial
rules."[31] Additionally, such property-owning farmers were naturally independent, answering, in Jefferson's words, only to heaven, [and] to their
own soil and industry."[32] It followed naturally that the cultivators of the soil
would be the most patriotic citizens of the republic, "tied to their country
and wedded to it's liberty and interests by the most lasting bands."[33] As
Jefferson described it in the *Notes*, these independent farmers provided a
constant source of republican renewal, venturing forth at the first sign of
corruption to exercise their inherent civic virtue. "Generally speaking," he
concluded, in a succinct statement of agrarian republicanism, "the proportion which the aggregate of the other classes of citizens bears in any state to
that of its husbandmen, is the proportion of its unsound to its healthy parts,
and is a good enough barometer whereby to measure its degree of corruption."[34]

Ultimately, agrarian pastoralism assumed a political economy of moral
self-sufficiency. Remarkable as it may seem today, agrarians like Jefferson
considered the primary purpose of an economic system to be the creation of
virtue rather than wealth. Simply put, the principal product of this economy was the character of the producer. In the agrarian vocabulary, terms
like "industry," "enterprise," and "investment" were personal attributes.
Similarly "labor" was a moral concept, implying dedication or diligence.
Even "property" was understood in terms of personal character, a sign, in
Calvinist terms, of inner grace, or a manifestation, in Lockean fashion, of
self-control. To agrarians like Jefferson, the tie between the cultivator and
the land was intimate and intense, an aesthetic bond rather than an economic nexus. Treating the land as a source of surplus or speculation or
considering production as mere profit could only destroy this spiritual relationship, and in the process corrupt not only personal morality but public
virtue as well. According to agrarian theory, commerce begot excess, excess
led to moral weakness, and weakness was certain to bring on tyranny. Put
bluntly, these Jeffersonians saw the transition from self-sufficiency to market capitalism as a process of corruption. The only antidote to this decline
was to rely on the hardy independence of the liberty-loving yeoman: "It is

[31] Jefferson to Peter Carr, 10 August 1787, in *Papers*, 12: 15.
[32] Jefferson, *Notes on Virginia*, in *Writings*, 3: 269.
[33] Jefferson to John Jay, 23 August 1785, in *Papers*, 8: 426.
[34] Jefferson, *Notes on Virginia*, in *Writings*, 3: 269.

the manners and spirit of a people," Jefferson explained, "which preserve a
republic in vigour."[35]

Agrarian politics was designed to encourage this moral economy. As a
historical and philosophical principle, agrarians counterpoised rural innocence to urban corruption. In the late eighteenth century, the primary symbol of moral corruption was the European city, which, with its teeming
masses and extremes of wealth and poverty, seemed a perfect antithesis to
the autonomy and equality of the yeoman farmer. Jefferson spoke graphi-
cally in the *Notes* of this urban corruption: "The mobs of great cities," he
contended, "add just so much to the support of pure government, as sores
do to the strength of the human body."[36] Thus, he sought to construct policies that would prevent, or at least forestall the process of urbanization,
along with the industrialization that was sure to accompany it. In this regard, as Henry Nash Smith has shown, he saw the West as a safety valve,
offering the urban laboring classes an escape from the poverty and subser-
vience of the city. In the vast western spaces, the resentments and social
pressures that characterized an advanced industrial economy would be
vented, diffusing harmlessly instead of building toward class conflict. It followed that the open lands promised to act as a deterrent to the evils of a
degenerated political system, obviating the social oppression and political
tyranny that were required to control the urban masses. Jefferson commented on the essential role of the western lands in ensuring the agrarian
character of the American economy: "While we have land to labour then,"
he continued in the *Notes*, "let us never wish to see our citizens occupied at
a workbench, or twirling a distaff."[37]

As to manufacturing, agrarians suggested that Americans rely on traditional mercantile ties: "let our work-shops," Jefferson went on authorita-
tively, "remain in Europe."[38] In fact, to the most ardent among them, Jefferson sometimes included, the American West provided the nation with an
opportunity for perfect economic self-sufficiency. It was his heartfelt wish,
he confided in a 1785 letter to a European correspondent, that Americans
should "practice neither commerce nor navigation, but to stand with respect to Europe precisely on the footing of China."[39]

The Agricultural Market

At the same time, nearing the end of the eighteenth century, other four-
stage thinkers had begun to concentrate on the third form of society, the

[35] Ibid.
[36] Ibid.
[37] Ibid.
[38] Ibid.
[39] Jefferson to G. K. van Hogendorp, 13 October 1785, in *Papers*, 8: 633.

agricultural market.[40] According to their theory, this stage was dominated by an early agricultural commerce, in which farmers produced crops and manufactured household items not only for their personal use but also for purposes of trade. Nevertheless, in this early market state, agricultural production predominated, and manufacturing consisted of domestic articles and the simplest of shop goods. By contrast, excess and luxury, the "fripperies" and "superfluities" that characterized an advanced industrial economy, were all foreign to the agricultural market. In other words, this stage was itself a higher version of the middle ground, in which people were able to remain simple and virtuous, while becoming at the same time more civilized and, within limits, more comfortable.[41] Adam Smith himself had argued that this revised middle state was the most natural and profitable for growing societies. By way of example, he pointed to the American colonies, where agriculture was still preferable to manufacturing. He described the existing situation in *The Wealth of Nations*.

> When an artificer has acquired a little more stock than is necessary for carrying on his own business in supplying the neighbouring country, he does not, in North America, attempt to establish with it a manufacture for more distant sale, but employs it in the purchase and improvement of uncultivated land. From artificer he becomes planter . . . who cultivates his own land, and derives his necessary subsistence from the labour of his own family, is really a master, and independent of all the world."[42]

Among American thinkers, this agricultural market stage was best described by Dr. Benjamin Rush, who in an essay extolling the economic potential of his home state of Pennsylvania placed the coming of agricultural commerce in broad philosophical perspective. To Rush, the first stage of society was represented by the early hunters who lived as savages, wandering through the wilds in barbaric solitude. In time, these primitive hunters moved on, to be replaced by settlers who created stable agricultural communities, living in houses of logs or boards, cultivating the land, and raising families. Without question, Rush considered this second species as representative of a higher stage of society. Yet unlike Crèvecoeur, he did not view these first agrarians as entirely virtuous, for what Crèvecoeur thought of as liberty, Rush saw as license. Thus, in Rush's rendition, these not-so-virtuous yeomen were unwilling to support a church, refused to bear the burden of taxes, and spent much of their time attending political protest meet-

[40] See Meek, *Social Science*, pp. 107–27.
[41] On the transition, see McCoy, *Elusive Republic*, pp. 32–40.
[42] Adam Smith, *An Inquiry Into the Nature and Causes of the Wealth of Nations*, 1776, ed. Edwin Cannan (New York: Modern Library, 1937), p. 359.

ings. In essence, they were flawed through an excess of independence. Far preferable, he claimed, was the succeeding state, in which self-sufficient and unruly settlers were replaced by more prosperous, more respectable farmers, who owned extensive lands, built comfortable and solid homes, constructed fences, paid their taxes, and valued the protection of the laws. For Rush, these landed entrepreneurs were the true inhabitants of the middle state. "It is," he wrote, "in the third species of settlers only, that we behold civilization completed—It is to the third species of settlers only, that it is proper to apply the term of *farmers*."[43]

Agricultural market thinkers presumed a more advanced stage of agricultural development. In place of the traditional pastoral, they chose to describe the land as more settled and secure, with fields cleared, marshes reclaimed, and thickets removed. In the center of this agricultural middle landscape stood their archetypical American, the industrious and prosperous commercial farmer. Among those who described this stage, the most influential may have been Benjamin Franklin who, in his "Information to Those Who Would Remove to America," written in 1782 but reprinted frequently and widely throughout the mid-1780s, depicted American society as perfectly poised between savagism and civilization, in what he called a stage of "happy Mediocrity."[44]

Like Crèvecoeur, Franklin contrasted American innocence to European corruption. His agricultural market perspective, however, although at first sight similar to Crèvecoeur's agrarian theory, was in fact strikingly different. For example, the cosmopolitan Franklin showed almost no interest whatsoever in the bucolic beauties of the American countryside. Instead, his depictions of the new land were dispassionate and functional, with references to the "salubrity of the Air, the healthiness of the Climate, the plenty of good Provisions."[45] More often he spoke of the land in purely physical terms, as "vast Forests still void of Inhabitants" or "an hundred Acres of fertile Soil full of Wood."[46] As to liberty and equality, those essential ingredients of Crèvecoeur's agrarianism, he was equally matter-of-fact. To the hard-headed Franklin, independence seemed less moral than economic, a product of republican virtue to be sure but, more important, of an expanding economy, "there being," he explained, "no Restraints preventing strangers from exercising any Art they understand, nor any Permission nec-

[43] Benjamin Rush, M.D., "An Account of the Progress of Population . . . ," n.d., in *Essays, Literary, Moral and Philosophical* (Philadelphia: Thomas and Samuel F. Bradford, 1798), p. 221.

[44] Benjamin Franklin, "Information To Those Who Would Remove to America," 1782, in *Writings*, 8: 604.

[45] Ibid., 608.

[46] Ibid., 607.

essary."[47] As to equality, Franklin relied on the principle of economic opportunity: "Multitudes of poor People from England, Ireland, Scotland, and Germany, have . . . in a few years become wealthy Farmers, who, in their own Countries, . . . could never have emerged from the poor Condition wherein they were born."[48]

Throughout his essay, an expansive Franklin described a flourishing agricultural market society, with inexpensive land and industrious labor combining to turn self-sufficiency into surplus. Manufacturing would be simple and small in scale, with artisans being drawn to the land either as farmers or as producers of domestic products to be used in the agricultural areas. As a result, Americans could keep their virtue while acquiring wealth. Thus, Franklin's agricultural market, although less idealized than Crèvecoeur's agrarian society, was nonetheless an ideal middle state. God himself had announced his approval, the profit-minded Franklin conjectured, "by the remarkable Prosperity with which He has been pleased to favour the whole Country."[49]

Implicit in agricultural market thinking was a somewhat ambiguous, though fairly sophisticated, social theory. Following Crèvecoeur, Franklin chose to describe the transformation that occurred in the act of coming to America, addressing his essay explicitly to those who would wish to emigrate. Yet unlike Crèvecoeur, with his promise of transatlantic renewal, Franklin made clear that not all Europeans could count on being transformed into Americans. In fact, Franklin ventured somewhat superciliously that most Europeans misunderstood America's promise, holding "mistaken Ideas and Expectations" of free land and easy living.[50] The truth was, he assured his Old World readers, that the New World offered little if any unearned wealth, but much in the way of opportunity. Thus it encouraged neither landed noblemen nor ambitious place-seekers, but sought instead artisans and farmers who would serve the country through ambition and hard work. In moving to America, these emigrants would find their lives transformed, for they would no longer be despised by their aristocratic betters but honored by their republican fellow citizens. Franklin captured the idea neatly: In America, he wrote, "people do not inquire concerning a Stranger, *What is he*? but, *What can he do*? If he has any useful Art, he is welcome; and if he exercises it, and behaves well, he will be respected by all that know him."[51]

Far from denying environmental factors, Franklin wrote at length of the

[47] Ibid., 608.
[48] Ibid.
[49] Ibid., 614.
[50] Ibid., 603.
[51] Ibid., 606.

importance of the open lands. At the same time, however, he stressed the relationship between land and labor, the fact that land was cheap and labor dear, and hence that through their own diligence and with the help of their neighbors, poor farmers could become wealthy planters in only a few years. "In short," he wrote, underlining the overridding importance of individual industry, "America is the Land of Labour."[52] In his own utilitarian way, Franklin too was describing a kind of rebirth, suggesting along the way that his "new man" had a distinctly commercial character: "if they are poor," he promised, "they begin first as Servants or Journeymen; and if they are sober, industrious, and frugal, they soon become Masters, establish themselves in Business, marry, raise Families, and become respectable Citizens."[53]

As to political theory, agricultural market thinkers suggested a revised form of republicanism. Agrarian republicanism was premised on the concept of civic virtue, with its assumption that citizens would sacrifice their own self-interest for the greater common good. Agricultural market theorists did not deny the principle, but suggested that civic virtue alone was not enough to assure republican freedom. Noah Webster made the case in a 1787 essay, in which he lamented the limitations of classical republican theory: "*Virtue*, patriotism, or love of country," he stated flatly, "never was and never will be, till men's natures are changed, a fixed, permanent principle and support of government."[54] Instead of virtue, Webster suggested that in an agricultural country the real source of republican freedom was found in the independence and equality that arose from the widespread ownership of property. Property, he proposed, was the real basis of both freedom and power. Thus, those agricultural states in which the distribution of land was most equal were not only the most free, but also the most stable, having neither arrogant aristocracy to oppress nor aggrieved democracy to rebel. It followed that property was the essential ingredient of republican government, the "very *soul of a republic*."[55] In a sweeping revision of classical theory, Webster concluded that civic virtue could only be established through the equal ownership of land. "The system of the great Montesquieu," he declared, "will ever be erroneous, till the words *property or lands in fee simple* are substituted for *virtue*, throughout his *Spirit of Laws*."[56]

The political economy of the agricultural market assumed the compati-

[52] Ibid., 607.
[53] Ibid. 608.
[54] A Citizen of America [Noah Webster], *An Examination into the Leading Principles of the Federal Constitution* (Philadelphia: Prichard and Hall, 1787), p. 47.
[55] Ibid.
[56] Ibid.

bility of civic virtue and commercial profit. Market thinkers did not for a moment deny that the agricultural life could be a source of moral virtue. On the contrary, in the words of the urbane Tench Coxe, himself a life-long resident of the city of Philadelphia, agriculture promoted morality "by keeping our people from the luxuries and vices of the towns."[57] Additionally, however, and equally important, agriculture was the foundation of the American economy. Coxe calculated that nine of ten Americans of his time were involved in agricultural production.[58] For the remainder, the few who made their livings by manufacturing, navigation, or trade, agriculture provided an absolutely essential source of raw materials, including grains for distilling and food processing; hemp and timber for shipbuilding; and flax, leather, and wool for the production of clothing.[59] In Coxe's words, agriculture was "the spring of our commerce, and the parent of our manufactures."[60]

Moreover, to Coxe the relationship between agriculture and the marketplace was complementary. With its limitless natural resources, including not only the endless open lands but also an adequate climate, rich soil, navigable rivers and deep harbors, America offered a setting in which agriculture and commerce were destined to advance together. In fact, in a 1787 address to Philadelphia's Friends of American Manufactures, a kind of early amalgamation of the Chamber of Commerce and the National Association of Manufacturers, Coxe showed how agriculture was the means not only of commerce but also of manufacturing. Referring to the power of wind, water, fire, and domesticated animals, he speculated that in America nature could provide the sources of energy that in Europe were consigned to human labor.[61] By relying on local resources, American producers could provide goods that were not only better—he cited the superiority of sunbleached American homespun to chemically treated Irish linen—but also cheaper.[62] Above all, rural manufacture would be domestic manufacture, producing simple and useful products for sale in local markets.[63] In this economic middle state, agriculture would be complemented, not corrupted, by manufacturing. The American states, Coxe concluded benignly, "cannot

[57] Coxe, "An Enquiry into the Principles, on Which a Commercial System for the United States of America Should Be Founded," 1787, in *View*, p. 7.

[58] Ibid., p. 6.

[59] Ibid., pp. 7–8.

[60] Ibid., p. 7.

[61] Coxe, "An Address to an Assembly of the Friends of American Manufactures," 1787, in *View*, pp. 38–42. See also Marx, *Machine in the Garden*, pp. 150–69.

[62] Coxe, "An Address," in *View*, p. 47. See also "An Enquiry," in *View*, p. 18, where Coxe refers to the "clear air and powerful sun of America."

[63] See Coxe, "An Address," in *View*, pp. 46–47.

make a proper use of the natural advantages of the country, nor promote her agriculture and other interests without manufactures."[64]

Finally, the agricultural market would encourage virtue and wealth alike. Among economic thinkers of the time, few were as sensitive to the threat of corruption as Coxe. Repeatedly in his writings he decried extravagance and wastefulness, denouncing in particular the importation of luxury items, including "buttons, buckles, broaches, breast-pins, and other trinkets."[65] At the same time, the banker-businessman Coxe tempered his concern about corruption with an ardent interest in economic growth. Thus, unlike those corruption-conscious republicans who made the case for sumptuary laws, Coxe called on Americans to forbear from purchasing luxury items, while at the same time creating their own more functional versions of these imported goods. In this way, he wrote in best booster fashion, "our dresses, furniture and carriages would be fashionable, because they were American and proper in our situation, not because they were foreign, shewy or expensive."[66] Like Franklin, Coxe envisioned an economic middle ground in which manufacturing would be small in scale and simple in operation, with labor remaining in the countryside, partaking of the wholesome life of rural America. In fact, paradoxical as it seems, Coxe could repeat the Reverend Belknap's 1785 argument that it was only by introducing more manufactures that Americans could constantly renew their agricultural virtues. The coming of an agricultural marketplace, including domestic manufacturing, he reiterated, borrowing Belknap's words, would "lead us once more into the paths of public virtue by restoring frugality and industry, those potent antidotes to the vices of mankind."[67]

Throughout the 1780s, proponents of the agricultural market sought to create an economic system in which development and expansion took place in close harmony. Like their agrarian counterparts, thinkers such as Franklin and Coxe saw the city as a symbol of corruption. Unlike the agrarians, however, they saw the countryside not as an alternative but as an antidote to urban decay. That is, agricultural market thinkers viewed the West as part of an expanding system in which the growth of eastern population inspired the opening of western lands. Excess urban population would be funneled out of the cities and into the countryside. In the rural areas, emigrants would take up not only farming but also commerce and manufacturing. With agricultural surplus and trade, rural population would increase, presumably creating villages and towns. Over time, this excess population would in turn find itself once again moving further westward. In short,

[64] Coxe, "An Enquiry," in *View*, p. 21.
[65] Coxe, "An Address," in *View*, pp. 49–50.
[66] Ibid., p. 50.
[67] Ibid., p. 53.

unlike agrarians who pictured an essentially static system of self-sufficient farming as opposed to mercantile city life, agricultural market thinkers envisioned a dynamic economy in which population moved steadily from the cities into the countryside, and from east to west.

As long as the western lands remained open, the system would remain harmonious. Before to the mid-1780s, the outlook seemed good, for even if the population doubled every twenty-five years, as Franklin had proposed in a widely accepted calculation, the extent of existing lands suggested that this growth could be contained for "many Ages."[68] To those like Coxe, this happy harmony of agriculture, commerce, and simple manufacturing offered the best of all possible systems: "It will consume our native productions[,] . . . improve our agriculture, . . . accelerate the improvement of our internal navigation and bring into action the dormant powers of nature and the elements[,] . . . and will give us real independence by rescuing us from the tyranny of foreign fashions, and the destructive torrent of luxury."[69]

Commerce and Industry

By the close of the century, still other writers had come to the conclusion that society could be found at its best only in the state of advanced civilization, represented in the four-stage theory by an economy of commerce and industry.[70] According to the theory, this fourth and highest stage was characterized by both an extensive market and a sophisticated industrial system, in which division of labor, mechanization, and large-scale investment allowed for the production of "finer" goods, including luxury items. No longer satisfied with the mere staples of household manufacture, consumers in this final stage sought out the little luxuries that could only be obtained through mass industrial production.[71] In the process, the coarse clothing and functional furniture of the agricultural market gave way to the latest fashions and most opulent furnishings. Furthermore, with the leisure and wealth of this higher economic stage, the liberal and fine arts were able to flourish. The result would be a more comfortable and more cultured life. Among European writers, Mandeville had gone so far as to celebrate this highest stage unequivocally, praising luxury even where it crossed over into licentiousness and vice.[72] But far more persuasive was David Hume, who

[68] Benjamin Franklin, "Observations Concerning the Increase of Mankind," 1751, in *The Papers of Benjamin Franklin*, ed. Leonard W. Larabee (New Haven, Conn.: Yale University Press, 1959–), 4: 228.

[69] Coxe, "An Address," in *View*, p. 53.

[70] See Meek, *Social Science*, pp. 177–229.

[71] On "necessaries and conveniences," see McCoy, *The Elusive Republic*, pp. 44–45.

[72] On Mandeville, see ibid., pp. 25–27.

contended that civilization did not inevitably breed corruption. In essence, Hume saw this fourth stage as a higher middle ground, civilized but uncorrupted. "Thus *industry*, *knowledge*, and *humanity*, are linked together by an indissoluble chain," he wrote, "and are found, from experience as well as reason, to be peculiar to the more polished, and, what are commonly denominated, the more luxurious ages."[73]

Among American writers, William Barton, a long-time Philadelphia associate of Coxe, may have been most active in making the philosophical case for this higher state of society. Writing under the pseudonym An American, Barton set out to criticize existing conceptions of development, condemning agrarians and agriculturalists alike for their idealized presentations of human history. According to An American, a totally self-sufficient people could exist "in the rudest state of mankind only."[74] In fact, he speculated that such self-sufficiency had never really existed at all, for human beings, however egoistic, were social creatures, and man through his wants and weaknesses was a "social animal."[75] He went on to observe that social life was economic life, for "the very origin of society" lay in a "reciprocity of services" and an "interchange . . . of property."[76] Thus commerce was essential to every society, "coeval," in Barton's terms, "with man himself."[77] At the same time, as simplicity gave way to civilization, and essentials were extended to encompass all manner of needs and wants, barter would be replaced by commercial intercourse, including money and the use of credit. To Barton, the source of this commercial wealth lay in agriculture, which he saw not as a source of self-sufficiency or self-respect, but of self-interest, with the possession of land being "the most valuable species of property."[78]

In a 1787 essay, Barton went on to argue for the establishment of a state loan office in which circulating medium based on the amount of landed wealth would be used to promote more agriculture, allowing for the improvement and purchase of lands, and hence for the creation of ever greater agricultural surplus. Agriculture was America's "principle manufacture": an "uncultivated soil," he observed, "is of as little use, as a diamond in the bosom of the mine."[79] Yet Barton went well beyond his colleague and patron Coxe in arguing that agriculture was not an economic end in itself, but

---

[73] David Hume, "Of Refinement in the Arts," 1752, in *Essays: Moral, Political, and Literary*, ed. T. H. Green and T. H. Grose (New York: Longmans, Green, 1898), 1: 302.

[74] [William Barton], "The True Interest of the United States, and Particularly of Pennsylvania, Considered," *American Museum*, 2, 1 (July 1787): 23.

[75] Ibid., p. 23.

[76] Ibid.

[77] Ibid.

[78] Ibid., p. 29.

[79] Ibid., p. 29; 32.

rather the means to the higher goal of a more advanced commercial society.
By cultivating the soil, the farmer-capitalists would enrich both themselves
and their country, for ultimately, Barton suggested, agriculture created
wealth, and wealth "encourages industry and genius; promotes arts and
manufactures; enlivens commerce; gives the means of comfortable subsistence to the poor; and enables all classes of people to contribute to the support of government, and establishment of public credit, by a regular and
liberal payment of taxes."[80]

For these champions of commerce and industry, the American landscape
was a source of economic treasure. Their descriptions evoked not bucolic
tranquillity but constant change and dynamic energy, with harbors and
highways being built, settlements and towns appearing along the roads and
waterways, and cities alive with commercial activity. The symbol of this
more mechanized state was the mechanic, and its most ardent champion
may have been a 1787 writer who went by the pseudonym A Plain, But
Real Friend to America. Writing in the *American Museum*, the anonymous
Friend offered an unrepentantly utilitarian view of the West. In America
nature was benevolent, "profusely liberal," in his phrase.[81] Yet the genius
of the land lay not in its agrarian beauty or even its agricultural fertility, but
in its commercial potential, its "raw materials proper for manufactures."[82]
In the lap of the western lands lay even the resources required to produce
articles of great refinement, the "ingredients," Friend somewhat surprisingly offered, "requisite for foreign luxuries."[83]

Fundamentally, this Friend was concerned that Americans reject the existing assumption that new nations like their own would be required to rely
on other, more mature states for their manufactured goods. The land alone,
rich in resources, seemed to suggest otherwise. At the same time, he observed that America boasted human resources as well, merchants and me-
chanics who were able and willing to create a more advanced economy, but
who, constrained by shortsighted policies, languished in idleness and poverty. By tapping these untold resources, Americans could break through
into a higher stage, leaping, as it were, from infancy into economic maturity.
Released from idleness and poverty, workers would gain both respect and
newfound riches. Freed from dependency on European mercantilism, the
new nation would find itself more independent and more influential in the
world. The Friend summed up bluntly: "What countries are the most flourishing and most powerful in the world? Manufacturing countries. It is not

[80] Ibid., p. 33.
[81] A Plain, But Real Friend to America, "On American Manufactures," *American Museum*,
1, 2 (February 1787): 117.
[82] Ibid.
[83] Ibid.

hills, mountains, woods, and rivers, that constitute the true riches of a country. It is the numbers of industrious mechanic and manufacturing as well as agriculturing inhabitants."[84] That a country of farmers and shepherds was not as valuable as one of artisans and manufacturers was an undeniable fact, he continued, "known to every politician in Europe."[85] America, Friend concluded in typical straight-from-the shoulder fashion, should learn this lesson: she "will never feel her importance and dignity, until she alters her present system of trade."[86]

As to the American economy, commercial capitalists such as the unknown Friend pointed to the increasing importance of the artisan. Contrary to established opinion, he explained, American agriculture had definite economic limitations, for current means required cultivation of extensive lands in order to realize marginal profits. To purchase land, not only for themselves but also—and in the long run more critically—for their children, farmers would be forced to the frontier. This Friend put the problem simply: "We cannot all be cultivators of land, because every father has it not in his power to give every one of his sons a tract of land."[87] By removing to the frontier, they would be so far from arteries of trade that they would find production unprofitable. Friend described the plight of those farmers who were forced westward, "to wander in the woods and wilds of the back country."[88] Almost as often, he suggested, and much more tragically, they could be found returning to Europe in search of land for themselves and their children. By contrast, the encouragement of industry would revitalize not only the economy, but also society itself through the immigration of Europe's most competent and desirable citizens. In the steps of Crèvecoeur and Franklin, Friend told how the act of immigration would create a new class of citizen, as Europe's "industrious poor" was transformed into America's "clothiers, fullers, hatters, saddlers, black and white smiths, cutlers, shoemakers, &c. &c. &c."[89]

At the same time, immigration would speed the transformation from an agrarian to an urban society. Arriving Europeans would "settle new towns and villages throughout the country," suggested the Friend, and would be instrumental in founding infant industries "on the banks of those fine rivers and streams which now wear a horrid, deserted aspect."[90] To the forward-

[84] Ibid., p. 119.
[85] Ibid.
[86] Ibid.
[87] A Plain, But Real Friend to America, "On American Manufactures," *American Museum*, I, 1 (January 1787): 17.
[88] Ibid., p. 19.
[89] Ibid.
[90] Ibid.

looking Friend, the creation of cities and the encouragement of manufacturing were absolutely essential. Unreservedly, and without qualification, he
called on Americans to build an advanced economy: "We should not then
see such sparse scattered settlements, but appear like the countries in some
parts of Europe, full of people, and as industrious as a bee hive."[91]

This commercial theory required a radical revision of republican political
theory. Where agrarians like Jefferson had argued that freedom required
self-sacrifice, and agricultural market thinkers like Coxe had contended that
it could be made compatible with self-interest, commercial republicans took
the thesis a long leap forward, boldly proclaiming that liberty and luxury
were perfectly congruent. In an essay dedicated to John Adams, a writer
identified as A Citizen of the United States rejected outright the ancient
republican axiom that civic virtue had been found only in the early Greek
city-states. As a general rule, this Citizen argued, the earliest states were in
fact far from virtuous. Born, he wrote, in "cimmerian darkness," they were
barbaric and chaotic creations, whose errors and imperfections had left the
world to struggle through "many centuries of sufferings."[92]

Unaccountably, the classical republics had over time come to be vener-
ated, and "fondly but unjustly lavished under the poetical imagery of a
golden age."[93] As a result, modern writers, including republican writers,
had been burdened with the preposterous notion that virtue could exist only
in settings of extreme simplicity, or as the Citizen put it somewhat more
cynically, "that honesty and barbarism are concommitants."[94] In fact, the
situation was quite the opposite, for it was only with the passage from rudeness to refinement that real virtue became possible. Thus the progress of
the species, long seen as a decline into corruption, was in fact as Hume had
depicted it, a step upward in the history of humanity in which, in the Citizen's words, "the noblest truths are unfolded by the improvement of human
reason."[95]

Not coincidentally, the coming of a more civilized life brought with it
excess and inequality. Here again the Citizen called for a revised republicanism, cooly contending that inequality was, at least to his mind, "perfectly
natural."[96] The laws of nature provided that effort and talent be rewarded,

[91] Ibid.
[92] A Citizen of the United States, "Political Sketches, Inscribed to His Excellency, John Adams . . . ," *American Museum*, 2, 3 (September 1787): 222, 224. This essay was written some-
time in late 1784 or early 1785.
[93] Ibid., p. 227.
[94] Ibid.
[95] Ibid., p. 230.
[96] Ibid., p. 232.

and that great efforts and talents be rewarded greatly. Thus, to this Citizen, luxury was both natural and moral, as well as perfectly compatible with republican freedom. "The truth is," he announced in a sweeping rejection of classical republican principles, "liberty and the completest complication of the laws, and the fullest dispersion of luxury through every vein of the body politic, are in all degrees and respects compatible with each other."[97]

To such committed capitalists, the elements of political economy had little room for what the Scottish philosophers called moral sentiment. William Barton for example made passing references to the moral necessity of industry and economy. But his primary concerns were clearly economic. Although never rejected in principle, virtue seemed in practice to be secondary to the more important project of making the nation economically sound. In general, Barton preferred to speak in terms of public policy, calling on the American governments—as distinct from the American people—to promote the introduction of manufacturing and trade and to protect existing industries through protectionist legislation. In his vocabulary, terms like "industry" and "economy" appeared more often as economic forces than moral traits, and "labor" itself became an impersonal, sociological term, as in his phrase "the price of labour."[98]

As to the traditional condemnation of corruption, along with the fear of Europe's debauched splendor, Barton rejected these outright. America's policy, he argued in his "Essay on the Promotion of American Manufactures," was to emulate Europe's model: "All the principle advantages that Europeans can derive from manufactures and mechanic arts," he wrote, "may be obtained by their introduction."[99] In fact, he maintained that Americans had no choice in following Europe, for whether they approved or not, the growth of population demanded that the economics of the new nation would change drastically. He emphasized the importance of this growing population: "what, then, is to become of this vast increase of the inhabitants of our towns? They cannot all be labourers: and but a small part can engage in husbandry . . . consequently, the greater part must apply to trades and manufactures or starve."[100] An additional consideration was the influx of European immigrants who either by capacity or choice were un-

97 Ibid., p. 234. See also Ralph Lerner, "Commerce and Character: The Anglo-American as a New-Model Man," *The William and Mary Quarterly*, 3rd ser., 36, 1 (January 1979): 3–26. Lerner (p. 19n.) uses the term "commercial republicans," but applies it more broadly than here, referring, for example, to Jefferson as a commercial capitalist.

98 William Barton, Esq., "Essay on the Promotion of American Manufactures," *American Museum*, 2, 3 (September 1787): 258.

99 Ibid.

100 Ibid.

suited to become farmers. Finally, in a striking amalgamation of cynicism and concern, Barton considered the economic future of a still largely untapped labor pool, those "numbers of industrial poor, unfit for hard labour, and likewise women and children."[101]

As to public policy, the proponents of commerce and industry were eager to encourage an economy that was both independent and integrated. Commercial theorists admitted that agriculture would long remain an important source of natural wealth. Like proponents of the agricultural market, they contended that agriculture and manufacturing would be of mutual benefit, for rural products would provide the raw materials for urban industries. Nevertheless, as the Board of Managers of the Society for the Promotion of Manufactures and the Useful Arts explained in an open letter to the people of Pennsylvania, agricultural production was not enough, for in producing agricultural goods for shipment abroad, American farmers became subject to "the fluctuating wants of other countries, the caprice of foreign princes, and the interruptions of war."[102]

Far better would be a system in which agricultural products were consumed at home by the growing population of America's cities. In a remarkable passage, the Board of Managers called openly for urbanization: "A people, employed wholly in the cultivation of lands, must always be a weak one: because its wealth and population must continue in a scattered state."[103] To these promoters of industry, it followed that the West presented a problem for the new nation, because "the cheapness of its western lands," they wrote, "will prevent our numbers from accumulating, if they are not induced to keep together, by towns and their neighborhood."[104]

Yet for economic progressives like those of the Pennsylvania Society, the solution to the problem lay not in closing off the the western lands, but in building up America's eastern manufactures, funneling excess population from the farms to the cities, and tying rural to urban areas by roads and waterways. In essence, they sought to place the resources of the frontier at the service of a national economic system. Incongruously enough, the American West was the key to an advanced industrial economy. With it, wrote A Plain, But Real Friend, far from remaining on the level of China, American industry could be placed "on the same footing as the manufactures of Europe."[105]

[101] Ibid.

[102] "Address of the Board of Managers of the Pennsylvania Society for the Promotion of Manufactures and the Useful Arts," *American Museum*, 2, 4 (October 1787): 361.

[103] Ibid.

[104] Ibid.

[105] A Plain, But Real Friend to America, "On American Manufactures," *American Museum*, 1, 3 (March 1787): 192.

Expansionism and the Idea of the Nation

Long before 1783, expansionism had been a fact of American life. Throughout the seventeenth century, Puritans had propounded the idea that they had a God-given mission to settle the western lands, taming the wilderness and converting its inhabitants. Eighteenth-century colonials carried on the concept, often substituting nature for providence, arguing that the physical presence of the open lands served as proof that Americans were predestined to civilize and develop the West. In the Revolution, the territories became a symbol of independence, representing the right to settle beyond the western boundaries established by British colonial rulers. After 1783, however, and the reopening of the West to settlement, the role of the territories became a critical political issue. With Independence and the end of colonial restrictions, settlers had gone west at an astonishing rate. Reports told of what Richard Henry Lee called "powerful emigrations," roads lined with wagons and rivers clogged with every imaginable form of boat.[106] Astonished observers spoke with awe, and sometimes with trepidation of the "rage for emigrating."[107] Whatever their views, Americans of the time agreed that the West would be a power to be reckoned with in shaping the new nation. As John Jay put it, "the seeds of a great people are daily planting beyond the mountains."[108]

In the debates that ensued, agrarians described the future of the West as an agrarian utopia. In their early postwar writings, they presented the open lands in classic pastoral terms, as a continuing source of moral regeneration. Typical was *The Golden Age; or the Future Glory of North America*, written in 1785 by an anonymous Jeffersonian, a somewhat sententious prose poem in which America's future was revealed to a simple yeoman who, through the intercession of America's "guardian angel," was fantastically transported through time.[109] The poem began with the standard statement of the potential for corruption inherent in all republics. However, it went on to give assurance that in America this corruption was "not likely to happen very soon."[110] The reason for the delay was the safety valve of the American West, offering the possibility of constant renewal through continuous expansion. From the top of a convenient mountain, the yeoman was able to foresee the future, looking first to the eastern lands, populated with "spa-

---

[106] Richard Henry Lee to [James Madison], 20 November 1784, in *Letters*, 2: 300.

[107] Jay to William Bingham, 31 May 1785, in *Correspondence*, 3: 154. See also Jensen, *The New Nation*, pp. 111–13.

[108] Jay to William Bingham, 31 May 1785, in *Correspondence*, 3: 154. See Jensen, *The New Nation*, pp. 114–15.

[109] Celadon, *The Golden Age: or, Future Glory of North-America* . . . (n.p., 1785). See also Marx's discussion in *Machine in the Garden*, pp. 106–107.

[110] Celadon, *Golden Age*, p. 7.

cious cities and a great many thriving towns," but also "diversified with
lofty hills and flowery dales."[111] Indeed, the eastern half of the continent
remained largely rural, "a thick conjunction of farms, plantation, gardens,
orchards, vineyards, &c."[112] Turning west, the yeoman viewed the endless
expanses of the western territories, savage but sublimely rich. As time
rolled by, settlers moved westward, taming the wilds. In this beatific Jeffersonian vision, however, the western lands remained an agrarian garden,
"a beauteous world," as the anonymous writer put it, "rising out of a dreary
wilderness."[113]

Throughout the 1780s, agrarians would contend that these open lands
were certain to remain indefinitely in this self-sufficient stage. In his "Observations on Demunier's Manuscript," written in 1786, Jefferson noted
that America's present population was ten persons to the square mile. At
the same time, he predicted that this figure would hold indefinitely, for "experience has shewn us that whenever we reach that[,] the inhabitants become uneasy, as too much compressed, and go off in great numbers to
search for vacant country."[114] Figuring that America's existing lands constituted about a million square miles, he calculated conservatively that the
present boundaries would be filled within forty years.[115] Quite prophetically, Jefferson was also able in 1786 to look to the additional four million
square miles extending westward beyond the Mississippi, suggesting that
these lands would be the first to be settled once the present boundaries had
been passed.[116] In any case, he made clear that while America would be
settled, and settled rapidly, it would be on farms and in small communities.
While still subscribing to the republican concern with corruption, Jefferson's vision of an endlessly expanding agrarian West led him to have few
fears. In fact, as Appleby has argued, his version of agrarian expansionism
was remarkably optimistic. Looking ahead with confidence, he wrote to Madison late in 1787, "I think our governments will remain virtuous for many
centuries; as long as they are chiefly agricultural; all this will be as long as
there shall be vacant lands in any part of America."[117]

Responding to the rapid settlement taking place, agrarians began to create a set of policies for westward expansion. Throughout the early 1780s,
small farmers and land-poor planters, burdened by heavy debts and increas-

[111] Ibid., pp. 10; 11.
[112] Ibid., pp. 10–11.
[113] Ibid., p. 11.
[114] Jefferson, "Observations on Demunier's Manuscript," 22 June 1786, in *Papers*, 10: 57.
For a similar view from the perspective of a European observer, see J. P. Brissot de Warville,
New Travels in the United States of America. Performed in 1788 (New York: T. & J. Swords,
1792), pp. xxi, 482n.
[115] Jefferson, "Observations," in *Papers* 10: 57.
[116] Ibid.
[117] Jefferson to Madison, 20 December 1787, in *Papers*, 12: 442.

ingly onerous taxes, had gone west, spurred on by land companies and eager speculators.[118] Moving west in search of debt relief and lower tax rates,
they seemed often all too eager to break the ties that bound the new territories to the existing states. The separatist movements in areas like Maine
and the Franklin region of North Carolina, along with the western rebellions of the period, not the least of which was the one led by Shays, stood as
vocal testimony to the desire for greater western autonomy.[119] Exacerbating
the problem was the inability of established state governments to agree on
a national policy for settling and governing the West. The territorial politics
of the period soon degenerated into petty conflicts and sometimes serious
confrontations, with local residents, land companies, and state legislatures
vying for control over the new lands.[120] In most cases, self-interest was
strong enough to muddle any clear political divisions. But in general, as
Robert Berkhofer has shown, those who endorsed Jefferson's agrarianism
tended to emerge from these debates favoring a western land policy that
assumed an economy of self-sufficient farming, a politics of local sovereignty
with fairly extensive powers ceded to the territories, and an admission procedure that would provide for numerous new states of small (no larger than
150 miles square) and essentially equal size.[121] Roughly embodied in the
Ordinance of 1784, which was the product of a Congressional committee
report written by Jefferson himself, these features became the primary ingredients of the earliest national land policy. Agrarians argued that to follow any less liberal program would alienate the West, exacerbating the separatist trend and possibly even damaging the ties of national union.
Jefferson explained the strategy in a 1786 letter to James Monroe: "Treat
them as fellow citizens. They will have a just share in their own government, they will love us, and pride themselves in an union with us."[122]

The essence of the agrarian platform was its localism. From Aristotle to
Montesquieu, republican theorists had held that freedom could exist only
in small states, whereas despotism was most appropriate to extensive empires. By extending its boundaries, the small republic would create a situation where people of large fortune and little moderation could gain power.
"It is ascertained by history," George Mason stated flatly, "that there never
was a government over a very extensive territory without destroying the

[118] See Jensen, *The New Nation*, pp. 112–13.

[119] See Peter S. Onuf, *The Origins of the Federal Republic* (Philadelphia: University of Pennsylvania Press, 1983), pp. 33–46.

[120] See ibid., pp. 149–85.

[121] Robert F. Berkhofer, Jr., "Jefferson, the Ordinance of 1784, and the Origins of the American Territorial System," *The William and Mary Quarterly*, 3rd ser., 29, 1 (January 1972): 231–
62.

[122] Jefferson to James Monroe, 9 July 1786, in Papers, 10: 113. See Jensen, *The New Nation*,
pp. 352–54.

liberties of the people."[123] Thus, agrarian writers made the case for smaller, self-governing states. Applied to the western lands, they tended to assume that the loose federal structure of the Articles would provide a flexible forum for administering the new territories. Above all, they were inexorably opposed to any policy in which a strong central government controlled vast tracts of territory. Harvard's James Winthrop, a champion of the classical polis, ridiculed the very concept of an extended republic: "The idea of an uncompounded republick, on an average, one thousand miles in length, and eight hundred in breadth, and containing six millions of white inhabitants all reduced to the same standard of morals, or habits, and of laws, is itself an absurdity."[124]

For these agrarian localists, Rome remained the archetype of the virtuous republic corrupted by its lust for imperial expansion. Writing as Roman republicans, using pseudonyms such as Agrippa, Brutus, Cato, and Cassius, these small-scale republicans warned of the certain loss of freedom that would accompany national greatness. Was it possible, asked the New York pamphleteer Cato, that some people could not "believe that an American can be a tyrant?" To this Cato, it seemed not only possible but, with expansion, altogether inevitable. Thus, he could conclude that "great power connected with ambition, luxury, and flattery, will as readily produce a Caesar, Caligula, Nero or Domitian in America, as the same cause did in the Roman empire."[125]

Proponents of the agricultural market saw the West in more ambivalent and more complex terms. In their postwar predictions, these writers seemed to be searching for a middle way that would allow both agrarian simplicity and economic comfort. Connecticut's young patriotic poet David Humphreys spoke for them in his 1786 poem *On the Happiness of America*, where he attempted to foresee the role of agriculture in the creation of a future American civilization. To Humphreys, agriculture would from that time be the primary source of America's greatness.

> Hail, agriculture! by whose parent aid
> The deep foundations of our states are laid;
> The seeds of greatness by thy hand are sown;
> These shall mature with thee and time alone;
> But still conduct us on thy sober plan,
> Great source of wealth, and earliest friend of man.[126]

[123] George Mason, address to the Virginia convention, 4 June 1788, in *Debates*, 3: 30.

[124] Agrippa [James Winthrop], letter to the *Massachusetts Gazette*, 3 December 1787, in *Complete Anti-Federalist*, 4: 77.

[125] Cato, letter to the *New York Journal*, 22 March 1787, in *Complete Anti-Federalist*, 2: 118.

[126] David Humphreys, *A Poem on the Happiness of America*, 1786, in *The Miscellaneous Works of David Humphreys* (New York: T. & J. Swords, 1804), p. 39.

At the same time, he was eager to point out the enormous commercial potential of American agriculture. In particular, he referred to the resources available for creating a commerical navy, calling on Americans to take to the seas. His poem depicted a free and open worldwide marketplace in which seamen traded agricultural products for European and Asian commerical goods.

> European artists send their midnight toil
> For crude materials of our virgin soil.[127]

To Humphreys, this global marketplace was the highest stage of agricultural commerce, allowing Americans to maintain their own simplicity while availing themselves of the world's wealth and culture. He concluded in this spirit, calling on future citizens to remain virtuous in spite of their prosperity.

> Ne'er may our sons for heaps of useless wealth,
> Exchange the joys of freedom, peace, or health,
> But make e'en riches to their weal conduce,
> And prize their splendour by their public use![128]

For the agricultural market theorists of the 1780s, the American West held an ambiguous future. In *The Elusive Republic*, McCoy described the problematic quality of the agricultural market ideal. Focusing on the figure of James Madison, he showed how those who sought to combine agriculture and commerce found themselves racing against time to maintain the tenuous balance between agrarian virtue and urban corruption.[129] As Madison saw it, the West would not forever remain an agrarian landscape, but rather, with the rising tide of immigration, would before long become far more heavily populated.[130] Whereas Jefferson had argued that America's existing territory would be settled in forty years, Madison calculated twenty-five.[131] In addition, whereas Jefferson envisioned a sparsely settled republic of ten persons to the square mile, Madison apparently thought in terms of a much higher density, in which a "great majority of the people will not only be without landed, but any other sort of, property."[132] Most important, Jefferson could be concerned by the coming of an advanced economy, but Madison was clearly alarmed, because he assumed its arrival would be in the not very distant future: "We see in the populous Countries

---

[127] Ibid., p. 43.

[128] Ibid.

[129] See McCoy, *The Elusive Republic*, pp. 120–32.

[130] See ibid., pp. 126–27.

[131] See James Madison, "Power to Levy Direct Taxes; the Mississippi Question," 12 June 1788, in *Papers*, 11: 125.

[132] Madison, address to the federal convention, 7 August 1787, in *Records*, 2: 204.

in Europe now," he would tell the federal convention, "what we shall be hereafter."[133]

For agriculturalists like Madison, the rapid settlement of the West posed particularly serious problems. With Independence, agriculture had boomed, as Americans moved from an exclusively British to a potentially worldwide agricultural market. In response, eastern creditors, controlling most of the available capital, had sought to tie western farmers to an improved system of commercial farming, lending money to expand production, favoring large farmers over smaller ones, buying crops cheap and selling them dear. As a result, commercial farmers in the areas most accessible to transportation multiplied and thrived, while self-sufficient farmers, borrowing repeatedly in order to expand, grew poorer and more desperate.[134] By 1787 it was clear that this economic strategy was creating enormous potential for conflict along the frontier. An additional dispute resulted when eastern processors encouraged overland trade at the expense of the easier and more lucrative river traffic to New Orleans; westerners reacted with rage to the Jay–Gardoqui negotiations, which threatened to limit their rights to navigation on the Mississippi for twenty to thirty years.[135] These specific problems were aggravated by a rising eastern pessimism, encouraged by separatist movements and increasingly bitter sectional rivalries, over the ability of the eastern states to maintain their traditional ties to the western territories.[136]

By 1786, the Ordinance of 1784 had come under fire for its inability to provide an orderly transition from territory to statehood, and political leaders began to seek alternatives. Returning from a western tour undertaken at the behest of Congress, James Monroe for one called for a radically revised system in which commercial agriculture would be fostered by large land sales, political control would be exercised by strong territorial governors, and admission procedures for statehood would be clearly established and exclusively controlled by Congress. As Peter Onuf showed in his *Origins of the Federal Republic*, these policies would come to fruition in the Northwest Ordinance of 1787. Onuf demonstrated that the forces combining to create the Ordinance were many and varied. Not the least of these forces was the anxiety of those like Madison and Monroe, who found themselves desperately seeking some means to control the West without alienating it.[137] Congressman Richard Henry Lee stated the problem, arguing that it was essential "for the security of property among uninformed, and

---

[133] Madison, address to the federal convention, 26 January 1787, in *Records*, 2: 124.
[134] See Jensen, *The New Nation*, pp. 111–15.
[135] See ibid., pp. 171–73.
[136] See Onuf, *Origins*, pp. 163–71. See also Jensen, *The New Nation*, pp. 352–54.
[137] See Onuf, *Origins* p. 170.

perhaps licentious people, as the greater part of those who go there are, that a strong toned government should exist, and the rights of property be clearly defined."[138]

Implicit in the Northwest Ordinance was an early example of federalist theory. In the essays of Hume, Madison had found the suggestion that liberty was not incompatible with extensive territory. In fact, given a federal structure in which local and national concerns could be addressed in independent but mutually supportive institutions, the liberty of the small polis could be reconciled with the power of the large state. In the case of the western territories, Madison and others had seized upon the suggestion of Monroe that they be divided into three to five large divisions. With sixty thousand citizens required for statehood, these dramatically expanded states would achieve admission to the union much sooner than under Jefferson's plan. By exercising careful control throughout the prestate period, Congress could fend off separatism, while allowing local authorities considerable control. Above all, as Onuf pointed out, by dropping the provision that existing states could effectively veto the admission of new ones, the Ordinance committed the West to the control of Congress, while still securing the legal rights of settlers.[139]

For agricultural market thinkers, the system offered several advantages. Most important, it would allow rapid expansion, as Americans raced westward in an attempt to secure the virgin lands needed to balance the rise of the commercial cities. Congress would receive expanded powers in opening the West, particularly in dealing with adversaries like Spain. The central government could better regulate agricultural trade by securing open markets around the world. At the same time, local liberties would be protected. Writing as A Landholder, Connecticut's Judge Oliver Ellsworth stated the position with stunning simplicity in an open letter to America's farmers: "A Federal government of energy, . . ." he wrote, mincing no words, "will preserve your liberty and riches."[140]

Finally, those embracing the cause of commerce and industry foresaw America's future as an advanced economy. In his epic poem *The Vision of Columbus*, published in 1787, the youthful Joel Barlow spoke for these thinkers. Following the anonymous Jeffersonian's *The Golden Age*, and Humphreys's *On the Happiness of America*, Barlow's *Vision* offered a mythic foretelling of America's future, complete with angel perched on the "Mount of Vision." In contrast to the pastoral future of the Jeffersonian epic, however, Barlow's Columbus, while beholding all of the spiritual powers of na-

[138] Richard Henry Lee to George Washington, 15 July 1787, in *Letters*, 2: 425.
[139] See Onuf, *Origins*, pp. 168–71.
[140] A Landholder [Oliver Ellsworth], letter to the *Connecticut Courant*, 5 November 1787, in *Essays*, p. 141.

ture, looked beyond these to the sources of commercial wealth—agricultural surplus for trade, timber for shipbuilding, precious stones and ores for manufacturing. Furthermore, unlike the predominantly agricultural future foreseen in Humphreys's ode, Barlow pictured an industrialized, urbanized America. With the angel's aid, Columbus was treated to a rapid flight through time, as before his eyes bays became harbors, roads and turnpikes stretched out across the land, and canals and waterways created an inland trading market.

> Where inland realms for ages bloom'd in vain,
> Canals, long-winding, ope a watery flight,
> And distant streams and seas and lakes unite.[141]

In Barlow's vision, the American West was a surprisingly urbanized utopia, with towns and cities rising along the roads and waterways.

> On each long strand unnumber'd cities run,
> Bend their bright walls and sparkle to the sun.[142]

Like Humphreys, Barlow stressed the importance of international trade, and showed American ships plying the seas in search of open markets. At the same time, however, and perhaps reflecting his financial ties to an Ohio land company, he envisioned the creation of continental markets as well, a thriving inland commerce extending "from sea to sea."[143] Above all, and consistent with his self-professed role as one of America's leading men of letters, Barlow depicted a civilized society, boasting its own art, poetry, and science. All told, an advanced economy offered the best possible means to secure this civilized state. Commerce and industry, he observed in an accompanying note, provided "the best possible system to produce the happiness of creatures."[144]

For those most eager to create an advanced economy, the role of the West was to some extent ironic. As Merrill Jensen has shown, many merchants remained strongly committed to a profitable system of transatlantic trade. Speculators in eastern lands sometimes saw the opening of the western territories as harmful to their vested interests. Conservative creditors feared that the West might become a debtor haven.[145] As a result, many eastern commercialists were in fact ardent antiexpansionists who, like the crusty

---

[141] Joel Barlow, *The Vision of Columbus* (Hartford, Conn.: Hudson & Goodwin, 1787), p. 246.

[142] Ibid., p. 255.

[143] Ibid., p. 201.

[144] Ibid., p. 243n.

[145] See Jensen, *The New Nation*, pp. 171–72.

Massachusetts conservative Rufus King, wanted to have as little as possible
to do with the West.[146]

At the same time, however, there were those who, although looking eastward to European markets, could still recognize the economic and strategic
importance of the West. Not least of these were the rising manufacturers of
the middle states, who depended heavily on western materials and markets.
Their economic interest led them to call for a stronger national union, proposing an early "American system" that would rely on the inland rivers and
overland routes to create a national trading union. Concomitantly, the creation of this stronger economic system required a more vigorous political
system, and many of these economic nationalists found themselves in alliance with the political nationalists who were making the case for an expanded central government.[147]

Among the latter, as Gerald Stourzh has shown, was Alexander Hamilton. Although he looked eastward in his thinking, and showed little enthusiasm for westward expansion, Hamilton consistently championed the
American interest in securing control over Mississippi navigation and the
port of New Orleans.[148] Whatever his aversion to the frontier, he recognized
that the West was essential to transforming America into a world power.
On this point, he felt no reservations, as he had admitted as early as 1782
in the "Continentalist": "There is something noble and magnificent in the
perspective of a great Federal Republic, closely linked in the pursuit of a
common interest, tranquil and prosperous at home, respectable abroad."[149]

To Hamilton the importance of the West lay in America's standing in the
world. In this regard, he saw the territories as troublesome and even threatening. Like so many Americans of the time, Hamilton was concerned about
the state rivalries that sparked conflict throughout the West, the "discord-
ant and undecided claims," as he would write in *Federalist* 7, that created
"an ample theatre for hostile pretensions."[150] He recognized clearly the economic importance of the territories, and stressed in particular the significance of controlling navigation on the Great Lakes and the Mississippi.[151]
More important, Hamilton was acutely aware of the strategic problems
posed by the West, where Britain and Spain seemed to exercise a free hand,

[146] See ibid.

[147] On the early nationalists, see Merrill Jensen, "The Idea of a National Government During
the American Revolution," *Political Science Quarterly*, 53, 3 (September, 1943): 356–79.

[148] See Gerald Stourzh, *Alexander Hamilton and the Idea of Republican Government* (Stanford,
Calif.: Stanford University Press, 1970), pp. 193–96. Stourzh notes a 1790 statement in which
Hamilton refers to the Spanish possessions on "our right" and the British possessions (Canada)
on "our left." See p. 195.

[149] Hamilton, "The Continentalist, no. IV," July 1782, in *Papers*, 3: 106.

[150] Hamilton, *Federalist* 7, in *The Federalist Papers*, pp. 60; 61.

[151] See Hamilton, *Federalist* 11, in *Federalist Papers*, p. 87.

maintaining garrisons and stirring up Indian resentments, and leaving America, in Hamilton's words, "exposed in a naked and defenseless condition to their insults and encroachments."[152]

Most important of all, as Stourzh has shown, Hamilton realized that the West was the bone of contention that encouraged the growing sectional conflict of the day.[153] Throughout the 1780s, Northern merchants and Southern planters had sought to enhance their respective political and economic power by aligning with the West. By 1787, Hamilton could see that this sharp sectional division stood as the greatest threat to national power. Thus, he contended that a national land policy designed to maintain sectional equilibrium was essential, probably following the model of the Northwest Ordinance, which had introduced the principle of coupling new Northern and Southern states. In any case, for Hamilton the territories were the key to national unity: "If these states are not united under a federal government, they will infallibly have wars with each other: and their divisions will subject them to all the mischiefs of foreign influence and intrigue. . . . The western territory is an obvious and fruitful source of contest."[154]

Thus, for Hamilton and his fellow nationalists, the West was a source of both sectional conflict and national power. Their position was problematic, for in order to secure the East, and in particular to maintain the balance between North and South, they found themselves relying on the West. Under the circumstances, Hamilton himself could be at best a somewhat reluctant expansionist.[155] Among his allies, however, there was considerably more enthusiasm. For example, John Dickinson could refer, in terms that were exceedingly unusual in the philosophical parlance of the time, to "an extensive republican empire."[156] Others dilated on America's future, seeming to forget republican fears of corruption in their fantasies of "opulence and power."[157] Interestingly, these enthusiastic expansionists looked to Rome for instruction, but not to the Roman republic. Instead they chose pseudonyms like Numa, the legendary king of ancient Rome, Fabius, the patrician dictator and general of the second Punic War, or even, in the case of one New Yorker, Caesar. For all of these nationalists, Hamilton included, the critical connection would be the Constitution, through which the American states would take their proper place in the world, creating "one

[152] Hamilton, *Federalist 24*, in *Federalist Papers*, p. 162.

[153] See Stourzh, *Alexander Hamilton*, pp. 115–16.

[154] Hamilton, "Extract from Colonel Hamilton's Speech in a Committee of the Assembly of New-York, on the 18th of February, 1787 . . . ," *American Museum*, 1, 6 (June 1787): 454.

[155] See also Stourzh, *Alexander Hamilton*, pp. 191–93.

[156] John Dickinson, "Letters of Fabius, no. VIII," 1788, in *Political Writings*, 2: 143.

[157] Columbus, "Reflections on the Policy and Necessity of Encouraging the Commerce of the Citizens of the United States of America . . . ," *American Museum*, 2, 3 (September 1787); 274.

great American system," as he would write in *Federalist* 11, "able to dictate the terms of the connection between the old and the new world."[158]

In fact, the economic debates of the decade would become crystallized in the debates over the federal Constitution. The tie between agrarianism and Antifederalism is subtle. Nevertheless, with some important exceptions, Antifederalists tended to cling with tenacity to the tenets of agrarian localism, arguing that republican freedom could exist only in states of strictly limited territory. Nothing "short of despotism," Pennsylvania's high-strung Antifederalist identified as Centinel suggested, could bind "so great a country under one government."[159] The assumption that republican politics could exist in a continental state was so much at odds with established doctrine that some Antifederalists found it impossible to give the proposal serious consideration. It was, an astonished Patrick Henry protested, "an idea extremely ridiculous."[160] Nor was their skepticism unfounded, for the examples of history suggested that republican liberty could not survive in consolidated states. "You might as well attempt," declared an opponent of the Constitution, "to rule Hell by Prayer."[161] Given these predispositions, Antifederalists could be certain that the national government outlined by their Federalist counterparts was a plan of imperial expansion. "It points to the time when the states shall all be consolidated into one empire," announced North Carolina's Joseph McDowell; "it is calculated to melt them down into one solid empire," warned his colleague William Lenoir; it was, stated the salty Bostonian known by the pseudonym John DeWitt, "nothing less than a hasty stride to Universal Empire in this Western World."[162] As these Antifederalists viewed it, the Constitutional system was not merely a plan for liberty and union. Instead, as Virginia's aristocratic William Grayson declared, it was something more ominous, "a contest for dominion—for empire."[163]

Among Federalists, the relation between political economy and political theory was at times ambiguous. But as McCoy has shown, at least some part of early federalist theory can be understood as an attempt on the part of proponents of agricultural commerce to reconcile agrarian and commer-

[158] Hamilton, *Federalist* 11, in *Federalist Papers*, p. 91.

[159] Centinel, letter to the *Independent Gazetteer*, 5 October 1787, *Complete Anti-Federalist*, 2: 141.

[160] Henry, address to the Virginia convention, 5 June 1788, in *Debates*, 3: 47.

[161] Thomas Wait to George Thatcher, 22 November 1787, cited in Main, *The Antifederalists*, p. 129.

[162] Joseph McDowell, address to the North Carolina convention, 30 July 1788, in *Debates*, 4: 211; William Lenoir, address to the North Carolina convention, 30 July 1788, in *Debates*, 4: 202; "John DeWitt," letter to the *Boston American Herald*, 5 November 1787, in *Complete Anti-Federalist*, 4: 25.

[163] William Grayson, address to the Virginia convention, 14 June 1788, in *Debates*, 3: 365.

cial considerations by creating a constantly expanding state.[164] Throughout the 1780s, agricultural thinkers had faced the intractable argument that republican freedom could not exist in large states. As late as 1787, Dr. Rush had to admit that "There is but one path that can lead the United States into destruction; and that is their extent of territory." With a federal form of government, however, Rush thought it just possible that "even this path may be avoided."[165] Inspired by Hume and their own anxieties about sectionalism, they turned increasingly to the idea of a greatly expanded federal state, a federated republic that could extend, as the enthusiastic George Nicholas of Virginia would put it, to "almost any extent of territory."[166]

Finally, for the champions of commerce and industry who would swell the Federalist ranks, the creation of an advanced economy required a constantly expanding nation. At the very least, the West provided the means by which the agricultural South could be brought into closer cooperation with the increasingly industrial North. Thus these economic modernizers would find themselves drawn inexorably into the Constitutional camp, as federalists and nationalists became allies in creating a continental republic. For these nascent Federalists, the American Constitution promised to place the new nation securely on the path to world power. As delegate Francis Corbin would explain to the Virginia convention, "A government of this kind may extend to all the western world; nay, I may say, *ad infinitum.*"[167]

In contesting the fate of the western lands, so important to the politics of the mid-1780s, Americans continued to align themselves into clearly identifiable camps. By 1787, the alliance of agriculture and commerce that would become the backbone of the Federalist party had already appeared. Indeed, out of the rising clamor for a convention, a Federalist party, committed to significant reform, was already emerging. More or less in response, Antifederalists could be found organizing as well.

Every bit as important, with the calling of the Philadelphia convention, a Federalist philosophy, or at the very least a Federalist persuasion was being created. Its creation signaled a radical revision in American republican thought, for in defining a concept of development that allowed the nation to advance economically and geographically at the same time, Federalists can be seen as redefining the very idea of the republic itself. Breaking

[164] See McCoy, *Elusive Republic*, p. 131.

[165] Benjamin Rush, "Address to the People of the United States . . . ," 1787, in *Principles and Acts*, p. 235.

[166] George Nicholas, address to the Virginia convention, 10 June 1788, in *Debates*, 3: 247. On Hume's influence, see Douglass Adair, "That Politics May be Reduced to a Science," in *Fame and the Founding Fathers*, ed. Trevor Colbourn (New York: W. W. Norton, 1974), pp. 93–106.

[167] Francis Corbin, address to the Virginia convention, 7 June 1788, in *Debates*, 3: 108.

free from the assumptions of classical republicanism, they began to formulate a more modern political theory, one premised on the belief that America
could be not only as large, but as great and as free as its citizens chose to
make it. Antifederalist thinkers would resist, but from that time the idea of
the small republic seemed somehow to lose its luster.

Nevertheless, in 1787 the extended republic remained only a grand theoretical proposition. At Philadelphia, Federalists would be required to
bring this audacious theory into political reality. If nothing else, creating
the Constitution would be an extraordinary experiment in republican politics. Thus they turned to assess the meaning of this totally new kind of
political experience. And Antifederalists turned as well, to meet them.

PART THREE

Creating a Contemporary Politics

∢5∢

EXPERIENCE

Examples, Precepts, and Theorems

WITH THE CONVENING of the Philadelphia convention, reformers turned to the problems associated with creating a contemporary politics. The events of the mid-1780s, the conflict and confusion, had been in one sense liberating. For by 1787 political observers could see that there was almost no agreement on the direction that events seemed to be taking. More important, there was nothing approaching consensus on an appropriate response, no common ground on which to build the basis of reform. In the absence of precedent or common agreement, the most determined of the reformers were forced to rely increasingly on their own initiative, sallying forth, sometimes blundering forth, in search of a more present-oriented politics. With the calling of the federal convention, they crossed the Rubicon, having from that time no choice but to revise their politics. In temporal terms, the Constitutional convention can be seen as symbolizing that instant of awareness described by Pocock in which a people becomes conscious of its mortality and takes steps to confront it. The convention was at the center of America's "Machiavellian moment," because it was there that champions of the new Constitution took up the unprecedented task of transcending time, as they reached beyond precedent to create a present-oriented politics.

For decades the argument has been made that the most compelling characteristic of the Constitution's framers was their contemporaneousness, their willingness to address the immediate issues of the day. From Max Farrand to Richard Hofstadter and Daniel Boorstin, scholars have contended that the creation of the Constitution, far from an excursion into timeless theory, was in fact an exercise in expediency, the product of bargaining and timely compromise.[1] In a 1961 article, John P. Roche put the case so persuasively that it has become commonplace among historians and political scientists to describe the delegates to the Philadelphia convention as

---

[1] See Max Farrand, *The Framing of the Constitution of the United States* (New Haven, Conn.: Yale University Press, 1913); Richard Hofstadter, *The American Political Tradition and the Men Who Made It* (New York: Vintage Books, 1948); and Daniel J. Boorstin, *The Genius of American Politics* (Chicago: The University of Chicago Press, 1953), pp. 66–98. Boorstin (p. 96) may have put it best: "And no part of our history is more familiar, than the story of how the framers of the federal Constitution achieved a solution: by compromise on desires rather than by agreement on a theory."

119

some of history's most pragmatic politicians.[2] As proof of their commitment to the here and now, John Dickinson's famous statement in the federal convention frequently has been cited: "Experience must be our only guide. Reason may mislead us."[3]

Over the years this present-oriented theory of politics has had its critics. Intellectual historians led by Douglass Adair have contended that Constitutional politics was based not only on the participation in immediate events but also on an extensive and informed reading of historical sources. In his celebrated essay on "Experience Must Be Our Only Guide," Adair described the pervasive influence of historical method on the late eighteenth-century republicans who constructed the Constitution.[4] To Adair and his students, "experience," including even that of the pragmatic Dickinson, implied history.

Likewise, political philosophers like Martin Diamond have argued that the debate over the Constitution should be seen primarily as a battle between competing versions of political philosophy. Although Diamond was only one of many such writers, his well-crafted writings were instrumental in reminding his fellow political theorists not only of the importance of concepts like federalism, separation of powers, and mixed regimes, but also of the absolutely crucial role that ideas of liberty, equality, and efficient government played in the founding.[5] To Diamond, the concept of "experience," far from instrumental and transitory, was based on an intimate and extensive knowledge of the timeless truths of republican political theory.

A third group of critics has included those political scientists, notably Robert Dahl, who pointed to the presence of an early form of scientific method implicit in Constitutional thought. In his *A Preface to Democratic Theory*, Dahl argued that Madisonian theory, although undeniably historical and philosophical in its origins, could best be understood as a scientific theorem, a set of hypotheses, definitions, and logical inferences derived from basic axiomatic propositions. To Dahl and his students, the American Constitution, the classic example of Madisonian thinking, was above all a scientific instrument, a somewhat flawed but exceedingly logical and system-

    [2] John Roche, "The Founding Fathers: A Reform Caucus in Action," *American Political Science Review*, 55, 4 (December 1961): 799–816.

    [3] John Dickinson, address to the federal convention, 13 August 1787, in *Records*, 2: 278.

    [4] See Adair, " 'Experience Must Be Our Only Guide,' " in *Fame and the Founding Fathers*, pp. 107–23.

    [5] See Martin Diamond, "What the Framers Meant by Federalism," in *A Nation of States*, ed. Robert A. Goldwin (Chicago: Rand McNally, 1961), pp. 24–40; "The Declaration and the Constitution," *The Public Interest*, 41, 3 (Fall 1975): 39–55; "The American Idea of Equality," *The Review of Politics*, 38, 3 (July 1971): 313–31; and "The Separation of Powers and the Mixed Regime," *Publius*, 8, 3 (Summer 1978): 33–43.

atic method of governing.[6] Thus, thinkers like Dahl have tended to see the "experience" of Constitutional creation as an early example of political science, an application of scientific methodology to the political world.

Although proponents of these three perspectives have generally found little in common, the differences between them have been greatly exaggerated. In truth, experience was a rapidly changing concept in 1787, and convention delegates relied on each of these perspectives, sometimes simultaneously, in creating the Constitution. Furthermore, the concept was immensely controversial, with Antifederalists and Federalists holding strikingly different definitions. Indeed, to some degree supporters and opponents of the Constitution distinguished themselves from one another by their respective uses of the term. Thus however pragmatic and practical, the debates of the federal and early state conventions were at least in part theoretical and temporal, for in order to create a politics based on their own experience, Americans had first to determine not only the character of that experience but the very meaning of political experience itself.

Historical Examples

In the eighteenth century, Americans were predisposed to look to history to find political models. Throughout the colonial period, political thinkers had relied heavily on the preeminent examples of the ancient constitution and the common law.[7] With Independence, they began to become more selective in their use of colonial precedents, adopting those legal and political antecedents that seemed applicable to the new nation, while rejecting others as inappropriate or outmoded. Their selective use of the past was not unusual, for eighteenth-century theoreticians tended to see history as a storehouse of examples, any one of which could be lifted out of time and placed in the present, providing a comparison between historical experience and contemporary events.[8] This emulatory form of history was as old as the political rhetoricians of the early Greek democracies. In its modern form, it had been adopted by republican theorists from Machiavelli to Montesquieu. In fact, it was a historical method peculiarly suited to republican politics, for it provided civic-minded republicans with conspicuous models of civic virtue: statesmen to emulate, speeches to imitate, and actions to copy. Antifederalists and Federalists alike entered the Constitutional debates holding this historical concept of "experience." Throughout the debates, they would continue to speak of "the experience of ages," "all the experience of the

[6] See Robert A. Dahl, *A Preface to Democratic Theory* (Chicago: University of Chicago Press, 1956).

[7] See Colbourn, *The Lamp of Experience*, pp. 3–20.

[8] Ibid.

world," or even "experience . . . from the beginning of the world to this day."⁹ In fact, delegates of all persuasions turned regularly to the examples of the past. As Dedham's weary Thomas Thacher would tell the Massachusetts convention, they had at every stage "quoted ancient history, and applied it to the question now under debate."¹⁰

Antifederalists in particular championed this emulatory history, returning repeatedly to the past in search of examples. In going to history, they went first, in the usual republican way, to the ancient republics, and especially to early republican Rome. But just as often, Antifederalists looked back even further, recalling with some regularity the very earliest examples of republican politics, the city-states of fifth-century Greece. In their much-beloved Montesquieu, they found the Greek polis of the Periclean Age presented as a republican prototype, a state that had combined an abiding respect for personal liberty with a strong commitment to public service.¹¹ Antifederalists embraced this Greek example, relying on the essays of Plutarch and the histories of Herodotus and Thucydides to school themselves in the advantages of polis politics. Many of them chose classical Greek pseudonyms for their public pronouncements, writing as Nestor, Lycurgus, Timoleon, and even Plato. In the examples of the fifth-century republics, these Antifederalists found a perfect politics, a model of government, as the South Carolinian Rawlins Lowndes observed with his usual oratorical flair, that "had stood the test of time and experience."¹²

Steeped in republican history, Antifederalists were predisposed to advocate a classical conception of republican politics. Fundamentally, they assumed that a republic could exist only in a state of limited territory, homogeneous population, and self-sufficient economy. "It is ascertained, by history," observed Mason, "that there never was a government over a very extensive country without destroying the liberties of the people."¹³ The earliest political forms, suggested Winthrop, writing as Agrippa, were small, self-sufficient republics. Certainly the most stable states, like the system that Moses devised when he led the Israelites out of Egypt, relied on this "face-to-face" form of politics. In fact, all known historical examples, ancient and

⁹ Patrick Henry, address to the Virginia convention, 9 June 1788, in *Debates*, 3: 164; Henry, address to the Virginia convention, 24 June 1788, in *Debates*, 3: 591.

¹⁰ Thomas Thacher, address to the Massachusetts convention, 4 February 1788, in *Debates*, 2: 146–47.

¹¹ On the importance of Montesquieu, see Donald S. Lutz, "The Relative Influence of European Writers on Late Eighteenth-Century American Political Thought," *American Political Science Review*, 78, 1 (March 1984): 189–97.

¹² Rawlins Lowndes, address to the South Carolina convention, 17 January 1788, in *Debates*, 4: 290. See also, on the republican reading of the classics, Richard M. Gummere, *The American Colonial Mind and the Classical Tradition* (Cambridge, Mass.: Harvard University Press, 1963).

¹³ George Mason, address to the Virginia convention, 4 June 1788, in *Debates*, 3: 30.

modern alike—what Agrippa called "the experience of mankind"—showed
that the best of all political systems was the small republic.[14] According to
Antifederalists, only small republics could inspire loyalty among their citizens, what Mason referred to as "the love, the affection, the attachment of
the citizens to their laws, to their freedom, and to their country."[15] In turn,
only small republics could count on their citizens to sacrifice for the common good, and to defend their nation against its enemies. It followed that
only small republics would be durable enough to survive and thrive over
long periods. As proof, Antifederalists cited the Greek republics, the Dutch
states, the Swiss cantons, and, more recently, the American colonies themselves. The classical republic, Mason concluded to the federal convention,
had proved its worth "in all ages."[16]

Of course, not all eighteenth-century Americans read their history in
quite this way. In fact, certain thinkers preferred a more skeptical reading
of the past, according to which historical events were often seen as mistakes
or failures that contemporary students would do well to avoid in their own
times. This cautionary form of history was also the product of a long intellectual heritage, having been introduced by Hellenistic Greeks like Polybius and perfected by Romans such as Cicero. Among early moderns, it had
been embraced by scientists like Francis Bacon, who argued that ancient
Greece and Rome represented the world's childhood, whereas modern Europe, availing itself of all earlier learning, constituted its old age. The assault
on past authority was led by philosophers like Descartes, who boasted that
he had forgotten all the classical literature he had ever read, and Hobbes,
who sneered at Aristotle and believed that political theory had begun with
his own efforts. It would continue in the literary debates known variously
as the "Quarrel Between the Ancients and Moderns" and the "Battle of the
Books."[17] In any case, by the end of the eighteenth century it had become
common to hear thinkers criticizing the classical states. The character of
these small states, lamented Virginia's classically educated Governor Edmund Randolph, comprised a "mournful history."[18]

In the Constitutional debates, Federalists in particular relied on this cautionary reading of the republican past. Within the Federalist ranks were

[14] Agrippa, letter to the *Massachusetts Gazette*, 29 January 1788, in *Complete Anti-Federalist*,
4: 106.
[15] Mason, address to the federal convention, 4 June 1787, in *Records*, 1, 112.
[16] Ibid.
[17] See E. G. Bourne, "The Use of History Made by the Framers of the Constitution," *Annual
Report of the American Historical Association*, 1896, 1: 225; Peter C. Hoffer, "The Constitutional Crisis and the Rise of a Nationalistic View of History in America, 1786–1788," *New York
History*, 52, 3 (July 1971), 305–23; and Jones, *Ancients and Moderns*, pp. 119–47.
[18] Edmund Randolph, address to the Virginia convention, 7 June 1788, in *Debates*, 3: 87.

many skilled students of history. For example, Madison would admit in the Virginia convention to using the "whole history of ancient and modern republics" to argue the excellence of the Constitution.[19] In fact, not only Madison and Hamilton but almost every vocal Federalist relied at some point on historical arguments to make their cases. Yet the Federalist conception of history was radically different from that held by their Antifederalist counterparts. Federalists found little to admire in the experience of the fifth-century democracies. Instead they saw much to avoid, for in place of liberty and virtue, they discovered the worst forms of personal oppression and popular tyranny. At best, the classical republics furnished "no other light than that of beacons," as Madison reported, "which give warning of the course to be shunned, without pointing out that which ought to be pursued."[20] John Adams put it somewhat differently, arguing in his *Defence* that the ancient polis should serve as a "boudoir," a room of mirrors in which young states, like young people, could see the reflection of their flaws, and then proceed to remedy them.[21] Whatever the metaphors, Federalists agreed that classical history provided an abundance of negative examples. The new American nation, counseled the redoubtable John Marshall, should make use of this history to "avail itself of the misfortunes of others," and thereby "gain knowledge from that source without fatal experience."[22]

Federalist historians used cautionary history to demonstrate the weakness of the small republic. Good government, they argued, could exist only where debate was disinterested and rational. According to their reading of the past, earlier republics had been hopelessly unsuited to such reasoned discourse. The size of the small republic alone had magnified the influence of unreason, leading to a politics that was intense and erratic. In such small states, suggested Charles Pinckney, one of South Carolina's most ardent advocates of social order, "the people are easily assembled and inflamed— are always exposed to those convulsive tumults of enfatuation and enthusiasm which often overturn all public order."[23] In fact, the face-to-face republic made genuine liberty impossible, in that within its borders factions developed easily, majorities oppressed minorities with little resistance, and the good of the whole was inevitably sacrificed to the good of a powerful few. By the same token, small republics could just as easily fall victim to majoritarian tyranny. According to Hamilton's interpretation of the Greek democracies, "When they assembled, the field of debate presented an ungov-

[19] James Madison, address to the Virginia convention, 16 June 1788, in *Debates*, 3: 87.

[20] Madison, *Federalist* 37, in *Federalist Papers*, p. 226.

[21] John Adams, *Defence*, in *Works*, 4: 469.

[22] John Marshall, address to the Virginia convention, 10 June 1788, in *Debates*, 3: 225.

[23] Charles Pinckney, address to the South Carolina convention, 14 May 1788, in *Debates*, 4: 327.

ernable mob, not only incapable of deliberation, but prepared for every enormity."[24] In these "hothouse" republics, passion caught fire easily, leading first to anarchy, then tyranny, as it became, in Hamilton's words, "a matter of contingency, whether the people subjected themselves to be led blindly by one tyrant or by another."[25] In short, Federalist writers saw the classical polis as fatally flawed. "It has been observed, by an honorable gentleman," an agitated Hamilton angrily told the New York delegates, "that a pure democracy, if it were practicable, would be the most perfect government. Experience has proved that no position in politics is more false than this. The ancient democracies . . . never possessed one feature of good government. Their very character was tyranny; their figure, deformity."[26]

In the state ratifying conventions, Federalists began to go beyond even this cautionary history. No Federalist denied that there had been a few effective republican governments. Some were willing to admit that there had been very excellent republics, "stupendous fabrics reared on the basis of liberty," as Hamilton called them, which had, in at least "a few glorious instances," survived and even "flourished for ages."[27] Yet even when these examples existed, Federalist delegates questioned their applicability to eighteenth-century America. As Hamilton described them in *Federalist* 8, the early Greek republics had been states at war, or living under threat of invasion. For all practical purposes, they had been military camps in which public service had been universally enforced. To Hamilton, these martial states seemed completely unlike the peaceful and prosperous nations of their own day: "The industrious habits of the people of the present day," he ventured, "absorbed in the pursuits of gain and devoted to the improvements of agriculture and commerce, are incompatible with the condition of a nation of soldiers, which was the true condition of the people of those republics."[28] It followed that the examples of these early armed republics had little to offer modern peacetime nations.[29] With this in mind, Federalist thinkers began to question the very legitimacy of such historical precedents. In the course of the conventions, it became germane for the first time to discuss just how much, if at all, the political examples of antiquity applied to what Madison called "the peculiar situation of the United States."[30]

[24] Alexander Hamilton, address to the New York convention, 20 June 1788, in *Debates*, 2: 253.

[25] Ibid., 253-54.

[26] Ibid., 253.

[27] Hamilton, *Federalist* 9, in *Federalist Papers*, p. 72.

[28] Hamilton, *Federalist* 8, in *Federalist Papers*, p. 69.

[29] Hamilton had made this argument as early as 1782. See his "'The Continentalist, no. VI," 4 July 1782, in *The Works of Alexander Hamilton*, ed. Henry Cabot Lodge, 2d ed. (New York: G. P. Putnam's Sons, 1903-1904), 1: 282.

[30] Madison, address to the Virginia convention, 16 June 1788, in *Debates*, 3: 87.

Philosophical Precepts

At the end of the eighteenth century, political history began to give way to a less historical, more philosophical reading of republican politics.[31] The eighteenth century was an age of vast colonial empires, not tiny independent city-states. Even the most committed republicans had to admit that classical politics in its purest form was exceedingly rare in the modern world, existing only in tiny mountain redoubts like San Marino or the Swiss cantons. As a result, political thinkers were forced to face the intractable fact that history would not always offer appropriate examples. Delaware's Dickinson led the way in distinguishing history from present-day politics. "Experience," he suggested, had two forms, "long experience," by which he meant the distant past, as recorded in history, and "short experience," meaning the more immediate past, the memory of recent events.[32] When pressed, Antifederalists as well as Federalists were fully prepared to admit that these two concepts of experience were distinct and often unrelated. As the Antifederalist Benjamin Randall confessed to the Massachusetts convention, "the quoting of history" was to his mind "no more to the purpose, than to tell how our forefathers dug clams at Plymouth."[33]

Nevertheless, Antifederalists tried valiantly to retain a place for their beloved classical republic. Most conceded that the ancient polis was far removed from their own world of modern nation-states. Yet they continued to refer to the importance of the small republican state, presenting the polis less as historical precedent than philosophical ideal. Antifederalists pointed out that the classical democracies, like their modern counterparts, had existed in the midst of large and powerful empires. Indeed, through the creation of confederacies like the Amphictyonic Council and the Achaean League, these small republics had managed to protect themselves against the larger monarchies around them. When pressed, Antifederalists admitted that the ancient confederacies had been tenuous and often unstable. Yet they persisted in speaking of them in the most idealized terms: "The most perfect harmony and friendship subsisted between them," as Monroe described the Achaean League, "and they were very active in guarding their liberties."[34] Like other republicans before them, Antifederalists assumed that human nature was unchanging and universal: Americans, as the New York pamphleteer Cato observed, were "like other men in similar situations."[35] From this it followed that certain fundamental assumptions would

[31] See Bailyn, *Ideological Origins*, pp. 22–54.

[32] Dickinson, address to the federal convention, 13 August 1787, in *Records*, 2: 278.

[33] Richard Law, address to the Connecticut convention, 9 January 1788, in *Debates*, 2: 200.

[34] James Monroe, address to the Virginia convention, 10 June 1788, in *Debates*, 3: 210.

[35] Cato, letter to the *New York Journal*, 22 November 1787, in *Complete Anti-Federalist*, 2: 118.

apply equally to all states and to all times. So it was that they pictured the principles of the the polis as ideal truths, axiomatic precepts suggested by, though somewhat divorced from, historical examples. In the course of the Constitutional debates, they began to turn to this more theoretical perspective on the past, looking to "universal principles," as Patrick Henry called them, that held "in all nations and ages."[36]

Federalists were less eager to maintain a role for these republican axioms. Indeed, in the conventions they became increasingly suspicious of the use of such precepts. Unlike their Antifederalist opponents, Federalists did not assume the universal character of the human condition. Instead, their comparative reading of historical and contemporary sources stressed the dissimilarity of environments. Americans, these Federalists maintained, were neither Greeks nor Romans. At best, according to the youthful Christopher Gore of Massachusetts, it was questionable "whether any conclusions can be fairly drawn" from such distant examples.[37] At worst, the Harvard-educated Gore told his colleagues, "such sources can have no weight in considering things so efficiently different."[38] Furthermore, historical precedent aside, even the philosophical precepts derived from such dissimilar sources were of questionable value. Whether they liked it or not, as Judge Richard Law told the Connecticut convention, the experience of other nations was "very different from ours."[39]

Predictably, Federalist writers would take a critical view of the role of confederation politics. Applying their own more skeptical reading of the past, they found the experience of the classical confederacies to be much less positive than Antifederalists had implied. Federalists were perfectly willing to admit, according to Hamilton, writing in *Federalist* 9, that the confederacies of Greek republics had experienced moments of peace and harmony. But these instances were but "occasional calms" that only served as "short-lived contrasts" to the "furious storms" that came later.[40] In his own extensive study of ancient and modern confederacies, Madison had found that confederation government, far from promoting harmony, had "in every instance, been productive of anarchy and confusion."[41]

Federalist theorists went so far as to suggest an inherent incompatibility between the liberty of the small state and the stability of the confederation. In every known confederacy, there had been a tendency to dissolution, as the constituent states increased their independence at the cost of the confed-

[36] Henry, address to the Virginia convention, 14 June 1788, in *Debates*, 3: 385.

[37] Christopher Gore, address to the Massachusetts convention, 22 January 1788, in *Debates*, 2: 66.

[38] Gore, address to the Massachusetts convention, 15 January 1788, in *Debates*, 2: 17.

[39] Law, address to the Connecticut convention, 9 January 1788, in *Debates*, 2: 200.

[40] Hamilton, *Federalist* 9, in *Federalist Papers*, p. 71.

[41] Madison, address to the Virginia convention, 7 June 1788, in *Debates*, 3: 129.

eration's central power. Eventually all had fallen victim to this centrifugal tendency. "When we examine history," James Wilson summed up persuasively to the Pennsylvania delegates, "we shall find an important fact, and almost the only fact which will apply to all confederacies: —They have all fallen to pieces, and have not absorbed the government."[42]

In the face of high-minded, high-sounding precepts, Federalist historians described themselves as offering these painful but incontestable facts. Hamilton in particular used this approach in *Federalist* 9, where he argued that Montesquieu's assumptions in the *Spirit of the Laws* were the product of uncritical speculation, his propositions being "supported by neither principle nor precedent," and hence "in the main, arbitrary."[43] Hamilton's own historical review had produced "extensive exceptions" to Montesquieu's principles,[44] and he used these historical exceptions to disprove philosophical rules. They "serve to prove," he wrote, "that there is no absolute rule on the subject."[45]

In the Constitutional debates, Federalist theorists thus could be found creating a more empirical approach to political theory. Over time, their arguments tended to become increasingly particularistic, inductive, and practical. According to Federalist delegates, they themselves relied only on "well-known facts."[46] Their Antifederalists counterparts, by contrast, were guilty of using "vague inferences," what Hamilton called those "airy phantoms that flit before the imaginations."[47] In truth, Federalists relied as much on philosophical principle as did their Antifederalist counterparts. At the heart of their thinking, however, lay interest rather than virtue. By relying on this more tangible, more measurable premise, Federalists could present their political philosophy as grounded in cold, hard political reality, the product of empirical evidence alone. Their arguments, declared Jay, came "from plain facts. Here is no sophistry, no construction, no false glosses, but simple inferences from the obvious operation of things."[48]

Federalists described the debates themselves as a clear contest between theory and practice. Antifederalism, Hamilton argued, was an ethereal philosophy, "the deceitful dream of a golden age."[49] Although sound in theory, it was weak in application—"virtuous in speculation," as Dr. Rush would

[42] James Wilson, address to the Philadelphia convention, 4 December 1787, in *Debates*, 2: 463.

[43] Hamilton, *Federalist* 9, in *Federalist Papers*, p. 75.

[44] Ibid., p. 76.

[45] Ibid.

[46] James Iredell, address to the North Carolina convention, 25 July 1788, in *Debates*, 4: 39.

[47] Hamilton, *Federalist* 8, in *Federalist Papers*, pp. 68; 71.

[48] John Jay, address to the New York convention, 21 June 1788, in *Debates*, 2: 285.

[49] Hamilton, *Federalist* 6, in *Federalist Papers*, p. 59.

put it, but "absurd in practice."[50] Federalism, on the other hand, was based on the "practical maxim" that there was no philosophical perfection, no "happy empire of perfect wisdom and perfect virtue."[51] Thus Federalists presented their own philosophy as the product of actual practice, "the more substantial prospects," as Hamilton concluded, "of dangers, real, certain, and formidable."[52] By the close of the conventions, they could be found describing an almost total break between theoretical and instrumental reasoning. Theory aside, these practical politicians described the Constitution as the product of pragmatic decision making, arrived at, in the words of Hamilton, by "attaching ourselves purely to the dictates of reason and good sense."[53]

The result was a revised view of political experience. While Antifederalists continued to hold to classical principles, Federalists began to look more often to the evidence obtained from contemporary facts. Thinkers like Madison warned delegates not to allow an excessive reliance on historical precepts—what he called a "blind veneration for antiquity"—to overrule the knowledge of their own situations, "the lessons of their own experience."[54] Others, including New York's Chancellor Robert Livingston, denounced the use of philosophical principles altogether, preferring to make use of what he called "facts within our knowledge."[55] Still others went even further, emphasizing the exclusive importance of current issues. What mattered alone, counseled James Wilson, was "our own experience."[56]

Yet Federalists found that facts alone, however persuasive, were not enough to provide legitimacy to their newly formed Constitution. As the debates ground on, Antifederalists continued to use both history and philosophy to criticize the Federalist argument. The lack of either historical or philosophical referents was to them a telling indictment of the new Constitution. Virginia's Henry for one could think of no more serious flaw than the lack of historical antecedents. "The whole history of human nature cannot produce a government like that before you," he told the Virginia convention.[57] In the same manner, Antifederalists condemned the Constitution for its violation of traditional republican precepts. The absence of such standards, they contended, left the Constitution without any authoritative

[50] Benjamin Rush, "On the Defects of the Confederation," 1787, in *Selected Writings*, p. 28.

[51] Hamilton, *Federalist* 6, in *Federalist Papers*, p. 59.

[52] Hamilton, *Federalist* 8, in *Federalist Papers*, p. 71.

[53] Hamilton, *Federalist* 70, in *Federalist Papers*, p. 425.

[54] Madison, *Federalist* 14, in *Federalist Papers*, p. 104.

[55] Robert Livingston, address to the New York convention, 27 June 1788, in *Debates*, 2: 342.

[56] Wilson, address to the federal convention, 20 June 1787, in *Debates*, 5: 219.

[57] Henry, address to the Virginia convention, 23 June 1788, in *Debates*, 3: 579.

source of legitimacy. Thoughtful Federalists were willing to concede the case. The new Constitution, Madison observed, was "in a manner unprecedented; we cannot find one express example in the experience of the world. It stands by itself."[58] Frequently Madison spoke of the uniqueness of the new Constitution: "a new and more noble course," "no parallel in the annals of human society," "no model on the face of the globe."[59] His repetition of the theme suggested a certain pride, but also a certain insecurity. A few Federalists were willing to admit their anxiety. In a speech delivered during the waning days of the federal convention, the octogenarian Benjamin Franklin told how the Constitutional debates provided "proof of the imperfection of Human Understanding."[60] So it was that having denied the role of both historical precedent and philosophical precept, Federalists found themselves searching for some other source of legitimacy. "We indeed seem to feel our own want of political wisdom," Franklin suggested, "since we have been running about in search of it."[61] Nearing the close of the convention, those like Franklin seemed to be searching desperately, "groping as it were in the dark to find political truth, and scarce able to distinguish it when presented to us."[62]

Scientific Theorems

Before the Constitutional convention, eighteenth-century republicans considered political philosophy and political science to be synonymous terms.[63] Republican thinkers described science as a collection of experiments, carried out over long periods, from which timeless principles had been derived. In this sense, "experience" was the product of past experimentation. Essentially their political science was based on three such time-tested experiments: mixed government, separated powers, and an early form of checks and balances. Theorists from Machiavelli and Harrington to the Commonwealth Whigs had held that there would always be a division between the one, the few, and the many. In the American colonies, where politics seemed to consist primarily of a struggle between the king's governors, aristocratic elites, and democratic citizens, the idea of mixed government was almost second nature.[64] As to separation of powers, which found its classical statement in the writings of Montesquieu, several of the American states

[58] Madison, address to the Virginia convention, 5 June 1788, in *Debates*, 3: 94.

[59] Madison, *Federalist* 14, in *Federalist Papers*, p. 104.

[60] Franklin, address to the federal convention, 28 June 1787, in *Records*, 1: 451.

[61] Ibid.

[62] Ibid.

[63] See Adair, " 'That Politics May Be Reduced to a Science,' " in *Fame and the Founding Fathers*, p. 94.

[64] See Wood, *Creation*, pp. 197–202.

had explicitly written the principle into their constitutions.[65] The result of this colonial heritage was that mixed government and separated powers became to some extent intermingled. Both before and after the Revolution, American republicans would tend to see the executive as a kind of monarch, the senate as a collection of aristocrats, and the lower house as the principal source of popular representation.[66] In addition, republicans from Aristotle to Jean Louis de Lolme had maintained that there was a natural antipathy between the different elements of government, and that the alliances and conflicts that developed between them led to a rough system of countervailing checks. By the 1780s in America, the ideas of mixed government, separated powers, and checks and balances had become hopelessly entangled, so that thinkers could frequently be found arguing that each of the branches of government should not only represent separate constituencies and hold separate functions, but also have independent powers strong enough to check the initiatives of the other branches. For Antifederalists and Federalists alike, these concepts were fundamental precepts, the first principles of what they called the "science of government."[67]

Nevertheless, Antifederalists practiced this republican science in its purest, most philosophical form. The historian Gordon Wood has gone so far as to argue that their political theory was in fact a form of classical philosophy.[68] Although Wood's case may be overstated, Antifederalists did tend to think of politics in terms borrowed from classical political theory. In particular, though they realized that America was uniquely democratic, they still described their society as a combination of monarchic, aristocratic, and democratic elements. After all, an executive was but another kind of king, a senate composed of the rich and influential but a variation on aristocracy. Besides, as Maryland's A Farmer put it in a letter to the *Baltimore Gazette*, the idea of mixed government had an impeccable heritage: "the most amiable and sensible of mankind seem to have made a stand in favour of a mixed government founded on the permanent orders and objects of men."[69] As to separated powers, every important Antifederalist embraced Montesquieu's hallowed principle. According to John Dawson, a Harvard-educated Virginian, "every schoolboy in politics" was convinced of its truth.[70] When it came to the concept of balance, Antifederalists were less certain. Many, in-

[65] Ibid., pp. 202–206.

[66] Ibid., pp. 206–14.

[67] David Ramsay, *The History of the American Revolution* (London: John Stockdale, 1793), 1: 357.

[68] See Wood, *Creation*, pp. 606–15. Wood's thesis has been challenged by Schmitt and Webking, "'Revolutionaries, Antifederalists, and Federalists,'" pp. 195–229.

[69] A Farmer, essay in the (Baltimore) *Maryland Gazette*, 25 March 1788, in *Complete Anti-Federalist*, 5: 41.

[70] John Dawson, address to the Virginia convention, 24 June 1788, in *Debates*, 3: 608.

cluding the prolific writer known as the Centinel, made the case for simple representative government, presumably on the order of the radically democratic Pennsylvania constitution.[71] Nevertheless, all Antifederalists believed in limiting the power of government, and to the extent that balances constituted checks, they tended to win Antifederalist favor.[72] Monroe, a leading Antifederalist in the Virginia convention, told his fellow delegates that they could look to history and philosophy alike to show that republican government must consist of three independent branches, each of which had a "repellant quality" that enabled it to "preserve itself from being destroyed by the other two; so that the balance was continually maintained."[73] Although somewhat hyperbolic, A Farmer was typical of Antifederalists in stating his commitment to this classical form of political science: "There is nothing solid or useful that is new," he declared flatly. "And I will venture to assert, that if every *political institution* is not fully explained by Aristotle, and other ancient writers, yet that, there is no *new* discovery in this the most important of all sciences, for ten centuries back."[74]

In the Constitutional debates, Federalists began to challenge this classical conception of political science. Earlier republican theorists had envisioned political life in static terms, as an almost geometrical pattern of fixed and standing social orders. In essence, they assumed that the elements of one, few, and many would combine in a finite number of triangular patterns of power: corrupt monarchs joining with power-hungry nobles to oppress the people; virtuous aristocrats and liberty-loving citizens confronting a tyrannical king; patriotic king and virtuous citizenry in alliance against a decadent nobility. Antifederalists continued to describe political relations using this same triangular terminology. In the Constitutional debates, however, Federalist thinkers introduced a more dynamic notion of politics, in which multiple social interests combined and competed to form an infinite pattern of alliances. In lieu of a sharp division between one, few, and many, they depicted a multitude of social groups pursuing independent demands: "a landed interest, a manufacturing interest, a mercantile interest, a moneyed interest, with many lesser interests," as Madison put it in *Federalist* 10.[75]

According to traditional theory, monarchs and nobles would combine all too often to oppress their liberty-loving subjects. By contrast, Federalists

[71] Centinel, letter to the (Philadelphia) *Independent Gazetteer*, October 1787, in *Complete Anti-Federalist*, 2: 136–43. See also Herbert J. Storing, "What the Anti-Federalists Were *For*," in *Complete Anti-Federalist*, 1: 55.

[72] See Storing, "What the Anti-Federalists Were *For*," in *Complete Anti-Federalist*, 1: 56–63.

[73] Monroe, address to the Virginia convention, 10 June 1788, in *Debates*, 3: 218.

[74] A Farmer, essay to the (Baltimore) *Maryland Gazette*, 29 February 1788, in *Complete Anti-Federalist*, 5: 17.

[75] Madison, *Federalist* 10, in *Federalist Papers*, p. 79.

pictured a continuing series of conflicts in which no single social order could gain superiority over the next. Indeed, as Madison developed the theory in *Federalist* 10, the more parties and interests the better, for, as he wrote, "you make it less probable that a majority of the whole will have a common motive to invade the rights of other citizens."[76] Under mixed government, the people had always been subject to oppression. In the Madisonian system, in which social groups were constantly combining and dividing, concerted action by any single interest became impossible, the potential for oppression was limited, and the rights of citizens were secured. Following Madison's lead, Federalist writers began to depict this multifactional politics as a decided improvement over the classical republican conception of mixed government. As James Wilson would boast to the Pennsylvania convention, "The ancients, so enlightened on other subjects, were very uninformed with regard to this."[77]

Similarly, Federalist theorists suggested their own revised version of the separation of powers. Where earlier republicans had held the view that different departments should pursue unrelated functions, Federalists envisioned a system of shared responsibilities. First and foremost, they did not assume that the three branches would represent distinct constituencies of king, nobles, and commons. Instead they argued that in the American republic, where all institutions answered ultimately to the people, power could be shared rather than divided. Moreover, whereas Antifederalists maintained that separated powers existed to limit institutional prerogatives, Federalists saw separation as a strategy that would increase each institution's powers, making it better able to pursue the public interest. At the same time, they held that no branch should be allowed to become dominant. In *Federalist* 51, Madison explained the theory by which institutions could be simultaneously strengthened and controlled: "Ambition must be made to counteract ambition. The interest of the man must be connected with the constitutional rights of the place."[78] By supplying those who administered the respective departments with the means and motives to resist the encroachments of others, Federalist theorists could create popular institutions that, while constantly in conflict with one another, would nonetheless be cooperating, whether they knew it or not, by pursuing policies that would secure the greater good. To these thinkers, such principles were entirely the product of modern political science, "wholly new discoveries," as Hamilton described them, that had "made their principal progress towards perfection in modern times."[79]

[76] Ibid., p. 83.
[77] Wilson, address to the Pennsylvania convention, 24 November 1787, in *Debates*, 2: 422.
[78] Madison, *Federalist* 51, in *Federalist Papers*, p. 322.
[79] Hamilton, *Federalist* 9, in *Federalist Papers*, p. 72.

Ultimately, Federalists sought to apply a revised concept of balance to the political world. As Wood described it, eighteenth-century republicanism had been based on a theory of potential energy.[80] Classical republicans held that all rulers would grow corrupt, and that the only insurance of freedom was for a people to stay vigilant, constantly on guard against corruption, ready to rebel. Periodically, citizens would be forced to throw off their corrupted rulers, replacing them with new, more virtuous ones. By contrast, Federalist theory was more kinetic, in that it pictured politics as a scene of constant motion, of multiple interests and overlapping institutions competing with one another in a continuing struggle for power.[81] In his *Defence*, Adams showed how the periodic conflict between kings, nobles, and people had led to a state of extreme imbalance, "perpetual alternations of rebellion and tyranny," as he described the early republics, "and the butchery of thousands upon every revolution from one to the other."[82] To Adams, the classical conception of balance was only a higher form of imbalance, a swinging pendulum that promised to alternate wildly between anarchy and tyranny. Nevertheless, even the gloomy Adams did not despair of a more perfect politics: "Some physicians," he wrote, "have thought, that if it were practicable to keep the several humors of the body in an exact *balance* of each with its opposite, it might be immortal; and so perhaps with a political body, if the *balance of power* could be always held exactly even."[83] Whereas Adams insisted on holding to the traditional concept of mixed government, Federalists led by Madison, relying on the idea of multiple interests, argued that the constant action and reaction of political groups would create a system that, while constantly in motion, would be extremely stable, "ever new," as Dickinson put it, "and always the same."[84] In short, in place of the periodic imbalance of classical philosophy, they offered the perpetual equilibrium of modern science, the "perfect balance," according to Hamilton, "between liberty and power."[85]

With this new form of political science, Federalists sought to create a timeless form of politics. Transcending any need for the lessons of the past, preventing any possibility of declension in the future, the American Constitution existed entirely in a theoretically perfect present. The discoveries of modern science had made it possible to bring the principles of the political realm into complete conformity with the laws of the natural world. Written

[80] See Wood, *Creation*, p. 606.
[81] Ibid. See also Neal Riemer, "The Republicanism of James Madison," *Political Science Quarterly*, 69, 1 (March 1954): 48–51.
[82] Adams, *Defence*, in *Works*, 4: 285.
[83] Ibid., 384–85.
[84] Dickinson, "Letters of Fabius, no. IV," 1788, in *Political Writings*, 2: 110.
[85] Hamilton, address to the New York convention, 25 June 1788, in *Debates*, 2: 316.

in "the language of reason and truth," based on principles "as fixed and unchangeable as the laws which operate in the natural world," the Constitution was intended to be a perfect system, "as infallible as any mathematical calculations."[86] Secure in their scientific faith, Federalists waxed euphoric on the superiority of the new Constitution; it was, as one said, the "best form of government that has ever been offered to the world."[87] Whereas other schemes had fallen into corruption and decline, a perpetually balanced federal Constitution seemed capable of continuing forever. With it, predicted an admiring Robert Davidson, the American states "shall resemble, the Solar System, where every obedient planet moves on its proper path, — never seeking to fly from, nor even approaching the great attractive orb, than the wise author of nature intended."[88] The federal Constitution was created to apply equally to every age, never running down, wearing out, or falling into disrepair. As far as these Federalist writers were concerned, the new republic could continue in this perfect state forever—"a system," Barlow rhapsodized, "which will stand the test of ages."[89]

Throughout the debates, Federalists would continue to argue that the Constitution was a theoretically perfect instrument. As the state conventions drew on, however, they came to admit the cold hard truth so often propounded by the Antifederalists—that the Constitution, however excellent in theory, might well be flawed in practice. Equally important, they realized that the case for ratification could be strengthened by embracing the Antifederalist demand for an amendment procedure. Thus, in Federalist rhetoric, "experience" began to undergo one final change, from experience as scientific truth to experience as scientific experimentation. In the later debates, experience was often used in this future tense. "Let us give it a trial," Tench Coxe would propose in 1788, "and when experience has taught us its mistakes, the people . . . can reform and amend them."[90]

Paradoxical as it seems, eighteenth-century science made allowance for both theoretical permanence and practical improvement. The application of

[86] The Friends of Union and just Government, *An Address to the Citizens of Pennsylvania* (Philadelphia: n.p., [1789]; Elizur Goodrich, D.D., *The Principles of Civil Union and Happiness considered and recommended. A Sermon* . . . (Hartford, Conn.: Hudson and Goodwin, 1787), p. 8; Hamilton, address to the New York convention, 28 June 1788, in *Debates,* 2: 366.

[87] Simeon Baldwin, *An Oration Pronounced Before the Citizens of New-Haven, July 4th, 1788* . . . (New Haven, Conn.: J. Meigs, 1788), p. 13.

[88] Robert Davidson, D.D., *An Oration on the Independence of the United States of America* . . . (Carlisle, Pa.: Kline and Reynolds [1787]), p. 15.

[89] Joel Barlow, *An Oration, Delivered in the North Church in Hartford . . . July 4th, 1787* . . . (Hartford, Conn: Hudson and Goodwin, [1787]), p. 19.

[90] Tench Coxe, "An Examination of the Constitution of the United States of America . . . ," 1788, in *Pamphlets on the Constitution of the United States* . . . , ed. Paul Leicester Ford (Brooklyn, N.Y.: n.p., 1888), pp. 153–54.

theory to practice had led to striking innovations in what scientists called "useful knowledge": astronomical discoveries had inspired new forms of navigation and cartography, the development of biological principles had led to improved agriculture, and chemical experimentation had advanced the quality of manufactured goods. In politics, the same seemed possible. The excellence of the Constitution, Virginia's George Wythe explained, "could not be denied by its warmest opponents."[91] Nevertheless, in its actual operation, there was always room for improvement: "experience was the best guide," Wythe continued, speaking as one of America's most distinguished legalists, "and alone could develop its consequences."[92] In the state conventions, experience frequently took on this subjunctive sense, with Federalists arguing that the Constitution should be viewed as perfect in theory, while open to improvement in practice. As an impatient Francis Corbin asked rhetorically in the Virginia convention, "What danger is there, then, to be apprehended from a government which is theoretically perfect, and the possible blemishes of which can only be demonstated by actual experience?"[93]

Thus, by the last of the debates, Federalist thinkers could claim that they had created a politics that would transcend time. Through their critical use of history, they had put an end to the unquestioned authority of the past. By relying on empirical evidence, they had established a political process that existed entirely in the present. With the concept of equilibrium, they had created a system that could in theory continue indefinitely. Finally, in the idea of experimentation, they had discovered the means to create a constantly improving future. As the historian Dr. David Ramsay would definitively conclude in his *History of the American Revolution*, the Federalist founders had placed the "science of politics on the footing with the other sciences, by opening it to improvements from experience, and the discoveries of future ages."[94]

As the ratifying conventions drew to a close, Federalists seemed increasingly to dominate the debates. By the late spring of 1788, ratification was already assured. Nevertheless, there remained New York and Virginia, those two balky giants, which while unable to prevent ratification itself, could extract significant concessions on amendments. As Antifederalists dug in, Federalists seemed increasingly confident, almost eager for what promised to be a formidable fray.

Their confidence was not unrealistic. For in the course of the federal convention, Federalist thinkers had made a compelling philosophical case. In

[91] George Wythe, address to the Virginia convention, 24 June 1788, in *Debates*, 3: 587.
[92] Ibid.
[93] Francis Corbin, address to the Virginia convention, 7 June 1788, in *Debates*, 3: 112.
[94] David Ramsay, *History*, 1: 357.

interpreting the meaning of political experience, they had created a Constitutional theory simultaneously grounded in historical events, constructed according to philosophical principles, and operating with scientific method and precision. With the acceptance of an amendment procedure, they could argue that their system would provide both permanence and the possibility of reform. The Constitution complete and the amendment process established, they could promise nothing less than perfection with progress. Antifederalists continued to cite their classical precepts, but in the face of this Federalist theory, they appeared increasingly anachronistic.

Yet in pointing toward amendment and future revision, the Federalists had introduced another issue altogether. The Constitution had been constructed, but remained to be brought into being. Alone, it was but a theoretical skeleton. Put into operation, it would become flesh and blood. Having transformed the republic in theory, Federalists turned to the more pressing problem of founding it in practice. On this point, on the issue of founding, Antifederalists would make their final stand.

‹6›

FOUNDING

Audacity, Ambition, Adaptability

IN THE DEBATES over ratification, convention delegates were forced to act politically in ways they had never acted before. If anything, they had practiced politics with an eye toward the past, constantly conscious of the importance of their heritage. From earliest times, citizens had been expected to keep alive original principles, passing on the legacy of the first founders to later generations. But with the creation of the Constitution, the situation had changed, for however intentionally or even knowingly, the drafters of the Constitution had radically reformulated the principles of their politics. It remained for the delegates to the state conventions to reject or ratify these new principles, choosing, in effect, to return to the precepts of the past, or to strike out in a different direction, creating a political theory more attuned to their own times, and to future times. Thus ratification required republicans to reconsider the concept of founding, and to reflect on its enduring effects, its meaning for both the present and the future.

In establishing their legacy as founders, the Federalist supporters of the Constitution were immensely successful. From virtually the time of the founding on, they have been described in glowing terms. Acting in the face of insurrection, seizing the time, the Federalist founders have been seen as political saviors who rescued America from the chaos of the Confederation by creating the incomparable federal Constitution, what John Fiske would call "this Iliad, or Parthenon, or Fifth Symphony, of statesmanship."[1] Forgoing ideology for practicality, these pragmatic politicians not only acted when others hesitated, but they acted with realism and common sense, with what Hofstadter labeled "a statesmanlike sense of moderation."[2] The Federalist founders were men of "elan and dash," filled with "verve and ardor," and having a "grandeur of scope unknown to any previous generation."[3] In short, these forward-looking founders looked to the future and, in so doing, left a lasting legacy, a "national framework," in Cecelia Kenyon's words, "which would accommodate the later rise of democracy."[4]

[1] John Fiske, *The Critical Period of American History, 1783–1789* (Boston: Houghton, Mifflin, 1888), p. 223.

[2] Hofstadter, *The American Political Tradition*, p. 15.

[3] Elkins and McKitrick, "Founding Fathers," pp. 206; 214; 203.

[4] Cecelia Kenyon, "Men of Little Faith: The Anti-federalists on the Nature of Representative Government," *The William and Mary Quarterly*, 3rd ser., 12, 1 (January 1955): 43.

By contrast, in opposing the Constitution, the Antifederalists seem to have relegated themselves to a legacy of shame. Many historians have failed to even mention their role in the debates, let alone to note the fact that they came close to carrying the day. Instead, most have chosen to describe them in distinctly unflattering terms. From the time of John Fiske, Antifederalists have been seen as complacent in the face of chaos, blind to the conflict and disorder that characterized the mid-1780s, "the most critical moment," as Fiske called it, "in all the history of the American people."[5] Similarly, they have been seen as negativistic obstructionists who set themselves against the new government while offering no alternative of their own, pursuing, in the words of one early twentieth-century historian, "merely a policy of negation."[6] Max Farrand popularized this line of criticism, arguing that the Constitution's opponents were failed founders, their attempts at statesmanship seeming to consist of little more than "trying to find excuses for their opposition."[7] "Realist" historians like Boorstin and Hofstadter honed the theme further, contending that the genius of the Federalist framers was their down-to-earth practicality, whereas the tragedy of their Antifederalist counterparts was their predisposition towards high-minded philosophical theorizing, what Boorstin called their intellectual "idolatry."[8] Perhaps most important, Cecelia Kenyon claimed that, along with their other faults, the Antifederalists were "men of little faith," elitist provincials who had no conception of the potential of the modern democratic state.[9] Elaborating on the theme, writers like Clinton Rossiter argued that the most telling Antifederalist fault was the inability to foresee the future development of the nation, their lack of continental "vision."[10] Even very recently, a sympathetic observer such as Herbert Storing could claim that the Antifederalists were ambivalent about the future of the nation. As Storing put it, "They did not fail to *see* the opportunity for American nationhood that the Federalists seized so gloriously, but they could not join in grasping it."[11]

Nevertheless, it is better and truer to see the Federalist founders not as so astonishingly superior to their Antifederalist counterparts, but as simply different. Federalists and Antifederalists alike were founders, as Storing

[5] Fiske, *Critical Period*, p. 55.

[6] Henry Jones Ford, *The Rise and Growth of American Politics* (New York: Macmillan, 1898), p. 101.

[7] Max Farrand, *The Fathers of the Constitution* (New Haven, Conn.: Yale University Press, 1921), p. 161.

[8] Boorstin, *Genius of American Politics*, p. 3.

[9] Kenyon, "Men of Little Faith," p. 3.

[10] See Clinton Rossiter, *1787: The Grand Convention* (New York: Macmillan, 1966), p. 57. See also Elkins and McKitrick, "The Founding Fathers," pp. 181–216.

[11] Storing, "What the Anti-Federalists Were *For*," in *Complete Anti-Federalist*, 1: 6.

himself has suggested.¹² But they were founders of different kinds, holding
fundamentally different definitions of founding. In large part, their views
reflected dissimilar notions of political action. They also implied divergent
expectations about the future. In the state ratification conventions, and especially in the later conventions, these differences would devolve into
heated conceptual conflict, and eventually into the final intellectual battle,
by which the Constitution's fate would be sealed.

Audacity

At the heart of the state debates lay deep disagreement over the need for
political action. For their part, Federalists saw the existing political situation as critical. At least, they used the term often in contemporary debate:
"the critical moment," "this critical period," "our situation is critical to the
greatest degree."¹³ As to the term's meaning, the case is also fairly clear.
From the time of Machiavelli, modern republicans had contended that there
were certain moments in history in which political action had special significance. As Pocock explained in *The Machiavellian Moment*, it was only
during these decisive moments that the power of fortune, the irrational or
unpredictable element in events, could be counteracted by human initia-
tive.¹⁴ These were the turning points of human history, "great eras," as
James Wilson wrote, "when important and very perceptible alterations take
place in the situation of men and things."¹⁵

Critical periods demanded action. As Federalists like John Jay described
them, they were transient and fleeting moments, "occasions when days,
nay, even when hours, are precious."¹⁶ Moreover, they demanded audacity,
for critical periods were by definition times in which action brought results,
"when exertion or neglect," in the words of Tench Coxe, "must produce
consequences of the utmost moment."¹⁷ Repeatedly Federalists argued that
failure to act would be consigning the new nation to certain disaster. At
times, their predictions were hyperbolic: "the frail and tottering edifice
seems ready to fall upon our heads and to crush us beneath its ruins," wrote

¹² Ibid., 3.
¹³ Alexander Hamilton, address to the federal convention, 29 June 1787, in *Debates*, 5: 259;
John Quincy Adams, "An Oration . . . ," 18 July 1787, in *Diary of John Quincy Adams*, ed.
Robert J. Taylor (Cambridge, Mass.: Harvard University Press, 1981), 2: 258; Marcus [James
Iredell], "Answers to Mr. Mason's Objections . . . ," 1788, in *Pamphlets*, p. 369.
¹⁴ See Pocock, *Machiavellian Moment*, pp. 156–82.
¹⁵ James Wilson, "Lectures on Law," in *The Works of James Wilson*, ed. Robert Green
McCloskey (Cambridge, Mass.: Harvard University Press, 1967), 1: 354.
¹⁶ John Jay, *Federalist 64*, in *Federalist Papers*, p. 393.
¹⁷ Coxe, "An Enquiry," in *View*, p. 4.

Hamilton in *Federalist* 15.[18] But rhetorical flourishes notwithstanding, they seemed to feel honest fear of a future left to what one writer called "necessity and chance."[19] Hence, Federalists could consider it their responsibility to present a plan—any plan—that afforded, in the words of the very rich and very worried Stephen Higginson, "even a gleam of hope."[20] Jay put it even more succinctly. Critical periods, he concluded, were "moments to be seized as they pass."[21]

By contrast, Antifederalists seemed surprisingly reluctant to take any action at all. Their stance was particularly surprising given the fact that their leaders conceded that events of the time required some kind of response. "I know our situation is critical," admitted the Federal Farmer, "and it behoves us to make the best of it."[22] In his *The Critical Period of American History*, possibly the most influential study of the Constitutional era, Fiske left the impression that Antifederalists opposed all attempts at constitutional reform. The truth is that many were strong advocates of revision. "It is no longer doubted," observed the New York Antifederalist Melancton Smith, "that the confederation, in its present form, is inadequate."[23] In fact, according to Patrick Henry, virtually all Antifederalists agreed that some sort of change was absolutely essential: "Every man says that something must be done."[24]

Yet in place of Federalist audacity, Antifederalists counseled prudence. Where Federalists were inclined to see critical situations as perilous, threatening imminent catastrophe, Antifederalists saw them as indeterminate, offering equal possibility of failure and success. Political action, it followed, could as often do harm as good. With characteristic equanimity, the Jovian Federal Farmer made the case in his first letter, reminding his readers that it was "natural for men, who wish to hasten the adoption of a measure, to tell us, now is the crisis—now is the critical moment which must be seized or all will be lost." This strategy, he allowed, had been used by tyrants in all ages. Federal Farmer warned of the consequence of undue haste: "The fickle and ardent," he suggested, "in any community, are the proper tools for establishing despotic government."[25] His caution was typical of Antifed-

[18] Hamilton, *Federalist* 15, in *Federalist Papers*, p. 113.
[19] Stephen Higginson to Nathan Dane, 3 March 1787, in "Letters of Stephen Higginson," *Annual Report*, 1: 753.
[20] Ibid.
[21] Jay, *Federalist* 64, in *Federalist Papers*, p. 393.
[22] The Federal Farmer, "Observations," 8 October 1787, in *Complete Anti-Federalist*, 2: 224.
[23] A Plebian [Melancton Smith], "Address," 1788, in *Complete Anti-Federalist*, 6: 135. See Fiske, *Critical Period*, pp. 55, 134–86.
[24] Patrick Henry, address to the Virginia convention, 24 June 1788, in *Debates*, 3: 595.
[25] Federal Farmer, "Observations," 8 October 1787, in *Complete Anti-Federalist*, 2: 226. On prudence, see Pocock, *Machiavellian Moment*, pp. 47–8, 238–39.

eralists, who, while admitting the need for revision, feared the indeterminate outcome of political reform. On the whole, they would have preferred to leave the solution to what one called "time and habit."[26] But at the very least, if action were to be taken, they insisted that their fellow citizens take time to "consider carefully."[27] As Federal Farmer advised sagely, before deciding on any plan, they should "enquire whether it will probably be a blessing or a curse to this people."[28]

At heart Antifederalists were conservative reformers. In keeping with classical republican theory, they held that corruption was inevitable, that even the best states would decline over time from freedom into tyranny. Also in accordance with this theory, they maintained that the purpose of political reform was to recapture the original liberty that had been lost over time. To Antifederalists as to generations of republicans before them, reform implied revision, the return to first best principles. Thus, they showed great respect, almost a kind of reverence, for precedent, what New York's A Countryman, writing in 1787 to the New York Journal, called fondly "the good old way."[29]

Above all else, Antifederalists were committed to maintaining the right of self-government won at such cost in the late Revolution. As Monroe put it in the Virginia convention, "We have struggled long to bring about this revolution, by which we enjoy our present freedom and security. Why, then, this haste—this wild precipitation?"[30] By extension, they argued that existing institutions had served well enough in protecting their liberties. The Articles of Confederation, according to Charleston's Judge Lowndes, was in fact a "most excellent constitution—one that had stood the test of time, and carried us through difficulties generally supposed to be insurmountable." Although most were not altogether pleased with its performance, Antifederalists accepted the present Confederation as their legitimate government. They therefore insisted that it be given all possible respect; constitutions should be treated, Lowndes reminded his colleagues, as "sacred things."[31] By contrast, they were predisposed to look on the proposed Federalist initiatives as illegitimate, a breach of the original contract that had established the republic. In this regard, certain Antifederalists pointed

[26] Centinel [Samuel Bryan], letter to the (Philadelphia) Independent Gazetteer, 5 October 1787, in Complete Anti-Federalist, 2: 137.

[27] An Old Whig, essay in the (Philadelphia) Independent Gazetteer, 1787, in Complete Anti-Federalist, 3: 39.

[28] Federal Farmer, "Observations," 8 October 1787, in Complete Anti-Federalist, 2: 226.

[29] A Countryman, letter to the New York Journal, 20 December 1787, in Complete Anti-Federalist, 6: 82.

[30] James Monroe, address to the Virginia convention, 10 June 1788, in Debates, 3: 222.

[31] Rawlins Lowndes, speech in the South Carolina legislature, 16 January 1788, in Complete Anti-Federalist, 5: 149; 150.

out that the Federalist proposals constituted a precedent for any and all future constitutions, including those that might establish the worst forms of
despotism. James Winthrop, writing as Agrippa, seemed to sum up their
brand of conservative reform: "The framing [of] entirely new systems," he
wrote, "is a work that requires vast attention; and it is much easier to guard
an old one."[32]

In the same manner, Antifederalists considered their current government
to be basically sound, and therefore reformable. Although few were inclined
to view their present situation as perfect, many pointed out that they were
living in peace and relative prosperity. At least some problems could fairly
be considered as caused by the late war, or by the newness of the postwar
system. For that matter, as Candidus observed in a letter to the *Boston Independent Chronicle*, some of their troubles, and notably their economic
woes, were the product of what he called "extraneous causes" and "private
imprudencies," and hardly the fault of government.[33] At least one somewhat more partisan commentator went so far as to argue that much of the
current dissatisfaction was incurred by the constant criticism of their Federalist foes.[34] All told, Antifederalists could contend in all good conscience
that their situation was really not so bad. Candidus made the case: "Let such
persons read the history of other nations," he told the critics, "and then
judge whether it is *impossible* that our situation should be worse."[35]

Additionally, inclined as they were to assume degeneration, Antifederalists had no reason to think that the new Constitution would offer any discernable improvement. Luther Martin of Maryland made this point in opposing ratification: "a short time might shew the new system as defective as
the old," he wrote with his usual cynicism, "perhaps more so."[36] The New
York pamphleteer Countryman, portraying himself as a simple but shrewd
farmer, preferred a homier style. How unwise it would be, he suggested, to
pull down a perfectly good old house in order to move, out of pride and
vanity, into a new one. How much more unwise if, though the new house
appeared large and fine on the outside, it was in fact not well finished
within, the foundation being bad, the roof leaky, and many of the posts
rotten. How much more sensible, concluded the doughty Countryman, to

[32] Agrippa [James Winthrop], letter to the *Massachusetts Gazette*, 22 January 1788, in *Complete Anti-Federalist*, 4: 103.

[33] Candidus, essay in the (Boston) *Independent Chronicle*, 6 December 1787, in *Complete
Anti-Federalist*, 4: 128.

[34] See Melancton Smith, address to the New York convention, 20 June 1788, in *Debates*, 2:
229.

[35] Candidus, essay in the (Boston) *Independent Chronicle*, 6 December 1787, in *Complete
Anti-Federalist*, 4: 126.

[36] Luther Martin, "The Genuine Information . . . ," 1788, in *Complete Anti-Federalist*, 2: 34.

continue peaceably in the old house, "mending it now and then, as it stands in need of it."[37]

Even while assuming the need for reform, Antifederalists were inclined to counsel delay. Following established republican theory, they believed that states traveled a cyclical course in which corruption led to revolution. Over time, sacrifice and patriotism would give way to selfishness and vice. Eventually corruption would become unbearable, and the consequence would be another flurry of reform, perhaps even another revolution. Jefferson had put the idea best in his statement that a little rebellion now and then was a good and necessary thing.[38] Until the proper moment for rebellion arrived, however, cyclical reformers were inclined to watch and wait. Thus, when Federalists seized the initiative, calling for the convention, insisting on total revision, and demanding rapid ratification, Antifederalists hesitated. The Federalist proposals, they argued, had come too soon in the cycle: "We are now, in a time of peace, without any real cause, changing our government," observed a dismayed William Grayson. "Let us therefore be cautious, and deliberate before we determine."[39]

Anxiety-ridden Federalists, fearing that with enough time most people would find something to dislike in the new document, took up the conscious strategy of overwhelming their opponents before they could begin to organize resistance. Antifederalist leaders like Elbridge Gerry of Massachusetts were well aware of the strategy, warning their colleagues that the Federalists were determined "to carry it thro by Surprise."[40] Forewarned or not, rank-and-file Antifederalists found themselves bewildered, "hurried on, like the driving of Jehu, very furiously," as an incensed Nathaniel Barrell told the Massachusetts convention.[41] To these believers in cyclical change, the time was simply not ripe for reform. Writing in the *Maryland Journal* as Caution, the highly respected Samuel Chase, a leader of Baltimore's legal community, urged that for the present they were "not pressed in point of time to determine on the subject." Antifederalists preferred to wait at least until the system began to show clearer signs of failure. After all, advised Caution, "no possible mischief or inconvenience can happen from delay."[42]

[37] A Countryman, letter to the *New York Journal*, 20 December 1787, in *Complete Anti-Federalist*, 6: 82.

[38] See Thomas Jefferson to James Madison, 30 January 1787, in *Papers*, 11: 93.

[39] William Grayson, address to the Virginia convention, 24 June 1788, in *Debates*, 3: 615.

[40] Elbridge Gerry to [James Warren?], 18 October 1787, cited in Robert Allen Rutland, *The Ordeal of the Constitution* (Norman, Okla.: University of Oklahoma Press, 1966), p. 21. See also Rutland, *Ordeal*, p. 307.

[41] Nathaniel Barrell, address to the Massachusetts convention, 5 February 1788, in *Debates*, 2: 160. Barrell would later reluctantly vote for ratification.

[42] Caution [Samuel Chase], letter to the *Maryland Journal*, 11 October 1788, in *Essays*, p. 328.

Although in hindsight their reticence may seem overly cautious, Antifederalists could hardly be blamed for complacency. On the contrary, their most often repeated fear was that sudden alterations might lead to further conflicts, what Federal Farmer called "tumults and disorders." In addition, because they assumed that all republics would eventually degenerate into tyrannies, they feared that precipitant action might well invite some kind of antirepublican reaction, as the "peaceable and better part of the community," in Federal Farmer's terms, became disposed to "accept any government, however despotic, that shall promise stability and firmness."[43] The result would be the worst of all possible outcomes—anarchy followed by tyranny. In point of fact, these were exactly the same fears expressed by their Federalist counterparts. Given this possibility, Antifederalists were prepared to endure much in the way of minor day-to-day dislocation. As a skeptical Richard Henry Lee put it in a letter to Governor Randolph, "to say that a bad government must be established for fear of anarchy, is really saying that we should kill ourselves for fear of dying!"[44]

Antifederalists expressed concern that the Federalist remedy might prove worse than the disease. Once a new constitution were put into place, they argued, it would be difficult if not impossible to revoke it. "Consider then duly before you leap," advised Centinel, "for after the Rubicon is once passed, there will be no retreat."[45] To Federalists, this hesitation seemed irresponsible. Yet Antifederalists could reasonably consider themselves as taking the responsible course. Where liberty was at stake, they contended, it was better to avoid failure, and the almost certain loss of the republic, than to seek the success of some indefinite improvements. "If a wrong step be now made," Henry warned the Virginia convention, "the republic may be lost forever. . . . A wrong step, made now, will plunge us into misery, and our republic will be lost."[46]

Ambition

In the state ratification debates, delegates came face to face with the issue of how to go about changing constitutions. Federalists seemed very much at ease with the problem. If anything, they were extraordinarily ambitious politicians. On their arrival at Philadelphia, supporters of constitutional reform had agreed on very little: most desired more power for the Confederation Congress, some preferred a new national government, a few even spoke for the abolition of the states. On most issues, they were hopelessly divided. In

[43] Federal Farmer, "Observations," 8 October 1787, in *Complete Anti-Federalist*, 2: 224.

[44] Richard Henry Lee to Edmund Randolph, 16 October 1787, in *Letters*, 2: 450.

[45] Centinel, letter to the (Philadelphia) *Independent Gazette*, 5 November 1787, in *Complete Anti-Federalist*, 2: 155.

[46] Henry, address to the Virginia convention, 4 June 1788, in *Debates*, 3: 22.

their desire for reform, however, Federalists found unity. Moreover, they found common ground in their willingness to revise existing institutions radically. Ironically, their greatest source of agreement may very well have been this willingness to dismiss summarily the existing Articles of Confederation, and to begin again with the federal Constitution. Indeed, there exists no better proof of the point than that once the final instrument was framed, and under the strong leadership of those like Madison, Hamilton, and Wilson, they became all but unanimous in their support for the new plan.

At the same time, Federalists made much of the absence of any comprehensive Antifederalist alternative. In particular, they derided Antifederalist incrementalism, referring to their proposals as small and insignificant, "a succession of expedients," as Hamilton put it with characteristic bluntness, "temporizing, impotent, disgraceful."[47] They also emphasized the inconsistencies within the Antifederalist camp. "Instead of agreeing in their objections," Wilson told the Pennsylvania convention, "those who make them bring forward such as are diametrically opposite. . . . Like the iron race of *Cadmus*, these opponents rise only to destroy each other."[48] In this respect, they argued that Antifederalists had no sense of statesmanship, no "liberal or enlarged plans of public good."[49] But the most telling Federalist argument was that their counterparts had no concern for the future, no interest in the influence of their deliberations on posterity. In creating the Constitution, they reminded their hapless counterparts, they were legislating not only for themselves, but "for generations unborn."[50] By installing an entirely new form of government, they would ensure liberty and order to future generations. At the same time, Federalists speculated, they would also win the respect and admiration of countless future citizens. "Posterity," predicted an expansive James Sullivan, writing as Cassius in a letter to the *Massachusetts Gazette*, "made happy by your wisdom and exertions, will honour and revere your memories."[51]

Antifederalist proposals did indeed seem unimpressive in comparison. On a number of issues, they took strong and consistently positive stands: the imperative of broad popular representation, the importance of state sovereignty, the need for a bill of rights. Yet most of their positions were phrased in negative terms: fear of consolidated government, opposition to

---

[47] Hamilton, *Federalist* 30, in *Federalist Papers*, p. 191.
[48] Wilson, address to the Pennsylvania convention, 30 November 1787, in *Debates*, 2: 450–51.
[49] Hamilton, *Federalist* 30, in *Federalist Papers*, p. 191.
[50] Alexander Tweed, address to the South Carolina convention, 20 May 1788, in *Debates*, 4: 333.
[51] Cassius, letter to the *Massachusetts Gazette*, 25 December 1787, in *Essays*, p. 48.

unlimited taxing authority, distrust of standing armies, condemnation of presidential power, disapproval of senatorial prerogatives, concern over legislative abuses. Their own suggestions for reform consisted of a few new laws and some revised institutions. As to any awareness of the long-term importance of their efforts, they were almost totally oblivious. When Federalists spoke of the need to legislate for the future, Antifederalists protested. The duty of the legislator, urged Melancton Smith, a hard-headed and practical Clintonian politician, was "to calculate for the present period, and not attempt to provide for the contingencies of two or three centuries to come." Antifederalist delegates expressed little confidence in their ability to foresee the future, let alone legislate for it. "In time," Smith went on, criticizing the proposed Constitution, "events might take place which no human wisdom could foresee, and which might totally defeat and render useless these provisions." In short, Antifederalists appeared to be at a loss in describing any enduring effects of their efforts. In government, Smith humbly told the New York delegates, "the present state of the country alone ought to be considered."[52]

Yet their stance is not exactly what it seems, for Antifederalists held a different conception of constitution than their Federalist colleagues. From Machiavelli to Montesquieu, republicans had maintained that government was based on a contract between rulers and ruled. Because they believed that rulers would always seek to extend their power, republicans tried to limit official prerogatives whenever possible. It followed that in creating constitutions, care had to be taken to list the precise limits of power. In the same manner, republican theory held that rulers would always seek to expand their influence at the expense of the liberties of the people. Thus the rights of citizens also had to be indelibly inscribed into constitutional law. As Wood has shown, the state constitutions of the Revolutionary era were cast in this republican mold, being written characteristically in an almost carping tone, as if admonishing rulers not to exceed the limits of their authority, while exhorting citizens to be distrustful of their leaders in protecting their freedom.[53] Similarly, in these documents the powers of officials were strictly limited, whereas the liberties of the people were extensively defined, often at extraordinary length. To Antifederalists, these republican constitutions, however carping or clumsily overwritten, were the best protectors of freedom. The fact that they were so specific posed no real problem, for when enough of these specific provisions had become dated, the constitution could be rewritten, and the state itself reconstituted.

[52] Smith, address to the New York convention, 1 July 1788, in *Debates*, 2: 381; 381–82; 382.

[53] See Wood, *Creation*, pp. 127–61.

Antifederalists expressed little concern over the fact that constitutions would go out of date. After all, the ultimate source of authority was the people, who had every right to revise their own government as the need arose. Jefferson himself, working on the premise that no generation could legally bind the next, proposed that every constitution be rewritten at least every thirty-four years.[54] Until then, the specificity of the document, along with its exacting detail, offered protection for the people. Federalists considered this conception of constitutionalism to be negative and narrow. Antifederalists preferred to describe it in more positive terms, as restricting power and protecting freedom. Said Henry, "It is our duty to rest our rights on a certain foundation, and not trust to future contingencies."[55]

Implicit in this concept of constitution was a classical republican idea of posterity. From the time of the Magna Charta, English opposition writers had relied on written documents to preserve and transmit specific liberties from generation to generation. As Wood has shown, the American colonial charters, replete with their bills of rights, were written with this transfer of liberties in mind. To the Antifederalists who followed in this tradition, constitutions were designed not to legislate for future citizens, but to protect them. Accordingly, far from feeling no responsibility for future citizens, Antifederalists seemed almost obsessed with their protection. The decisions of the conventions, for better or worse, would affect not only themselves, said Centinel, but also "posterity for ages to come."[56] Federalists and Antifederalists alike admitted the power of fortune in public affairs. Both assumed that the outcome of their actions could not be predicted. Both believed, in the commonly heard phrase, that their efforts could prove "a blessing or a curse."[57] Yet where Federalists tended to stress potential benefits, Antifederalists more often warned of possible calamities. Mason was typically somber: "The liberty or misery of millions yet unborn," he told the Virginia delegates, "are deeply concerned in our decision."[58]

Hence, unlike Federalists, who acted to effect a plan that they could later justify, Antifederalists sought to act in such a way as to avoid mistakes that they might later regret. As Lowndes put it, it was their responsibility to write laws that "cannot possibly do any injury to us or our posterity."[59] Where Federalists welcomed the role of republican prototype, Antifederalists responded very differently, seeming humbled by the thought that they

[54] See Jefferson to Madison, 6 September 1789, in *Papers*, 15: 393.

[55] Henry, address to the Virginia convention, 20 June 1788, in *Debates*, 3: 541.

[56] Centinel, letter to the (Philadelphia) *Independent Gazetteer*, 5 November 1787, in *Complete Anti-Federalist*, 2: 155. See Wood, *Creation*, pp. 268–73.

[57] Philadelphiensis [Benjamin Workman], essay in the (Philadelphia) *Independent Gazetteer*, 1787, in *Complete Anti-Federalist*, 3: 106.

[58] George Mason, address to the Virginia convention, 11 June 1788, in *Debates*, 3: 271.

[59] Lowndes, address to the South Carolina convention, 16 January 1788, in *Debates*, 4: 271.

might by their failure be consigning not only themselves, but all the world, and for centuries to come, to hopeless tyranny. Considering the circumstances of the time—the infancy of the republic, the absence of any precedent, the importance of their example to other nations, the effect of their decisions on future citizens—their concern was understandable. "The establishment of a new government is a matter of such immense magnitude," observed the scrupulous Benjamin Workman, writing as Philadelphiensis, "that any other human transaction is small indeed, when compared to it. Great circumspection is therefore necessary on this interesting occasion: The temporal, and in some measure, even the eternal happiness of millions of souls is involved in this important work."[60]

Finally, Antifederalists held a classical republican concept of law. Whig republicans had long been concerned about the exercise of arbitrary power. But American colonials in particular, having been subject to the whims of colonial judges and governors, found the power that lay in interpreting the law to be always onerous and often oppressive. With the Revolution, as Wood described, they sought to limit such discretion, checking the prerogatives of courts and officials through codification and precise legislative enactment. During the 1780s, while Federalists rankled under the proliferation of statutes, their Antifederalist opponents held tenaciously to the principle that law should be, in the terms of North Carolina's Timothy Bloodworth, "clear and unequivocal."[61] Thus, they saw the broad, flexible language of the new Constitution as an invitation to oppression. Grayson for example told the Virginia convention that he for one "did not believe there existed a social compact upon the face of the earth so vague and so indefinite as the one now on the table."[62] The result of such imprecision could only be a return to the arbitrary power of the colonial past. In the creation of a constitution, insisted James Galloway, another leader of the opposition in North Carolina, "no general, indeterminate, vague expression ought to be suffered."[63]

Thus, when Federalists maintained that the system of checks and balances built into the new Constitution would be enough to prevent any abuse of interpretation, Antifederalists replied that it was surely not enough to trust to what Henry called "checks on paper." In their insistence on precise and specific constitutions, Antifederalist theorists contended that the federal Constitution was too theoretical. In a stinging attack in the Virginia

[60] Philadelphiensis, essay in the (Philadelphia) *Independent Gazetteer*, 1787, in *Complete Anti-Federalist*, 3: 106.

[61] Timothy Bloodworth, address to the North Carolina convention, 25 July 1788, in *Debates*, 4: 68. See Wood, *Creation*, pp. 291–305.

[62] Grayson, address to the Virginia convention, 23 June 1788, in *Debates*, 3: 583.

[63] James Galloway, address to the North Carolina convention, 25 July 1788, in *Debates*, 4: 70.

convention, Henry derided its "specious, imaginary balances," its "rope-dancing, chain rattling, ridiculous ideal checks and contrivances." Far from the ideologues described by Boorstin and Hofstadter, the opponents of the Constitution saw themselves as the true realists of the time, insisting, in Henry's words, on a concept of law that provided for "real checks" and "real balances."[64] As the stolid Mason would put it, in republican constitution making, theories mattered little. What counted, he said, was "the plain meaning of the words."[65]

In sum, though they seemed to be incompetent framers, Antifederalists were in fact only framers of a different kind, who on their own terms were extremely efficient. Like most republicans before them, they believed that every generation had the right to legislate for itself. According to the theory, founders provided examples for later citizens to follow, not laws for them to obey. Future citizens would look back on the actions of the framers with admiration and emulation, but hardly with reverence. Under no circumstances did Antifederalists think of themselves as immortals winning undying fame for themselves. In fact, they were at their rhetorical best in scoffing at the pretentions of those all-too-ambitious Federalists who pictured themselves in the role of classical legislators. When the slightly dotty Franklin ventured to liken the Federalist framers to Moses and Aaron, and the new Constitution to the Decalogue, Antifederalists answered with sarcasm and ridicule. As for him, Abraham White told his colleagues in the Massachusetts convention, he "would not trust a 'flock of Moseses,'" if they were peddling the new Constitution.[66]

Douglass Adair has described the importance of the love of fame and the desire for political immortality in inspiring the Federalist founders.[67] For their part, Antifederalists seemed content to forgo fame in order to seek assurance that they would not live in infamy, considering it better to live the lives of humble republicans, and lose the chance for immortal praise, than run the risk of inviting future tyrants, and be cursed by posterity forever. The usually ponderous Cato captured their position in a short but sobering phrase: In legislating for the future, he reminded his colleagues, "you have a great name to lose."[68]

[64] Henry, address to the Virginia convention, 9 June 1788, in *Debates*, 3: 164; 5 June 1788, in *Debates*, 3: 54; 9 June 1788, in *Debates*, 3: 165; 5 June 1788, in *Debates*, 3: 54.

[65] Mason, address to the Virginia convention, 15 June 1788, in *Debates*, 3: 479.

[66] Abraham White, address to the Massachusetts convention, 14 January 1788, in *Debates*, 2: 28.

[67] See Adair, "Fame and the Founding Fathers," in *Fame and the Founding Fathers*, pp. 3–26.

[68] Cato, letter to the *New York Journal*, 22 November 1787, in *Complete Anti-Federalist*, 2: 117.

Adaptability

Ultimately, ratification required that delegates address the issue of adaptability, the capacity of a constitutional order to respond to changing conditions. Here the Federalist founders seemed surprisingly at ease in making the case for experimentation and flexibility. At the very least, they were prepared to place a good deal of faith in the people, whom they saw as capable, under the institutions established by the new Constitution, of seeking out not only their own best interests but also the greater public good. Assuming as they did the desirability of an extended sphere of government, they expressed little fear of either population growth or territorial expansion. Even more important, secure in their faith in a system of checks and balances, they spoke of the new nation in dynamic and forward-looking terms. "This is a Constitution for the *future* government of the United States," Stephen Cabarrus told North Carolina's convention. "It does not look back."[69] Although Federalists did not assume automatic progress, they did believe that their politics could be adapted to changing circumstances. All told, and taken in the context of their times, they looked quite confidently to the future: "We must bear in mind," Hamilton wrote in *Federalist* 34, "that we are not to confine our view to the present period, but to look forward to remote futurity."[70]

Antifederalists, in contrast, appeared to take a short-sighted view. In the state debates, they gave the distinct impression that they had little faith in popular government. Henry took the lead in emphasizing a pervasive wickedness, what he seemed to delight in calling "the depravity of human nature."[71] Antifederalists sought every possible means to limit the prerogatives of the people, criticizing the new government for its failure to provide adequate protection against majoritarian tyranny. Monroe, for example, criticized the Constitution on the grounds that he could "see no real checks in it."[72] As to any expanded vision of the nation, Antifederalists held to the time-honored principle that freedom could exist only in the face-to-face polis. The very idea of an extended republic, vast in population and territory, rich in economic resources, was to them a theoretical impossibility. They looked to the future of their rapidly developing, rapidly expanding state with trepidation. Thus, their dreams of futurity were more like nightmares, populated by what Kenyon called a "parade of imaginary horri-

[69] Stephen Cabarrus, address to the North Carolina convention, 29 July 1788, in *Debates*, 4: 184.

[70] Hamilton, *Federalist* 34, in *Federalist Papers*, p. 207.

[71] Henry, address to the Virginia convention, 12 June 1788, in *Debates*, 3: 327.

[72] Monroe, address to the Virginia convention, 10 June 1788, in *Debates*, 3: 219.

bles."[73] In the state conventions, Antifederalists warned of the time when
pagans would be voters, when Jews, Moslems, or even atheists might be
legislators, and when even the Pope himself could conceivably be elected
President. Kenyon seems to have been correct in suggesting that Antifederalists saw little reason to put any faith in future citizens. "The degeneracy
of mankind militates against such a degree of confidence," explained North
Carolina's General McDowall. "I wish to see everything fixed."[74]

Nevertheless, Antifederalists were not opponents of popular government.
In fact, they had an extreme, perhaps excessive faith in the people. Antifederalists spoke often, and in glowing terms, of the virtue of republican citizens. At the same time, they were perfectly willing to admit the failings of
their fellow men. Their republican theory, with its emphasis on corruption,
allowed this seeming contradiction, for Antifederalists did not distrust their
fellow republicans because they were vicious but because they were cor-
ruptible. New York's Smith put it bluntly (and perhaps prophetically given
his role as one of the founders of Tammany Hall): "Sir, in many countries,
the people pay money to corrupt themselves: why should it not happen in
this?"[75] Their references to human nature centered on the fear of political
degeneration. Many were directed explicitly at their all-too-corruptible rulers: "a general presumption that rulers will govern well," Cato wrote, "is
not a sufficient security."[76] But even when they spoke of their fellow citizens, Antifederalists made clear that their real fear was corruption. By becoming lax, allowing themselves to be tempted by luxury, citizens hastened
the decline of their republic. Antifederalists warned that future citizens
would be tempted to "sit down easy," becoming "cool and inattentive" to
the safety of their liberties.[77] Eventually they believed that these fallen republicans would lose all trace of virtue. Hence they sought to make advance
allowance for the corruption that was certain to come. As Grayson argued,
government ought to be established "on a supposition that men will be bad;
for it may be eventually so."[78] Antifederalists condemned human pride,
along with its ally power; they condemned complacency and vice; they condemned weakness. They seemed to distrust democracy, but in fact, they
feared degeneration. Henry summed up with typical eloquence, and for

[73] Kenyon, "Men of Little Faith," p. 15.
[74] Joseph McDowall, address to the North Carolina convention, 28 July 1788, in *Debates*, 4: 150.
[75] Smith, address to the New York convention, 25 June 1788, in *Debates*, 2: 314.
[76] Cato, letter to the *New York Journal*, 22 November 1787, in *Complete Anti-Federalist*, 2: 117.
[77] A Plebian, "Address," 1788, in *Complete Anti-Federalist*, 6: 135.
[78] Grayson, address to the Virginia convention, 21 June 1788, in *Debates*, 3: 563.

once, with very atypical brevity: "Virtue," he told the Virginia delegates, "will slumber."[79]

Antifederalists were at best ambivalent about the propects of a modern nation. Holding to the theory of the small, self-sufficient republic, they argued fiercely that national consolidation would lead inevitably to tyranny. In the debates, these delegates embraced what they took to be the true "federalist" position, first supporting a confederation of sovereign states, and then, as Storing has shown, arguing for the mixture of state and national sovereignty.[80] At no point did their commitment to local and state government lead Antifederalists to oppose the strengthening of certain national institutions. Instead, they opposed what they saw as consolidated national power. As Bailyn demonstrated, the first principle of Whig republicanism was that centralized power would always gain ground at the expense of local liberty.[81] Writing as A Plebian, Smith made the case, reminding his readers that national government "steals, by insensible degrees, one right from the people after another, until it rivets its powers so as to put it beyond the ability of the community to restrict or limit it."[82]

Thus, when the more committed nationalists in the Federalist ranks spoke of an extensive republic presided over by a strong centralized administration, Antifederalists were understandably frightened. The very notion, observed the Maryland democrat identified as A Farmer, "terrifies the minds of individuals into meanness and submission."[83] At heart, these classical republicans believed that a consolidated republic could not long endure. No "man of reflection," offered Federal Farmer, could even imagine that such a system could "move on harmoniously together for ages, or even for fifty years."[84]

At the time, given the already apparent problem of American sectionalism, the estimate probably seemed generous. Frequently Antifederalists described consolidation as leading not only to dissolution, but to some non-republican form of authoritarian government: "I am consoled," lamented a pessimistic Henry, "if American liberty will remain entire only for half a century."[85] The indisputable fact was that recorded history showed no single example of an extensive republican state. Under the circumstances, An-

[79] Henry, address to the Virginia convention, 9 June 1788, in *Debates*, 3: 165.

[80] See Storing, "What the Anti-Federalists Were *For*," in *Complete Anti-Federalist*, 1: 32.

[81] Bailyn, *Ideological Origins*, pp. 55–93.

[82] A Plebian, "Address," 1788, in *Complete Anti-Federalist*, 6: 130.

[83] A Farmer, essay in the (Baltimore) *Maryland Gazette*, 7 March 1788, in *Complete Anti-Federalist*, 5: 31.

[84] Federal Farmer, "Observations," 13 October 1787, in *Complete Anti-Federalist*, 2: 251; 252.

[85] Henry, address to the Virginia convention, 7 June 1788, in *Debates*, 3: 147.

tifederalists were on solid ground in describing an expanding republic as a
potential empire. The price of power, they calculated, was the loss of liberty: "those nations," summarized Henry, "who have gone in search of
grandeur, power, and splendor, have also fallen a sacrifice, and been the
victims of their own folly. While they acquired those visionary blessings,
they lost their freedom."[86]

It is true that Antifederalists provided little in the way of vision. Generally speaking, they preferred not to speculate about the future. "I have not
the art of divination," delegate William Lancaster told the North Carolina
convention. "In the course of four or five hundred years, I do not know how
it will work."[87] When they did try to foretell the future, however, they
spoke with foreboding. The specifics of the federal Constitution aside, Antifederalists had no reason to think that any single form of government
would prove durable enough to last for any length of time. In the course of
several centuries, Smith surmised, "two or three great empires might be
established, totally different from our own."[88] As for posterity, they expressed little confidence. In future periods, thought Mason, "the government will be administered by different people. We know what they are now,
but know not how soon they may be altered."[89]

As a result, Antifederalists saw little advantage in adapting to the future.
On the whole, the future seemed fairly unpromising to them. They put no
trust in the size of future governments, the power of future rulers, or the
vigilance of future citizens. Instead they looked with dread toward big and
distant government allied with big and distant economic interests, toward
irresponsible or immoral rulers, and toward well-intentioned but weak citizens who would stand by helplessly while their liberties were lost or stolen.
Thus, in the Antifederalist lexicon, adaptation was synonymous with retreat. They had no intention, as Lowndes concluded, "to risk the loss of
political existence on experiment!"[90]

Ultimately, Antifederalists did believe in adaptation. But their concept
was defensive, implying a means to protect themselves from potential harm.
Throughout the state debates they had made the argument for an amendment procedure, describing amendments as barricades thrown up by re-
treating republicans to slow the march of state power. Thus, when Federalists, coming late to the concept, began to embrace the amendment
procedure, contending that amendments could be used to correct mistakes,
and that the new republic could be improved over time, they protested.

[86] Henry, address to the Virginia convention, 5 June 1788, in *Debates*, 3: 47.
[87] William Lancaster, address to the Virginia convention, 30 July 1788, in *Debates*, 4: 215.
[88] Smith, address to the New York convention, 30 June 1788, in *Debates*, 2: 382.
[89] Mason, address to the Virginia convention, 14 June 1788, in *Debates*, 3: 426.
[90] Lowndes, address to the South Carolina convention, 16 January 1788, in *Debates*, 4: 271.

Errors once made would never be righted, Antifederalists countered, because powers once granted could never be revoked. Henry made the point with stinging sarcasm: "Evils admitted in order to be removed subsequently, and tyranny submitted to in order to be excluded by a subsequent alteration, are things totally new to me."[91]

As the conventions wore on and the critics dug in, Federalists began to argue that the only possible means to arrive at agreement would be first to establish the broad outlines of the system, and then amend it to everyone's satisfaction. Henry was incredulous: "You agree to bind yourselves hand and foot—for what? To get out. Is there no danger, when you go in, that the bolts of federal authority shall shut you in?"[92] Antifederalists had no illusion that power could ever be easily checked. In fact, though they fought doggedly for a bill of rights, they assumed that even the strictest constitutional limitations would not serve indefinitely to prevent the creation of standing armies, the rise of monied aristocrats, or the incessant growth of national power. Ultimately they saw the first ten amendments as a symbol, a source of political education, or a reminder to future citizens, not only of their rights, but also of their responsibilities. Antifederalists did not rely on progress to advance the cause of freedom. Instead they put their faith, what little of it they had, in the decency, and honesty, and public-mindedness of future citizens. As Pennsylvania's high-toned Federal Republican observed, whatever the future held, one truth would always endure, "that some degree of virtue must exist, or freedom cannot live."[93]

With ratification by Virginia and New York, their cause was all but lost. Yet while bested in the ratification struggle, Antifederalists were not altogether unsuccessful. By holding out for the inclusion of a bill of rights, by requiring a strong role for the state and local governments, and by insisting on broad-based popular participation, they had made the Constitution more palatable to the several states. Moreover, they had made it a sounder and, however ironically, a stronger document.

Still, their Federalist counterparts had won a stunning victory. As a matter of practical politics, they had swept the opposition before them. But in the realm of political philosophy, in the larger battle for the minds of their fellow citizens, Federalist thinkers had secured an even more spectacular triumph. In creating the Constitution, they had introduced an entirely new concept of constitutionalism. In securing the republic, they had reformulated republican theory, bending classical republican principles to modern liberal realities. And in founding the new nation, they had placed their

[91] Henry, address to the Virginia convention, 24 June 1788, in *Debates*, 3: 591.
[92] Henry, address to the Virginia convention, 9 June 1788, in *Debates*, 3: 174.
[93] A Federal Republican, letter to the *Pennsylvania Herald*, 28 October 1787, in *Complete Anti-Federalist*, 3: 76.

eighteenth-century republic on the path to what would become an age of
nationalism. In short, while Antifederalists had rescued at least some classical principles, saving them for the Constitution, the Federalist founders
had reached well beyond them, and had taken a giant step toward the creation of a modern way of thinking about politics.

For the founders, however, there would be little time to reflect on these
astonishing accomplishments. The Constitution had been created, but the
new nation remained to be brought fully into reality. Here supporters of the
Constitution faced the problem of building support for the new Constitutional order, instituting it not only on paper but also, and far more impor-
tantly, in the hearts and minds of citizens. In this attempt at creating legitimacy, they found themselves facing the problem of winning the loyalty of
their fellow Americans, and especially the Americans of the next generation. At the same time, their opponents, the Constitution's critics, along
with its few remaining foes, had their own plans for these future citizens.
Thus, while ratification brought to a close the debates of the 1780s, it announced the beginning of the bitter confrontations of the 1790s.

PART FOUR

Prefabricating the Future

·7·

POSTERITY

Creating Constitutional Character

BY THE FOURTH OF JULY 1788, ten states had ratified the Constitution, one more than the required majority, and Federalists across the land celebrated victory with parades and partisan speeches. In Philadelphia, thousands marched in procession, complete with bands, horsemen, and Indian chiefs. Pulled atop a horse-drawn carriage was a representation of the new union, a Corinthian-style temple supported by thirteen columns, with the figure of Plenty surmounting the dome. Orations, poetic odes, and toasts capped off the day, along with artillery salutes from warships in the harbor. Yet not all the celebrations were as enthusiastic: in Albany, New York, there was rioting, with Antifederalists publicly burning the new Constitution, and in Providence, Rhode Island, opponents routed the celebrants altogether, turning their commemoration of the Constitution into a Fourth of July memorial for the Revolution. The new Constitution had been adopted. But it remained for it to be accepted, winning the loyalty and respect of its citizens. And here, as the Antifederalist protests attested, the case was by no means closed. So it was that following ratification, supporters and opponents alike looked ahead with anxiety, attempting to foretell how the Constitution would fare in the 1790s and beyond, for themselves and for posterity.

In retrospect, the postfounding era has proved to be exceptionally elusive. To some students, the early 1790s was a time of peace, prosperity, and political consensus, a Constitutional Augustan Age in which Antifederalists retreated in shame, and Federalists everywhere ascended serenely to power.[1] To others, including those such as Marshall Smelser, John C. Miller, and John R. Howe, it was something else altogether, a time of instability and conflict, in which state was pitted against state, section against section, and especially party against party.[2] To others still, and most recently to Lance Banning, both of these were partly true. Banning depicted the post-Constitutional period as a paradoxical time in which consensus and

[1] See for example Richard Hildreth, *The History of the United States of America* (New York: Harper & Brothers, 1856), 6: 331–409.

[2] See Marshall Smelser, "The Federalist Period as an Age of Passion," *American Quarterly*, 10, 4 (Winter 1958): 391–419; John C. Miller, *The Federalist Era, 1789–1801* (New York: Harper & Row, 1960), esp. pp. 1–19; and Howe, "Republican Thought," pp. 147–65.

conflict were both present, and closely intertwined. Simply put, his argument was that Antifederalists, along with the Republicans who followed in their steps, had to accept the Constitution in order to fight its corruption by their Federalist foes. He summarized: "Paradoxically, then, it was the appearance of a deeply felt opposition to the policies of our first administration which assured the quick acceptance of the Constitution that had been committed to its care. More than the government itself, the opposition had to have an unchallengeable constitution on which it could rely."[3]

In fact, the situation was even more complex. To begin with, following ratification, American politics was very much in transition. After the Constitutional debates were completed, the Antifederalists and Madisonian Federalists of the 1780s all but disappeared as identifiable parties, not to be replaced by the Republicans and Hamiltonian Federalists of the 1790s until the conflict over Hamilton's economic policy in late 1792.[4] In between, party politics was inchoate, with important Antifederalists like Gerry, Randolph, and even Patrick Henry becoming Federalists; at the same time, leading Federalists, including no less than Madison himself, were in the process of becoming Republicans.[5] Hence, from ratification to late 1792 or early 1793, it is preferable to speak not of Antifederalists and Federalists at all, but of Constitutional opponents, or Opposition thinkers, made up mainly though not exclusively of old Antifederalists, and Constitutional supporters, or Constitutionalists, consisting mostly of old Federalists but including many former Antifederalists as well.[6]

In addition, the Constitutional system was by no means secure. Following ratification, Opposition and Constitutionalist forces can be seen as continuing the Constitutional debates. In the early 1790s, of course, the important issues had changed, for politics no longer centered on the Constitution itself, on the institutional shape and structure of American government, but rather on what might better be called Constitutionalism, the processes and procedures by which Americans would govern themselves. Here a sense of legitimacy was generally lacking, because quite aside from the question of whether they accepted the Constitution in principle, many thinkers of the time remained unwilling to accept it, unproven as it was, in practice.

This legitimacy had to be created. The critical figures in this effort were those champions of the Constitution who, beginning as early as mid-1787 but especially following ratification, worked relentlessly to win popular ac-

---

[3] Lance Banning, "Republican Ideology and the Triumph of the Constitution, 1789 to 1793," *The William and Mary Quarterly*, 3rd ser., 31, 2 (April 1974): 187.

[4] See Banning, *Jeffersonian Persuasion*, pp. 128–29.

[5] See ibid., pp. 114–15.

[6] See ibid., pp. 126–60.

ceptance for the new government. The task before these thinkers was to make the Constitution seem somehow second nature, an integral part not only of American politics but of the American psyche. To do this, they set about creating a Constitutional character, or Constitutional psychology, through which they sought to shape not only contemporary but future citizens. By instilling this psychololgy, they assumed that they could assure the continuing vitality of their politics. In other words, they believed that they could, in some sense, prefabricate the future of the republic.

Opponents were not altogether persuaded. They themselves championed a different political psychology, one radically opposed to this Constitutional character. Throughout the postfounding period, these opposing forces would confront one another, touting their respective conceptions of citizenship. But in truth they spoke less to one another than to another audience altogether, the succeeding generations of citizens. For at issue in the early 1790s was a highly problematic future, what they tended to call, albeit somewhat cynically, the "problem" of posterity.

The Problem of Posterity

From the moment of founding, supporters of the Constitution showed an acute awareness of the importance of the future. Founding took place in an instant, whereas implementation required years, decades, or centuries. The Constitution was written to last for ages, its precepts designed to endure, as John Adams had confidently predicted, for "many thousands of years."[7] It was clear to those who had witnessed the framing of the Constitution that they would not live to see its final outcome. "We, who are now actors on the theater of life," said the Revolutionary War veteran Dan Foster in a 1789 sermon to the Vermont legislature, "shall soon be called off; —a new set of comedians will rise and take our places."[8] By 1788, many of the founding generation, veterans of Revolution and Constitution alike, having entered public life fifteen or more years earlier, were already old for their day. "The evening tide of life is fast approaching," Dr. Samuel Whitwell all too prophetically told Boston's Society of the Cincinnati shortly before his death, "a few more days will remove us from the theatre of action. —Annually do our numbers diminish."[9] Death came to this heroic band as to anyone. "Though you are called Gods," the Reverend Josiah Bridge advised the leaders of Massachusetts in a 1789 election sermon, "yet you must

7 John Adams, *Defence*, in *Works*, 4: 297.

8 Dan Foster, A.M., *An Election Sermon; Delivered Before the Honorable Legislature of the State of Vermont . . . October 8th, 1789* (Windsor, Vt.: Alden Spooner, 1790), p. 22.

9 Samuel Whitwell, *An Oration Delivered to the Society of the Cincinnati . . . July 4, 1789* (Boston: Benjamin Russell, 1789), p. 18.

die like men."¹⁰ As to the result of the founding, they would never know.
The completion of the American experiment, Thomas Jefferson would con-
fide to his friend Edward Rutledge, would "require time, temper, wisdom,
& occasional sacrifice of interest; & how far these will be ours, our children
may see, but we shall not."¹¹

In 1788, Americans faced the irony of founding, the irrefutable fact that
ultimate political responsibility lies not with the founders who frame the
constitution, but with the citizens who live under the new government.
Regardless of persuasion, thinkers of the time were acutely conscious of the
problem, assuming that no future generation would equal that of the
founders, because no future age could expect to boast a Washington, Franklin, Hancock, and Adams: "posterity may have reason to rue the day," admitted Candidus, thought to be the aging Antifederalist Benjamin Austin,
"when their political welfare depends on the decision of men who may fill
the place of these worthies."¹² Even as the Constitution was being signed,
some were suggesting that, whether through ignorance or incompetence,
future citizens might well weaken its character, undermine its institutions,
or even destroy its fragile form altogether. When they looked to posterity
they saw little that was comforting. "In short my dear Friend you and I have
been indefatigable Labourers through our whole Lives," Adams confided
to Jefferson, "for a Cause which will be thrown away in the next generation,
upon the Vanity and Foppery of Persons of whom we do not know the
Names perhaps."¹³

The persistence of the classical republican concept of posterity made the
dilemma of founding even more extreme. Republican theory had long been
premised on the assumption that future citizens would be activists, that they
would oppose tyrants, guard against corruption, and fight to limit the
power of government. Yet the founders had argued that the new Constitution had put an end to the need for such activism. Indeed, the greatest fear
of supporters of the Constitution was that ambitious Americans would in
the future seek to play the roles of revolutionaries and constitutionalists
themselves, emulating the example of the framers by destroying their government and preempting their place as founders. In his "Discourses on
Davila," published in 1791, John Adams contended that the passion for

¹⁰ Josiah Bridge, A.M., *A Sermon Preached Before His Excellency John Hancock, Esq. Governor . . . of the Commonwealth of Massachusetts, May 27, 1789* . . . (Boston: Adams & Nourse,
1789), p. 47.
¹¹ Thomas Jefferson to Edward Rutledge, 24 June 1797, in *Writings*, 7: 154.
¹² Candidus, letter to the *Boston Independent Chronicle*, 6 December 1787, in *Complete Anti-
Federalist*, 4: 128–29.
¹³ Adams to Jefferson, 8 October 1787, in *Papers*, 12: 221. See also Madison, *Federalist 10*,
in *Federalist Papers*, p. 80.

distinction, the "desire to be observed, considered, esteemed, praised, beloved, and admired by his fellows," remained one of the most potent forces
in public life, "one of the earliest as well as the keenest dispositions discovered in the heart of man."[14] Adams knew only too well the power of the
desire for distinction, feeling it deeply, speaking almost reverently of the
love of fame as "the ruling passion of the noblest minds," yet sensing in it
danger from the popular demagogue, Hamilton's "man of irregular ambition."[15] Thus he argued that government must limit the influence of the
ambitious, not only preventing them from using their talents to destroy the
established order, but indeed capturing and expropriating their abilities,
setting one against another in a continuing struggle to win personal fame
that within the Constitutional system became a struggle to serve the public
good. It was, he wrote of the desire for distinction, "a principal end of government to regulate this passion, which in its turn becomes a principal
means of government."[16]

The Constitution's framers, relying on accepted Enlightenment assumptions, had insisted that ambition could be controlled by the introduction of
well-framed laws and institutions. Even in 1791 Adams would make the
case. But as early as 1787 some supporters of the Constitution had begun
to recognize a fundamental weakness in the assumption. The debate over
ratification made it even clearer that even the best of laws and institutions
would not be enough to assure wide acceptance for the Constitution. Especially following ratification, however, as politics began to degenerate into
partisanship and violence, supporters were forced to reconsider their most
basic suppositions, admitting that the creation of a political order alone
would not create orderly government. All the checks ever imagined, all the
balances ever devised could not restrain the ambition that lay in the hearts
of talented citizens. Laws, as the Reverend Peres Fobes would remark in a
1795 Massachusetts election sermon, "cannot reach the heart."[17] Effective
government relied not on written rules only, but on an unwritten ethic, the
shared expectations that make government necessary, the conventions that
make it acceptable, the agreements that make it work. This unwritten ethic
was the basis of political legitimacy, residing, New York's Reverend Sam-

[14] Adams, "Discourses on Davila," 1791, in *Works*, 6: 232; Hamilton, *Federalist* 72, in *Federalist Papers*, pp. 437; 440.

[15] Adams, "Davila," in *Works*, 6: 234. On Hamilton's "man of irregular ambition," see *Federalist* 72, in *Federalist Papers*, p. 440.

[16] Ibid. See Martin Diamond, "Democracy and *The Federalist*: A Reconstruction of the Framers' Intent," *American Political Science Review*, 53, 1 (March 1959): 67–68. On the desire for
distinction, see Adair, "Fame and the Founding Fathers," in *Fame and the Founding Fathers*,
pp. 3–26.

[17] Peres Fobes, L.L.D., *A Sermon, Preached Before his Excellency Samuel Adams, . . . May
27th, 1795 . . .* (New York: Thomas Greenleaf, 1795), p. 13.

uel Miller told his Wall Street church, "not in the words and letters of the *Constitution*; but in the temper, the habits, and the practices of the people."[18]

Thus in the years after ratification, supporters of the Constitution realized their responsibility to define not just what Americans thought about their government, but what they felt about it as well. Having constructed the Constitution, they set about to build Constitutional character, a personal commitment to government that would ensure the new order "with far more efficiency, and incomparably more ease," as Yale's new President Timothy Dwight would put it in a 1795 speech to the Connecticut Cincinnati, "than the post and the prison, the gibbet and the cross."[19]

Continuity

The first consideration in the making of this Constitutional character was the creation of a sense of continuity. Ordinarily, constitutions require a period of operation during which new governments can win the loyalty of their citizens. The founders had no illusion that their own new system would meet with unanimous or even wide acceptance. The debate in many of the states was long and rancorous, and the commitment to state sovereignty remained strong. Whether they liked it or not, they were forced to admit that time alone would tell whether the idea of federal government would win popular support. The new Constitution required a period of testing, during which its principles could be adopted, its institutions embraced, and its operations accepted. "TIME," as Hamilton had put it with some sense of resignation in the last of the *Federalist Papers*, "must bring it to perfection."[20]

In the years following the founding, however, supporters of the Constitution began to realize that they did not have the luxury of a long period of acceptance. Thus, they set about creating continuity, showing how American politics had been characterized since Independence by the continuous development of Constitutional principles. In essence, their task was to make the new Constitution seem old. Effecting this change would be no mean feat, for prior to ratification, the Constitution had been popularly considered to be an entirely new departure in republican government. Antifederalist writers never tired of noting the disparity between Revolutionary principles and Constitutional practices. The new Constitution, an impassioned

[18] Samuel Miller, A.M., *A Sermon, Preached in the New Presbyterian Church, New-York, July Fourth, 1795 . . .* (New York: Thomas Greenleaf, 1795), p. 23.

[19] [Timothy Dwight], *A Sermon, Delivered on the 7th of July, 1795, before the Connecticut Society of Cincinnati* (New Haven, Conn.: T. & S. Green, [1795], p. 16.

[20] Hamilton, *Federalist 85*, in *Federalist Papers*, p. 526.

Thomas Treadwell had told the New York convention, "departed widely
from the political faith of '76, when the spirit of liberty ran high and danger
put a curb on ambition."[21] Especially troubling to Antifederalists was the
inclusion of institutions like the Senate, which was reminiscent of English
aristocracy and seemed like a sure sign of revision to the system they had
rebelled against. Such aristocratic institutions, offered South Carolina's
Revolutionary War hero Captain Francis Kinloch, provided practical proof
that they were "getting back fast to the system we destroyed some years
ago."[22]

Even after 1788, however, certain critics continued to depict the Constitution as, if not America's counterrevolution, then at least a deviation from
Revolutionary principles. Typical was the talented Mercy Otis Warren,
whose three-volume *History of the American Revolution*, written during the
1780s and 90s (though not published until 1805), reminded readers that
the legacy of the Revolution had not perished. In describing the creation of
a Constitutional Opposition after 1788, she wrote:

There yet remained a considerable class of these firm adherents to the
principles of the revolution; they were strongly impressed with the necessity of an energetic government, and the weakness of the old confederation. . . . But they had not contemplated the introduction of new
projects, which were thought designed to enrich and enoble some of
the officers of the army, to create a splendid government, and to support the dignity of new orders in the state. These were articles that had
made no part of their creed.[23]

Interestingly enough, in the years before 1788 few supporters of the Constitution would have disagreed. In fact, the creators of the Constitution
themselves were eager to describe the Constitution as a non-Revolutionary
document. After all, the very genius of the Constitution had been that it had
announced a break with the mistaken assumptions of the past. Thus, they
had offered the new system as a correction for Revolutionary excesses, "the
proper antidote for the diseases of faction," as Madison had called it in *Federalist* 14.[24] Yet with the framing, foresighted thinkers led by Rush and
Barlow began to make another case altogether. Dr. Rush announced the
change in a 1787 oration entitled "An Address to the People of the United

[21] Thomas Treadwell, address to the New York convention, 1 July 1788, in *Debates*, 2: 401.

[22] Francis Kinloch to Thomas Boone, 26 May 1788, in "Letters of Francis Kinloch to
Thomas Boone," ed. Felix Gilbert, *The Journal of Southern History*, 8, 1 (February 1942): 105.

[23] Mercy Otis Warren, "History of the Rise, Progress and Termination of the American Revolution," 1805, in *Complete Anti-Federalist*, 6: 216.

[24] Madison, *Federalist* 14, in *Federalist Papers*, p. 99. See also Wood, *Creation*, pp. 273–82,
532–36, 606–15.

States." "There is nothing more common," he remarked, "than to confound the terms of *American Revolution* with those of *the late American war*. The American war is over: but this is far from being the case with the American revolution. On the contrary, nothing but the first act of the great drama is closed."[25] Always one to know which way the political winds were blowing, the politic Barlow echoed the theme, showing how rebellion and founding were in fact closely connected. The Revolution, he stated in his 1787 Hartford oration, "is but half completed. *Independence* and *Government* were the two objects contended for: and but one is yet obtained."[26] For these thinkers, Revolutionary politics presupposed Constitutional government. In fact, Revolution went hand in hand not only with creating the Constitution but also with building the nation. In any case, Rush was particularly eager to inform his audience that the struggle for freedom continued. In America's government, he wrote, "in her finances, in her trade, in her manufactures, in her morals, and in her manners, 'THE REVOLUTION IS NOT OVER!' "[27]

Following ratification this argument was frequently heard. Before 1788, Revolution and Constitution commonly had been seen as distinct events. Afterward, Constitutional historians led by Dr. Ramsay took up the task of showing how Revolution and Constitution were in fact inseparable. Thus, Ramsay would deliberately delay publication of his study of Revolutionary America until after ratification so that his *History of the American Revolution*, rather than conclude at the attainment of Independence in 1783, could continue on with a description of the Confederation period, including a survey of the events leading up to the Philadelphia convention, and ending with the text of the Constitution itself. According to Ramsay, the decisions of these years showed striking consistency, the transition from Revolution to Constitution having been carried out "without a sigh or groan."[28] The Constitution did not reject republican precepts but rather adopted and developed them. "The people of the United States gave no new powers to their rulers," he maintained, "but made a more judicious arrangement of what they had formerly ceded."[29] In this revisionist history, the Constitution, far from signaling a reversal of the Revolution, announced its culmination. "Till this period," confided the enthusiastic New Hampshire Federalist Aaron Hall in a 1788 oration, "the revolution in America, has never appeared to me to be completed; but this is laying on the cap-stone of the great American Empire."[30]

[25] Rush, "Address to the People of the United States," in *Principles and Acts*, p. 234.

[26] Barlow, *An Oration*, p. 8.

[27] Rush, "Address," in *Principles and Acts*, p. 236.

[28] Ramsay, *History*, 2: 344.

[29] Ibid., 341–42.

[30] Aaron Hall, M.A., *An Oration, Delivered at the Request of the Inhabitants of Keene, June 30*,

Constitutional historians made the Revolution look distinctly less revolutionary than before. That is, their arguments tended to place the Revolutionary War within a sequence of events culminating in the Constitutional convention, effectively picturing a violent revolt as a deliberate reform. Warren and the Opposition historians continued to stress the passionate idealism of the war. Barlow and the Constitutionalists, by contrast, spoke of its rationality and predictability. "This single circumstance . . . will stamp a peculiar glory on the American revolution, and make it as a distinguished era in the history of mankind," Barlow counseled; "that sober reason and reflection have done the work of enthusiasm, and performed the miracles of gods."[31] This was a radical reinterpretation, through which a theory of politics inspired by Revolutionary passion became in retrospect an idea of government informed by Constitutional reason. The preachers and orators who followed Barlow's lead described the American Revolution as another Glorious Revolution, a "revolution by reasoning," as the Reverend Hitchcock put it in a Fourth of July oration.[32] Contrary to popular opinion, Americans had not acted precipitously in 1776. Instead, Hitchcock informed his Providence, Rhode Island, audience, they had "*reasoned* before they have *felt*," following not the cry of impassioned protest, but "the *still small voice*, the voice of rational reflection."[33] In essence, these thinkers drained the blood from the Revolutionary War, reclaiming its ardor, stressing instead its "philosophic composure."[34] "No circumstance of whim or passion moved us," declared Major William Pierce in a Georgia Fourth of July oration, "no frantic zeal enraged us, —no cause of a popular demagogue inflamed us, . . . —no, —all was the result of reason."[35]

The result was a Revolution different from the one that had actually taken place. Unlike Opposition history, which showed the war being waged by separate and often divided colonies, Constitutional history described a continental strategy carried out by one united people. Moreover, whereas Warren continued to emphasize the time-honored theme that the war was fought for independence, Ramsay and his colleagues could be found arguing that it was meant to create a strong central government. As early as 1787, the New York pamphleteer Caesar had begun to argue that the desire for national government had been the war's primary purpose. Revolution-

---

1788 . . . (Keene, N.H.: James D. Griffith, 1788), pp. 6–7. See also Jensen, *The New Nation*, p. 96.

[31] Barlow, *An Oration*, p. 6.

[32] Enos Hitchcock, A.M., *An Oration: Delivered July 4, 1788* . . . (Providence, R.I.: Bennett Wheeler, [1788]), p. 11.

[33] Ibid.

[34] Alexander C. Macwhorter, *An Oration Delivered on the Fourth of July, 1794* . . . (Newark, N.J.: John Woods, 1794), p. 16.

[35] William Pierce, *An Oration, Delivered at Christ Church, Savannah, on the Fourth of July, 1788* . . . (Savannah, Ga.: James Johnston, 1788), pp. 5; 7–8.

aries, he had contended, "sought to obtain liberty for no particular State, but for the whole Union, indissolubly connected under one controlling and supreme head."[36] According to Ramsay, Americans before the war had felt little sense of national identity: "Country religion, local policy, as well as private views," he reflected, "operated in disposing the inhabitants to take different sides."[37] The common experience of British oppression had drawn them together, however, setting people "thinking, speaking and acting, in a line far beyond that to which they had been accustomed."[38] With the creation of national institutions like the army and the congress, and the appearance of national leaders like Hamilton and Madison, a national purpose began to be defined. Local prejudices gave way to continental loyalties, and out of the common experience of war emerged a united nation: "the great body of the people," Ramsay allowed, "as soon as reason got the better of prejudice, found that their best interests would be most effectually promoted by such practices and sentiments as were favourable to union."[39]

Having found the spirit of Constitutionalism long before the Constitution, supporters of the new system faced the task of explaining how that spirit had been waylaid along the road to strong government during the Confederation period. They proceeded to describe how the Confederation had been a misguided detour into excess and error. It must have come as a surprise to Americans of the time to learn how bad the Confederation had been. Opposition historians were willing to admit that the critical period was a time of confusion and uncertainty. Constitutionalists, by contrast, were candid about their plan to depict the Confederation as an age of calamity, with the Constitution as the document that redeemed the time of its terrible discontent. Ever the ideologue, Fisher Ames wrote a friend that he for one intended to convince Americans that before the federal convention "the corn would not grow, nor the pot boil."[40] Ames went on to tell how credit had expired, gold vanished, and property depreciated, how commerce had fallen off and produce dropped in value, how government had become totally inadequate. Only after it was over did people begin to realize how critical the critical period had been. "I believe it is not generally known on what a perilous tenure we held our freedom and independence during that period," the usually phlegmatic James Wilson had somewhat disingenuously reminded the Pennsylvania convention. "The flames of internal insurrection were ready to burst out in every quarter; . . . and from one end

[36] Caesar, letter to the *New York Daily Advertiser*, 17 October 1787, in *Essays*, p. 290.
[37] Ramsay, *History*, 2: 310.
[38] Ibid., 315.
[39] Ibid., 317.
[40] Fisher Ames to George Richards Minot, 23 July 1789, in *Works of Fisher Ames*, ed. Seth Ames (Boston: Little, Brown and Company, 1854), 1: 66.

to the other of the continent, we walked on ashes, concealing fire beneath our feet."[41]

While Constitutional historians left no doubt that the weakness of the Confederation had subverted the true tradition of American politics, they made it clear that in spite of this reversal, the spirit of strong national government had survived. Unlike Opposition history, which stressed the importance of liberty, Constitutional history took up the theme of union. Throughout the war, Americans had maintained their commitment to the nation, the tie that held the states together during troubled times. "Not that Confederation, but common danger, and the spirit of America, were the bonds of our union," Judge Edmund Pendleton had told the Virginia convention; "union and unanimity, and not that insignificant paper [the Articles of Confederation], carried us through that dangerous war."[42] Errors in government had been only temporary aberrations, the product of what Rush called "very unfavorable circumstances." The American states had just emerged from a corrupt monarchy, and their people were inexperienced in republican government. "Although we understood perfectly the principles of liberty," said Rush, "yet most of us were ignorant of the forms and combinations of power in republics." The nation was in the midst of war, the British army "in the heart of our country, spreading desolation wherever it went."[43] Under these circumstances, mistakes in government had become inevitable. It was not to be wondered, a reflective John Jay had declared, "that a government instituted in times so inauspicious should on experiment be found greatly deficient and inadequate to the purpose it was intended to answer."[44]

Happily, the Constitutional convention had reasserted the rationality that had all along been the true character of American politics. Opposition historians continued to recall the partisan conflict so common in the convention, but their Constitutional counterparts did yeoman labor in making politics look more like philosophy. The convention itself was pictured as a dispassioned philosophical gathering, "an assemblage of wisdom and philanthropy."[45] Party politicians were made out to be unbiased philosophers, "distinguished by their patriotism, virtue, and wisdom," "commanding all the sources of information," "unawed by fear, unbiassed by self-interest."[46]

[41] James Wilson, address to the Pennsylvania convention, 11 December 1787, in *Debates*, 2: 521. See also Frank I. Schechter, "The Early History of the Tradition of the Constitution," *American Political Science Review*, 9, 4 (November 1915): 707–34.

[42] Edmund Pendleton, address to the Virginia convention, 5 June 1788, in *Debates*, 3: 38.

[43] Rush, "On the Defects of the Confederation," in *Selected Writings*, p. 26.

[44] Jay, *Federalist 2*, in *Federalist Papers*, p. 39.

[45] Hitchcock, *An Oration*, p. 14.

[46] Jay, *Federalist 2*, in *Federalist Papers*, p. 39; Harrison Gray Otis, *An Oration, Delivered July 4, 1788* . . . (Boston: Benjamin Russell, 1788), p. 15.

Partisan debate became intellectual discussion. "In the mild season of peace," wrote Jay, "with minds unoccupied by other subjects, they passed many months in cool, uninterrupted, and daily consultation; and finally, without having been awed by power, or influenced by any passions except love for their country, they presented and recommended to the people the plan produced by their joint and very unanimous councils."[47]

Constitutional historians rewrote the history of the convention, depicting the Constitution as the product not of expediency and compromise, but of theory and philosophy. It was as if the founding had been the result of revelation by some Enlightenment deity. In Constitutional history, worldly politicians became themselves almost gods. The act of founding, the Newport, Rhode Island, lawyer William Hunter would conclude in a 1795 Fourth of July oration, "required minds, rarely gifted, and richly endowed, but a prudence, a forbearence, a discretion, too seldom bestowed on Mortals. —It almost required," he told his audience in the grand oratorical style for which he was known, "men to be like the God of the Stoics, all Intellect, and no Passion."[48]

Citizenship

The second element in the creation of Constitutional character was a new conception of citizenship. This reinterpretation required a new philosophy of political education. For one hundred years colonials had been schooled in classical republican theory, a training that had been one of the greatest inspirations to the American Revolution. Classical republicanism held that citizens were required to guard their freedom constantly, coming forward to fight when liberty was threatened and returning to their homes only when it was secured. In adopting these classical precepts, Revolutionary writers had looked especially to Rome, to those ancient republicans like Cato, Cicero, and Cincinnatus who embodied these ideals—modeling themselves on these classical characters, imitating their oratorical styles, adopting their names as pseudonyms. In the years before the Constitution it was still common to find veterans of the Revolution exhorting their children to rely on Livy, Plutarch, or Tacitus for the same precepts that they themselves had followed in Revolutionary days. Throughout the ratification process there were those who championed the classics, entreating others to "recur to the page of history" to find those "universal principles" that had

---

[47] Jay, *Federalist 2*, in *Federalist Papers*, p. 39.

[48] William Hunter, *An Oration, Delivered in the Baptist Meeting-House in Newport, July 4, A.D. 1795* . . . (Newport, R.I.: Henry Barber, 1795), p. 14.

"stood the shock of ages."[49] Afterward as well, Opposition thinkers, including many of these same Revolutionary veterans, would continue the commitment to this classical political education. As the aging Sam Adams would write in a letter to his cousin John, the role of "divines and philosophers, statesmen and patriots" was to educate their "*little boys* and *girls*" in the love of their country, "instructing them," he wrote sagely, "in the art of self-government, without which they never can act a wise part in the government of societies, great or small."[50]

After ratification, however, critics began to challenge the need for this kind of classical education. Throughout the conventions, delegates had argued that the examples of classical politics were at best inappropriate and at worst harmful to the realities of Constitutional government. With ratification, even bolder thinkers set out to eliminate altogether such assumptions from republican theory by purging their classical sources from republican education. Typical was Rush, who took the lead in what amounted to a campaign of censorship: "Let us try the effect of banishing the Latin and Greek languages from our country," he wrote in 1789. "They consume the flower of human life, and by enabling us to read agreeable histories of ancient crimes often lead us to imitate or to tolerate them."[51] The ancient languages were detriments to society, to be classed, Rush went on, with two of his own oldest enemies, "Negro slavery and spirituous liquors."[52] By 1791 he was arguing for the complete abolition of the classics from American education. "It is high time to cease from idolizing the idolatry of Greece and Rome," Rush wrote in his essay on the Latin and Greek languages. "Truth alone is knowledge, and spending time in studying Greek and Roman fictions, is only labouring to be more ignorant."[53]

According to Rush, classical education had little to offer a modern developing nation. Unlike Sam Adams, who continued to celebrate the Greek and Roman classics, Rush was eager to consign them to the back shelves of America's libraries. After all, ancient terms were inadequate to describe

[49] George Mason, address to the Virginia convention, 14 June 1788, in *Debates*, 3: 380; Patrick Henry, address to the Virginia convention, 14 June 1788, in *Debates*, 3: 386; Henry, address to the Virginia convention, 7 June 1788, in *Debates*, 3: 137. On classical education, see Richard M. Gummere, "The Heritage of the Classics in Colonial North America: An Essay on the Greco-Roman Tradition," *Proceedings of the American Philosophical Society*, 99, 2 (April 1955): 68–78; Charles F. Mullett, "Classical Influences on the American Revolution," *The Classical Journal*, 35, 2 (November 1939): 92–104; and Colbourn, *The Lamp of Experience*, pp. 21–25.

[50] Samuel Adams to John Adams, 4 October 1790, in *Works*, 6: 414.

[51] Rush to Adams, 15 June 1789, in *Letters*, 1: 516.

[52] Rush to Adams, 2 July 1789, in *Letters*, 1: 518.

[53] Rush, "Observations Upon the Study of the Latin and Greek Languages . . . ," 1789, in *Essays*, p. 34.

contemporary concepts. "Where shall we find Latin words to convey just ideas of the many terms which electricity—chemistry—navigation—and many other sciences have introduced into our modern languages?" he asked rhetorically.[54] Moreover, as a practical matter, old irrelevant classics could contribute little to the modern world. No American youth had need of "lectures upon the ruins of Palmyra and the antiquities of Herculaneum, or in disputes about Hebrew points, Greek particles, or the accent and quantity of the Roman language," Rush wrote as part of his plan for a federal university. Instead, "the youth of America will be employed in acquiring those branches of knowledge which increase the conveniences of life, lessen human misery, improve our country, promote population, exalt the human understanding, and establish domestic, social, and political happiness."[55]

To Rush, the enormous economic potential of the new nation was a crucial consideration. "Here the opportunities of acquiring knowledge and of advancing private and public interest are so numerous," he eagerly perceived, "and the rewards of genius are so certain, that not a particle of time should be mis-spent or lost. We occupy a new country. Our principal business should be to explore and apply its resources, all of which press us to enterprise and haste."[56] Put simply, the study of history, language, and classical literature consumed time better spent gaining command of agriculture, manufacturing, or international trade. "Under these circumstances," Rush concluded with inspired sarcasm, "to spend four or five years in learning two dead languages, is to turn our backs upon a gold mine, in order to amuse ourselves in catching butterflies."[57]

The Constitutional concept of citizenship was designed for nation building. Where Revolutionary republicans had emphasized political activism, a role appropriate to a revolutionary age, Constitutional thinkers called for private enterprise, a function absolutely essential to a time of development. The new Constitutional citizen, Rush explained in an essay entitled "Of the Mode of Education Proper in a Republic," was to be taught that "study and business should be his principal pursuits in life."[58] In lieu of civic virtue, these thinkers looked to self-interest. The good citizen was required, Rush continued his essay, to "love life, and endeavour to acquire as many of its

[54] Ibid., p. 35.
[55] Rush, "To the Friends of Federal Government: A Plan for a Federal University," 29 October 1788, in *Letters*, 1: 494–95.
[56] Rush, "Observations," in *Essays*, p. 39.
[57] Ibid. It should be noted that not all Constitutionalists made the case for the banishment of classical education. See for example John Adams replying to Rush, 13 and 15 October 1810, in *The Spur of Fame*, ed. John A. Schutz and Douglass Adair (San Marino, Calif.: The Huntington Library, 1966), pp. 170–71.
[58] Rush, "Of the Mode of Education Proper in a Republic," 1786, in *Essays*, p. 12.

conveniences as possible by industry and economy."[59] Constitutionalists held to an early utilitarian calculus in which the interest of each accumulated arithmetically to create the interest of all. Thus the new model American was required "to amass wealth," Rush declared, "but it must be only to encrease his power of contributing to the wants and demands of the state."[60] Above all, because private enterprise was a political obligation, these thinkers called on Americans to seek personal profit in the service of public prosperity: "A particular attention to the virtues of economy, temperance, and industry, are peculiarly necessary in a country like ours," New Hampshire's William Atkinson concluded in a 1791 Fourth of July oration. "The farmer who will make three ears of corn grow where nature gave only one, is more deserving of a statue than the conqueror of a world."[61]

In their essays, sermons, and speeches, Constitutionalists took up the task of creating private citizens. John Adams set the example for their efforts. The pre-Revolutionary letters of Adams to his wife had shown his determination to educate their children in the tenets of classical republicanism. As late as 1783, Adams was demanding that they take up the public life. But beginning about 1780, his correspondence began to show a nagging intimation that these principles had somehow become inappropriate. In the early letters, Adams had demanded republican frugality from his children, and even in the 1780s he was insisting that they despise the pursuit of personal fortune. As Adams made clear after 1780, however, the creation of wealth in the interest of national development was another matter altogether, for when the future of the country was at stake, Adams announced to his wife, "I would have my children attend to duits and farthings as devoutly as the merest Dutchman upon earth, if such attention was necessary to support their independence."[62] Of public life there was little said in the later letters, as Adams wrote increasingly of private affairs, how the ideal citizen was the "honest, sensible, humane man." Instead, Adams could be found in his later years regularly encouraging a notion of private enterprise far removed from his earlier advocacy of public virtue. In the last analysis, he confidently concluded, the man who lived "in a moderate simplicity clearly within his means, and free from debts or obligations, is really the most respectable man in society, [and] makes himself and all about him the most happy."[63]

[59] Ibid., pp. 11–12.

[60] Ibid., p. 12.

[61] William King Atkinson, *An Oration, Delivered at Dover, New-Hampshire, on the Fourth of July, 1791* . . . (Dover, N.H.: E. Ladd, 1791), p. 19.

[62] John Adams to Abigail Adams, 18 December 1780, in *Letters of John Adams, Addressed to his Wife*, ed. Charles Francis Adams (Boston: Charles E. Little and James Brown, 1841), 2: 76.

[63] Adams to Abigail Adams, 8 April 1783, in *Letters*, 2: 96.

In Constitutional thought, civic education was intended to promote a more stable politics. In encouraging stability, the writers and orators turned to a theory of obligation dramatically different from that found in classical republicanism. Revolutionary republicans, believing that the greatest threat to freedom came from the power of government, had looked skeptically at their rulers. Constitutionalists, on the other hand, maintained that such skepticism was unnecessary, that because duly elected officials relied on the ultimate authority of the people, their power could never pose a threat to freedom. Patriotic ministers led the way in arguing that freedom was secure only when citizens were obedient. The liberty of Americans under the Constitution consisted of "nothing more than obedience to the authority and majesty of the laws," as the Reverend Chandler Robbins described it in 1791, "—and laws, too, made by themselves."[64] Under the Constitution, leaders were representative and responsible. Hence, citizens had the obligation to respect them—"a *respectable* behavior," the eminently respectable Robbins went on, being "unquestionably due to those in authority."[65] Subordination ensured liberty, for "when the people are submissive to their laws and rulers," Israel Evans told a 1791 gathering of New Hampshire officials, "their liberties will be permanent."[66] Constitutional citizens, far from revolutionary, were champions of order, dedicating themselves, according to Bridge, to "the support of order, peace and good government."[67] They stayed away from protest and concentrated on the home; their primary responsibilities, as Rhode Island's Reverend Hitchcock summed them up in his 1793 moral tale *The Farmer's Friend*, were to establish the "best cultivated farm" and "best regulated family."[68] In short, as the widely respected theologian William Linn informed a New York audience, citizens had one overriding duty: "to be obedient subjects."[69]

Self-Control and Continuing Commitment

The final factor in Constitutional character was a psychology of control, through which the continuing commitment of future citizens could be as-

[64] Chandler Robbins, A.M., *A Sermon, Preached Before his Excellency John Hancock, Esq. Governour . . . of the Commonwealth of Massachusetts, May 25, 1791 . . .* (Boston: Thomas Adams, 1791), p. 27.

[65] Ibid., p. 25.

[66] Israel Evans, A.M., *A Sermon, Delivered at Concord, Before the Hon. General Court of the State of New-Hampshire . . .* (Concord, N.H.: Geo. Hough, 1791), p. 21.

[67] Bridge, *A Sermon*, p. 53.

[68] Enos Hitchcock, D.D., *The Farmer's Friend . . .* (Boston: I. Thomas and E. T. Andrews, 1793), p. 270.

[69] William Linn, D.D., *The Blessings of America. A Sermon, Preached in the Middle Dutch Church, On the Fourth of July, 1791 . . .* (New York: Thomas Greenleaf, 1791), p. 30.

sured. Following ratification, certain advocates of the Constitution came to the realization that politics was influenced by psychology, that the strongest political commitment was psychological, the best social control self-control. Thus, they set out to create a psychological theory to match their political thought, building a private constitution to complement the public one. This required a radical revision of existing theory, for republicans had long held that citizens were to be constantly vigilant, standing ready at any moment to defend freedom against tyranny. Throughout the Revolution, the responsibility of freedom-loving patriots had been to rouse themselves from their lethargy, girding their loins in times of despair and hardship, pressing on at times of success, keeping constantly in mind the ultimate ends of victory and independence. During the ratification debates the theme was continued, with Antifederalists like A Columbian Patriot, believed to have been Mrs. Warren, calling on citizens to rescue freedom from ever approaching tyranny, "calling on them," as Patriot wrote, "before they are compelled to blush at their own servitude, and to turn back their languid eyes on their lost liberties."[70] But after 1788, Opposition leaders could increasingly be found decrying the loss of the old republican spirit. Writing to his colleague and friend Elbridge Gerry, Mercy Warren's husband James, a proud and unrepentant old Revolutionary himself, told of his 1792 return to some of the scenes of the War of Independence:

> I have lately trod the sacred ground of Concord, where the noble resolution was taken to raise an army to oppose the mighty power of Britain. I visited with a degree of veneration the room where the Committee set. A thousand recollections, and a thousand reflections filled my mind. I saw but few of the old hands, and little of that noble spirit, and as little of those comprehensive views and sentiments which dignified those times. Thus I have lived long enough to feel pains too great for me to describe.[71]

Constitutional thinkers saw the situation quite differently. Whatever their thoughts on the role of republican citizens before the Constitution, they were determined to create controlled and committed citizens afterward. Barlow set the standard in his 1787 Fourth of July oration at Hartford, coining a phrase that would be quoted often by his contemporaries: "the noblest effort of human nature," he offered, was *the conquest of self*."[72] Self-sustaining government required self-regulating citizens. Thus, these

[70] A Columbian Patriot [probably Mercy Otis Warren], "Observations on the New Constitution, and on the Federal and State Conventions," 1788, in *Pamphlets*, p. 3.

[71] James Warren to Elbridge Gerry, 18 December 1792, in *A Study in Dissent*, ed. C. Harvey Gardiner (Carbondale, Ill.: Southern Illinois University Press, 1968), p. 251.

[72] Barlow, *An Oration*, p. 14.

thinkers seemed determined to create a "happy temper of mind" in which citizens would be "cheerfully obedient to their laws."[73] In 1788, their political education began to take on the attributes of psychological management. The new American, explained the Reverend Hitchcock, would "cheerfully submit to lawful authority," "encourage and support public officers," and "cultivate . . . those benevolent dispositions so necessary to . . . the preservation of peace and harmony."[74]

The creators of Constitutional character were determined to create a psychology to perpetuate their government. Their theory of personality internalized their model of politics. Assuming a political pattern of corruption followed by rebellion, Opposition thinkers presupposed a psychology in which skepticism was punctuated by periodic bursts of protest. Constitutionalists, relying instead on the Aristotelian model of excess and imbalance, sought a perpetually balanced middle state. Constitutional government, the Reverend Linn explained, was "the happy medium between oppression and licentiousness."[75] In the same way, Constitutional self-government offered a balance between psychological states, a medium of personal moderation. As early as 1725, in his *Dissertation on Liberty and Necessity, Pleasure and Pain*, the young Benjamin Franklin had applied the idea of balance to the psychological realm, devising a Newtonian psychology based on the principle of the pendulum, according to which every human emotion would move between poles of pleasure and pain, each sentiment seeking out its opposite as required by the laws of physics.[76] When people embraced pleasure, they condemned themselves thereby to equal pain, for the pendulum promised to swing back to its opposite state. Thus, those who insisted on ecstasy consigned themselves to despair, whereas those willing to accept moderate happiness suffered only limited sorrow. The ideal condition was the balanced pendulum, the psychological state in which pleasure was controlled, pain limited, and perpetual moderation assured. "Men should en-

73 Evans, *A Sermon*, p. 15.

74 Hitchcock, *An Oration*, pp. 18–19; 19. The development of this Constitutional psychology is seen best in the numerous election sermons of the period. See for example Samuel Miller, A.M., *Christianity the Grand Source, and the Surest Basis, of Political Liberty: A Sermon, Preached in New-York, July 4th, 1793* . . . (New York: Thomas Greenleaf, [1793]), p. 14; Nathan Williams, A.M., *Carefully to observe the signatures of Divine Providence, a mark of wisdom. Illustrated in a Sermon* . . . (Hartford, Conn.: Hudson and Goodwin, 1793), p. 22; Caleb Blood, *A Sermon Preached Before the Honorable Legislature of the State of Vermont; . . . October 11th, 1792* . . . (Rutland, Vt.: Anthony Haswell, [1792], pp. 32–33; and Timothy Dwight, D.D., *Virtuous Rulers a National Blessing. A Sermon, Preached at the General Election, May 12th, 1791* (Hartford, Conn.: Hudson and Goodwin, 1791), p. 36.

75 Linn, *The Blessings of America*, p. 17.

76 On Franklin, see *A Dissertation on Liberty and Necessity, Pleasure and Pain* (London: n.p., 1725), p. 15.

deavor at a *balance* of affections and appetites," wrote Adams, "under the monarchy of reason and conscience, within, as well as at a balance of power without."[77] The model Constitutional character was defined by this prudent balance, a "happy mediocrity," as one thinker put it, "an *animated moderation*."[78]

Yet some sought an even stronger psychology, arguing that balance was not enough, that if Newtonian physics had defined the shape of Constitutional government, post-Newtonian technology offered a better metaphor for Constitutional psychology. Dr. Rush in particular began at this time to make use of certain concepts from applied science. Opposition thought, the creation of a simple agrarian world, was individualistic and libertarian. Constitutionalism, the product of an increasingly technological society, seemed to stress homogeneity and social order. Education should be designed, Rush advised accordingly, to "render the mass of the people more homogeneous, and thereby fit them more easily for uniform and peaceable government."[79] Opposition writers could continue to emphasize personal freedom. By contrast, Constitutionalists had begun to talk more often of social uniformity, how the wills of the people had to be "fitted to each other" to "produce regularity and unison in government."[80]

The advocates of this psychology, like Americans of every previous period, believed that times of achievement would be followed by those of backsliding, with strong generations leading to weak ones, extraordinary parents to unexceptional offspring. They looked cynically at the next generation: "Wise men beget fools," warned a gloomy John Adams, "and honest men knaves."[81] Yet Constitutional thinkers seemed determined to banish the threat of generational decline. The new psychology required no ages of achievement and allowed none of backsliding. It promised to see to it that strong and weak generations, wise men and fools alike, would disappear, to be replaced by a succession of mediocre generations, an unending line of obedient citizens. With these prudent people, balanced government would never falter, holding instead to controlled, self-sustaining, perpetual moderation. The Constitution had created a Newtonian machine. To run it, Constitutional psychology provided Newtonian parts: "I consider it is possible," Rush concluded with astonishing frankness, "to convert men into

[77] Adams, *Defence*, in *Works*, 4: 407.

[78] David Osgood, A.M., *A Sermon, Preached at the Request of the Ancient and Honorable Artillery Company in Boston, June 2, 1788* . . . (Boston: Benjamin Russell, 1788), p. 6; Dickinson, "Letters of Fabius . . . , no. IX," 1788, in *Political Writings*, 2: 165.

[79] Rush, "Of the Mode of Education Proper in a Republic," in *Essays*, p. 8.

[80] Ibid., p. 15.

[81] Adams, *Defence*, in *Works*, 4: 396.

republican machines. This must be done, if we expect them to perform their parts properly, in the great machine of the government of the state."[82]

Nevertheless, just as these thinkers demanded moderation in the public life, they required extraordinary effort in the private. Indeed, the two realms were complementary, for public disinterest freed the citizen for private involvement. As early as 1780, John Adams had foreseen the argument. Looking well ahead, Adams predicted that political founding would be followed by socioeconomic improvement, which would be followed by cultural and artistic advances. Each stage would require appropriate efforts. He described the process in a letter to his wife concerning the education of their children. "I must study politics and war," he wrote, "that my sons may have liberty to study mathematics and philosophy. My sons ought to study mathematics and philosophy, geography, natural history and naval architecture, navigation, commerce and agriculture, in order to give their children a right to study painting, poetry, music, architecture, statuary, tapestry and porcelain."[83]

Political founding had already been secured. Cultural advances seemed at least a generation in the future. In the meantime, there remained the responsibility of socioeconomic development, the role of the next generation, which would act diligently in building the nation by developing its social life and establishing economic prosperity. In this regard, even conservative assessments suggested extraordinary potential. It was, Adams claimed, "like contemplating the heavens through the telescopes of Herschell. Objects stupendous in their magnitude and motions strike us from all quarters, and fill us with amazement!"[84] Constitutional government, having provided exceptional resources, insisted in return on exceptional efforts. Adams thought it little to ask of the next generation. "A profligate American youth," he wrote, "must be profligate indeed, and richly merits the scorn of all mankind."[85]

The Constitutional character had definite limits. According to the theory, Americans had the responsibility to build the private realm while remaining outside the public, keeping their role economic, not political. Even where citizens were allowed the chance for political action, it was limited, for they could advance their politics only incrementally, and any change they made would be presupposed by the principles of the Constitution. In fact, within the private realm itself innovation was incremental, progress being possible only when citizens suppressed any desire to reject the efforts of the previous

---

[82] Rush, "Of the Mode," in *Essays*, pp. 14–15. See also John F. Kasson, *Civilizing the Machine* (Harmondsworth: Penguin Books, 1977), pp. 28–36.

[83] John Adams to Abigail Adams, n.d. [fixed by content in 1780], in *Letters*, 2: 68.

[84] Adams, *Defence*, in *Works*, 6: 218.

[85] Ibid.

generation, giving up the demand for sudden or discontinuous change and consigning themselves to a cautious course of step-by-step development. This theory made allowance for economic innovation by doing away with political instability, and provided for reform by outlawing rebellion. Put simply, progress demanded prudence. The role of future Americans, intoned the Reverend Josiah Whitney, pastor of a large Brooklyn church, in a sermon delivered to the elected officials of neighboring Connecticut, was to make "a wise, and discreet improvement of our constitutional privileges."[86]

Apparently most Americans accepted the role assigned them by the makers of this Constitutional character, and many eagerly took up their new political status. With ratification, a period of protest, conflict, and uncertainty had apparently come to a close. Old Revolutionaries could continue to recall the Revolution, but Americans of all persuasions had long ago turned willingly, like Cincinnatus returning to the plow, to private enterprise. But especially among the young, the desire to look from public to private concerns was strong, for those of the postfounding generation in particular seemed to recognize that the end of an age of self-sacrifice marked the beginning of a period of self-interest. The new Constitutional psychology found a receptive audience among these young Americans. John Quincy Adams, age twenty-five, speaking as a representative of his generation in addressing a Boston audience filled with his father's peers, announced their acceptance: "From the present prosperous appearance of our public affairs," he confessed, "we may admit a rational hope that our country will have no occasion to require of us those extraordinary and heroic exertions which it was your fortune to exhibit."[87]

In effect, the new psychology stipulated that from that time, heroic politics existed only in the past, the duty of Americans being to revere the founders, remembering their illustrious deeds, applauding their magnificent government, and cherishing their hallowed Constitution. Opposition writers protested, reminding their readers of the all-too-human frailty of the founders. But Constitutional orators continued to encourage a psychology of respect and even reverence. This new political psychology secured immortality for the government the founders had handed down, "perpetuated in our posterity," as the Reverend Foster said, "to the latest age."[88] In the

[86] Josiah Whitney, A.M., *The essential requisites to form the good Ruler's Character, illustrated and urged. A Sermon, Preached . . . at Hartford, . . . May 8th, 1788* (Hartford, Conn.: Elisha Babcock, 1788), p. 35. See also Jean Yarbrough, "Federalism in the Foundation and Preservation of the Republic," *Publius*, 6, 3 (Summer 1976): 59.

[87] John Quincy Adams, *An Oration, Pronounced July 4th, 1793, at . . . Boston . . .* (Boston: Benjamin Edes & Son, 1793), p. 14.

[88] Foster, *An Election Sermon*, p. 24.

same way, it assured immortality for the founders, "whose prudence, integrity and virtue," Dr. Whitwell declared, "will ever make them renowned to posterity."[89] Finally, it promised immortality to the founding itself, Americans remembering it, revering it, remaining grateful always, according to Brooklyn's Reverend Whitney, for "the great, and good things which have been done for us."[90] To succeeding generations, it would be as if their fathers were always present, while they remained forever children: "Secure in their prosperity," wrote the aging James Sullivan, "they weep for joy, that Heaven hath given them—Fathers!"[91]

The preachers and orators made it clear that the framers of the Constitution alone deserved the godlike immortality attributed to founders. They did what they could, while critics protested in vain, to ensure that their children would live in the shadow of the founding. As early as 1783, John Adams had written to his sons concerning their responsibility to be private citizens, promising that if they ever shirked their duty, or offered even one word of complaint, he would disinherit them. "Work, you rogues, and be free," he arrogantly advised. "You will never have so hard work to do as papa has had."[92] As late as 1798, Adams was still repeating the theme, although by this time it had become a political argument, directed not to his own children but to all young Americans. Addressing a group of young men who had created a club to inspire youthful participation in politics, Adams was paternal and benign. Taking note of their enthusiasm and having, he said, no wish "to deny the ardor of curiosity," he lauded their intentions. But he went on to imply politely if superciliously that their efforts were futile, and even somewhat pathetic. "I will hazard a prediction," he concluded; "that, after the most industrious and impartial researches, the longest liver of you all will find no principles, institutions, or systems of education more fit, in general, to be transmitted to your posterity, than those you have received from your ancestors."[93]

The children of the founders accepted the status of mortals descended from demigods. But while most endorsed their new position, some admitted reservations. There was a definite cost in accepting the Constitutional character: for future Americans, the price was that they themselves would never be allowed to define a political role of their own. The framers had laid the basis for permanent government. "The seeds of Liberty are plentifully

[89] Whitwell, *An Oration*, p. 13.

[90] Whitney, *The essential requisites*, p. 35.

[91] Cassius [James Sullivan], letter to the *Massachusetts Gazette*, 25 December 1787, in *Essays*, p. 48.

[92] Adams to Abigail Adams, 8 April 1783, in *Letters*, 2: 95.

[93] John Adams to the Young Men of the City of Philadelphia . . . , 7 May 1798, in *Works*, 9: 188.

sown," as John Quincy Adams explained in his 1793 Boston oration, and promised "eventually [to] flourish with luxuriant profusion."[94] But in this promise of success lay a dilemma for future citizens, in that the republic would prosper with or without their efforts. The creators of the Constitution, having done their work all too well, had left future Americans no significant political role, an oversight, the younger Adams implied, that had consigned the citizens of succeeding generations to perpetual inferiority. Under the new system, Americans were never again to undertake extraordinary political actions, because from that time there were, at least in theory, no more revolutions to be fought and no more constitutions to be founded. Above all, from that time there was no more fame to be won: "The field is extensive; it is fruitful," explained Adams, "but the copious treasures of its fragrance have already been gathered by the hands of genius; and there now remains for the gleaning of mental indigence, nought but the thinly scattered sweets which have escaped the vigilance of their industry."[95]

Proponents of the new psychology had set out to end the menace of ambition, revoking from succeeding generations the chance for glory by purging from them the desire for fame. They did not falter in carrying out the task. The most painful punishment in life, John Adams wrote, was to be denied the opportunity for fame. The citizen without distinction was like the consumer without wealth, a creature not so much despised as neglected. "Mankind takes no notice of him," Adams wrote, echoing Adam Smith. "He rambles and wanders unheeded. In the midst of a crowd, at church, in the market, at a play, at an execution, or coronation, he is in as much obscurity as he would be in a garrett or a cellar. He is not disapproved, censured, or reproached; *he is only not seen*."[96] The founding generation had feared this obscurity, a fate, as Adams described it, "mortifying, painful, and cruel."[97] But Adams did not hesitate in leaving it as a legacy to the succeeding generations of Americans, who would be unacquainted with distinction and incapable of fame. Constitutional citizens were deferential, retiring, unobtrusive, in private life solid and respectable, in politics anonymous. After all, advised Connecticut clergyman Charles Backus in a 1793 sermon, there

[94] John Quincy Adams, *An Oration*, pp. 19–20.

[95] Ibid., p. 7. Adams's metaphor was adopted later by Abraham Lincoln in his address to the Young Men's Lyceum of Springfield, Illinois. But where Adams, speaking for the second generation of American republicans, counseled acceptance and resignation, Lincoln, representative of the next generation, argued ominously that the time was ripe for protest and a renewal of heroic action: "This field of glory is harvested, and the crop is already appropriated. But new reapers will arise, and *they*, too, will seek a field." Abraham Lincoln, "Address Before the Young Men's Lyceum of Springfield, Illinois," 27 January 1838, in *The Collected Works of Abraham Lincoln*, ed. Roy P. Basler (New Brunswick, N.J.: Rutgers University Press, 1953–), 1: 113.

[96] John Adams, "Davila," in *Works*, 6: 239.

[97] Ibid.

was always "much more to praise in the good man, who passes all his days in the vale of obscurity, than in some who are recorded as the boast of their nation or age."[98]

Nevertheless, they did not entirely eliminate the desire for fame. John Quincy Adams readily admitted that he and his peers were unprepared to follow the example of their parents. But that did not mean they were unable to match the deeds of the previous generation. The older generation would make a grave mistake, Adams told his listeners, to conclude "from the greater prevalence of private and personal motives in these days of calm serenity, that your sons have degenerated from the virtues of their fathers." Rather the opposite was true, it being, he supposed, "a subject of pleasing reflection" to them to know their children were their equals. The fire of ambition had not been extinguished in the hearts of young Americans. Instead, as Adams informed his audience, the flame burned low but brightly: "the generous and disinterested energies, which you were summoned to display, are permitted by the bountiful indulgence of Heaven to remain latent in the bosoms of your children."[99]

The Constitutional psychologists had done all they could to eradicate Revolutionary ambition. In his Boston oration, John Quincy Adams showed that they had not succeeded completely. Adams recalled for his Independence Day audience the events of the American Revolution. He spoke at length of the character of the Revolutionary patriots, their dedication to republican principles, their love of liberty. Then he assured his aging listeners that his own generation stood ready to emulate the example of these heroes. The Revolution had been fought and won, but liberty was fragile, never secure, and Americans were certain to be called on again to protect their freedom. Adams promised they would be ready "should the voice of our country's calamity ever call us to her relief."[100] In times of crisis, patriots would come forward to defend the old republican principles, resisting oppression, maintaining liberty. Adams swore to his audience that he and his generation would be among those patriots, that they would remain loyal to the memory of the Revolutionary generation, faithful to what he called "the precious memory of the sages."[101] Americans would not forget the heritage of Revolutionary republicanism. Rather, he promised they would keep alive the legacy of the Revolution, emulating their ancestors, defending the old principles, acting, Adams declared, "as the faithful disciples of those

[98] Charles Backus, A.M., *A Sermon, Preached Before His Excellency Samuel Huntington, Esq. L.L.D. Governor . . . of the State of Connecticut . . . May 9th, 1793* (Hartford, Conn.: Hudson and Goodwin, 1793), p. 6.
[99] John Quincy Adams, *An Oration*, p. 14.
[100] Ibid., p. 14.
[101] Ibid., pp. 14–15.

who so magnanimously taught us the instructive lesson of republican virtue."[102]

By 1793, the American Constitution was secure. Accepted on all sides as
legitimate, the new government could turn to the day-to-day demands of
governing. At the same time, far from the seats of power, citizens went
about their business quietly and prosperously, relieved no doubt that the
founding was finally over. Yet the Constitutional system, having been made
secure, was now stable enough to allow the resumption of party politics. As
Opposition and Constitutionalist faded, Republican and Federalist rose into
view, with partisans moving from persuasion to party with little predictability. While most Americans were celebrating the new Constitutional consensus, party leaders were already at odds, their disagreements as ardent as
ever before.

In the end, Constitutionalists had both succeeded and failed in creating
Constitutional character. From that time on, Constitutional citizens would
bear at least some of the attributes of modern liberalism, considering it their
primary responsibility to act in the private realm, pursuing their individual
interests and thereby building the country's economy. At the same time,
these citizens retained at least some semblance of classical republicanism as
well, remaining ready to do battle against the enemies of their freedom.
Ironically, the two sides of this civic character were related, for as the new
government gained legitimacy, Americans were able to be both friend to
the Constitution and foe to all its enemies, including those in the opposite
party. Political consensus, in short, not only allowed but even encouraged
partisan conflict.

Yet this Constitutional character would soon be tested. For with the
French Revolution, citizens would find themselves once more choosing
sides in what would become a protracted political conflict. With good reason, thinkers in 1794 would again consider the future. This time, however,
they would be looking not simply to the fate of their new nation, but to the
fate of the world as they knew it.

[102] Ibid., p. 15.

∗8∗

DESTINY

Prophecy and the Prophets of Progress

THE BATTLES OVER the Constitution behind them, Americans in the early 1790s looked ahead to what they hoped would be a period of harmony at home and peace in the world. Their illusions were soon shattered, for with the coming of the French Revolution in 1789, there began a decade of national and international turmoil unparalleled in American history. The French Revolution created repercussions that resounded throughout the Western world. Sympathizers and opponents everywhere could be found taking sides, their differences poisoning the domestic politics of virtually every interested state. But for Americans in particular, their nation new and untested, the situation seemed threatening. On the near horizon, they could foresee events both grand and terrifying, a European revolution that seemed certain to liberate much of the world, but that also seemed capable of sweeping back to rattle the foundations of their own revolutionary republic. So it was that Americans of the 1790s looked to the future, fearfully and hopefully seeking to catch some glimpse of their destiny—the new nation's eventual success or its ultimate failure.

Treatments of the 1790s have tended to overlook this element of expectation. Histories of the early republic have examined the influence of economic interests, state and sectional rivalries, social distinctions, and ideological disputes.[1] They have reviewed at some length the formative role of party organization.[2] At least one has considered the contribution of popular

[1] On the economic interests involved, see Charles A. Beard, *Economic Origins of Jeffersonian Democracy* (New York: Macmillan, 1915). On state and sectional rivalries, see Manning J. Dauer, *The Adams Federalists* (Baltimore: Johns Hopkins Press, 1953); Paul Goodman, *The Democratic-Republicans of Massachusetts* (Cambridge, Mass.: Harvard University Press, 1964); and Alfred F. Young, *The Democratic Republicans of New York* (Chapel Hill, N.C.: University of North Carolina Press, 1967). On social distinctions, see David Hackett Fischer, *The Revolution of American Conservatism* (New York: Harper & Row, 1965). On ideological disputes, see Richard Buel, Jr., *Securing the Revolution* (Ithaca, N.Y.: Cornell University Press, 1972); Linda K. Kerber, *Federalists in Dissent* (Ithaca, N.Y.: Cornell University Press, 1970); and Marshall Smelser, "The Jacobin Phrenzy: Federalism and the Menace of Liberty, Equality, and Fraternity," *The Review of Politics*, 13, 4 (October 1951): 457–82, and idem, "The Jacobin Phrenzy: The Menace of Monarchy, Plutocracy, and Anglophilia, 1789–1798," *The Review of Politics*, 21, 1 (January 1959): 239–58.

[2] See William N. Chambers, *The First Party System* (New York: Wiley, 1972); Noble E. Cunningham, *The Jeffersonian Republicans* (Chapel Hill, N.C.: University of North Carolina

political thought.[3] Yet the studies have said little if anything about the role of popular prediction, the fears and hopes that citizens held about the future.

Recently, however, a formidable phalanx of scholars has demonstrated that many thinkers of the time were predisposed to practice their politics with an eye to the future, viewing events through the lens of religious prophecy. Following the lead of Ernest Tuveson, scholars like J. F. Maclear, Robert Middlekauff, and William McLoughlin, along with Davidson, Hatch, and Bercovitch, have now established that at the end of the eighteenth century in America there was enormous popular interest in the prophetic books of the Bible.[4] In fact, as Maclear has observed, millennial ideas were "so common as to be canonical."[5] These frightening, fascinating prophecies promised that the end of the world would be preceded by a thousand-year kingdom of peace known as the millennium. The millennial theme was pervasive in religion, where ministers promised millennial states that ranged from the literal heavenly kingdoms of the Calvinist conservatives to the metaphorical earthly states of the dissenters and deists. Somewhat surprisingly, it was almost as common in politics, where political prophets could frequently be found using these prophecies concerning the fate of the world to make predictions about the future of their new nation, claiming that the creation of the Constitution would usher in a new era of peace and happiness, a political heaven-on-earth.[6]

Throughout the 1790s, these political millennialists, Federalists and Republicans alike, would be instrumental in inspiring a millennial politics, an

---

Press, 1957); idem, *The Jeffersonian Republicans in Power* (Chapel Hill, N.C.: University of North Carolina Press, 1963); Richard Hofstadter, *The Idea of a Party System* (Berkeley, Calif.: University of California Press, 1969); and Young, *The Washington Community*, pp. 65–83.

[3] See Howe, "Republican Thought," pp. 147–65.

[4] Millennialism in its American context is introduced in Tuveson, *Redeemer Nation*, pp. 1–25. See also Maclear, "The Republican and the Millennium," pp. 183–216; Middlekauff, *The Mathers*, pp. 320–49; William G. McLoughlin, "The Role of Religion in the Revolution," in *Essays on the American Revolution*, ed. Stephen G. Kurtz and James H. Hutson (Chapel Hill, N.C.: University of North Carolina Press, 1973), pp. 197–255; Davidson, *Logic of Millennial Thought*, pp. 12–36; Hatch, *Sacred Cause*, pp. 1–20; and Bercovitch, *American Jeremiad*, pp. 93–121. Important articles also include Ira V. Brown, "Watchers for the Second Coming: The Millenarian Tradition in America," *The Mississippi Valley Historical Review*, 39, 3 (December 1952): 441–58; David E. Smith, "Millenarian Scholarship in America," *American Quarterly*, 17, 3 (Fall 1965): 535–49; Nathan O. Hatch, "The Origins of Civil Millennialism in America," *The William and Mary Quarterly*, 3rd ser., 31, 3 (July 1974): 407–30; J. F. Maclear, "New England and the Fifth Monarchy: The Quest for the Millennium in Early American Puritanism," *The William and Mary Quarterly*, 3rd ser., 32, 2 (April 1975): 223–60; and Timothy L. Smith, "Righteousness and Hope: Christian Holiness and the Millennial Vision in America, 1800–1900," *American Quarterly*, 31, 1 (Spring 1979): 21–45.

[5] Maclear, "The Republic and the Millennium," p. 184.

[6] See Hatch, *Sacred Cause*, p. 23n.

early and very volatile version of nationalism that combined elements of interventionism, isolationism, and xenophobia. At the same time, other thinkers would rely on an expanded idea of progress to shape a more pragmatic brand of nonmillennial nationalism. Needless to say, proponents of these perspectives would repeatedly find themselves at odds. Cutting across party lines, millennialists and progressives offered radically dissimilar forecasts of the fate of the new nation. At least by implication, their predictions also suggested very different policies, as well as very different styles of politics. In any case, armed with ideas of prophecy and progress, these thinkers did battle in the mid- to late-1790s. At stake was the nation's future, the definition of its destiny.

Political Millennialism

At heart, millennialism is a theory of apocalypse. All millennialists believe that the end of the world is coming, and that a series of prescribed signs and preordained events will announce the beginning of the end. In some of the more radical biblical texts, such as the books of Joel, Isaiah, and Daniel, the signs are cataclysmic, including wars, earthquakes, and political revolutions. In other more moderate Scriptures, like the book of Micah, the events seem more subdued, as in the prediction that before the end there will be advances in piety, learning, and peace. All millennial Scripture seems to be consistent with the explanation found in the book of Revelation that a cosmological conflict will be joined on the plains of Armageddon, in which the forces of heaven led by the risen Jesus Christ will meet the powers of hell led by the Antichrist, Satan, or the devil. That battle is to end with the promised triumph of the armies of righteousness. With the victory at Armageddon, the devil is to be bound in chains and held captive for the thousand-year reign of peace. At the close of that millennial age, however, Satan will break loose again and, aided by the allied armies of darkness, confront the heavenly host once more on the field of battle. In this final conflict, Christ and his angels will triumph at last, the forces of evil will be banished forever, and the saints of all the ages will celebrate in chorus the glorious finale of Judgment Day.[7]

Such millennial prophecy has often been applied to politics. The appli-

[7] For an introduction to the concept, see Ernest Lee Tuveson, *Millennium and Utopia* (1949; reprint, Berkeley, Calif.: University of California Press, 1964), pp. 1–21; Tuveson, *Redeemer Nation* (Chicago: University of Chicago Press, 1968), pp. 1–25; and Hillel Schwartz, "The End of the Beginning: Millenarian Studies, 1969–1975," *Religious Studies Review*, 2, 2 (July 1976): 1–15.

cation, however, has been complex.[8] One version of millennialism has emphasized the Second Coming of a warrior Christ who would usher in with the sword the millennial period of peace.[9] This "premillennialism," with its assumption of apocalyptic conflict and world-ravaging war, has been a deeply pessimistic brand of prophecy.[10] At least in America, premillennialists have been found to be conservative and even reactionary in their politics.[11] In contrast, a second version has looked more often toward the thousand years of peace.[12] This "postmillennialism," which assumed that heaven-on-earth would be announced quietly, attained gradually, and marked by steady progress in religion, science, and the arts, has been supremely optimistic in its predictions.[13] Among Americans, postmillennialists have been described as pursuing progressive and reformist policies.[14]

Unfortunately, scholars have seldom ventured beyond the standard ideal types of either brand of millennialism. Yet as James W. Davidson has shown, millennialism in its truer and more common form has been a mixture of these strains.[15] Prophecy has seldom been pure, and the millennialists of most times have practiced neither premillennialism nor postmillennialism, but a complicated combination of both. Thus, Davidson found that many millennialists have managed to be simultaneously pessimistic and optimistic, pursuing an "afflictive model of progress" that allowed them to be, in effect, conservative and progressive at the same time.[16]

Even more unfortunate, all too many historians have not only divided millennialism into separate pre- and postmillennial parts, but have assigned each to its own political party, to Federalists and Republicans respectively. For example, in his *Religion and the American Mind*, Heimert compared the

[8] On the political background of early millennialism, see Norman Cohn, *The Pursuit of the Millennium*, rev. ed. (1961; reprint, New York: Oxford University Press, 1970), pp. 19–41.

[9] For premillennialism, see Harris, *All Coherence Gone*, pp. 86–118; Christopher Hill, *Antichrist in Seventeenth-Century England* (London: Oxford University Press, 1971), pp. 98–115; and William M. Lamont, *Richard Baxter and the Millennium* (London: Croom Helm, 1979).

[10] See Tuveson, *Millennian and Utopia*, pp. 22–70.

[11] See Smith, "Millenarian Scholarship," p. 539.

[12] On the concept of postmillennialism, see Peter Toon, "The Latter-Day Glory," in *Puritans, the Millennium, and the Future of Israel*, ed. Peter Toon (Cambridge: James Clarke, 1970), pp. 23–41.

[13] See Tuveson, *Millennium and Utopia*, pp. 113–203; Miller, "The End of the World," in *Errand*, pp. 221–34; and Maclear, "The Republic and the Millennium," pp. 188–200.

[14] See Smith, "Millenarian Scholarship," p. 539.

[15] On the contradictions inherent in the millennial model, see James West Davidson, *The Logic of Millennial Thought*, pp. 129–41, 279; idem, "Searching for the Millennium: Problems for the 1790's and 1970's," *The New England Quarterly*, 45, 2 (June 1972): 241–61.

[16] Davidson, *Logic of Millenial Thought*, pp. 131–32. See also Middlekauff, *The Mathers*, pp. 279–350; Bercovitch, *American Jeremiad*, pp. 3–30; and James H. Moorhead, *American Apocalypse* (New Haven, Conn.: Yale University Press, 1978), pp. 6–22.

pessimistic conservatism of the premillennial Federalist preachers with the optimistic progressivism of the postmillennial Republican politicians.[17] As Davidson has shown, however, the situation was otherwise, because irrespective of party, political millennialists combined pre- and postmillennial themes, mixing their predictions of failure and success.[18]

This dualistic form of millennialism was particularly well suited to the 1790s. The early national period was a time of enormous uncertainty, in which the future seemed to hold equal potential for disaster and triumph. Thus, the rhetoric of early nationalists could be deeply pessimistic, haunted by fears of international conflict and domestic disorder, and at the same time supremely optimistic, proud of the successful Revolution, boastful about the recent Constitutional founding, and captivated by the seemingly limitless potential of the new nation. Certain Federalists may have leaned more toward pessimism, and certain Republicans more toward optimism, but generally, supporters of both parties combined elements of each. For the contradictory 1790s, this contradictory millennialism was the perfect prophecy.

Interventionism

In 1789 Americans of all stripes could be found making the case for international intervention.[19] The Constitutional founding had announced the possibility of republican self-government. As the first new republican nation, the United States had the responsibility to export its perfect politics to all other countries, to "regenerate the old world."[20] Federalists and Republicans, conservatives as well as liberals, eagerly urged the extension of the Revolution, not only to France but to all oppressed people. "The sceptre of domination," intoned the Federalist editor Theodore Dwight to a gathering of the Connecticut Cincinnati, "trembles in the hands of every monarch in Europe."[21]

Whereas secular thinkers put their faith in progress, millennialists looked to prophecy to foretell the future role of America in the world. Prophecy held that the chosen nation had the mission to spread its true religion over the earth, ushering in a new age of faith and announcing the end of time.

[17] See Heimert, *Religion and the American Mind*, pp. 532–45.

[18] See Davidson, "Searching for the Millennium," pp. 254–61.

[19] See Strout, *American Image of the Old World*, pp. 42–43.

[20] John Mercer, *An Oration Delivered on the Fourth of July 1792* . . . (Richmond, Va.: T. Nicolson, [1792]), p. 17.

[21] Theodore Dwight, Esquire, *An Oration, Spoken Before the Society of the Cincinnati, of the State of Connecticut* . . . *on the 4th of July, 1792* (Hartford, Conn.: Hudson and Goodwin, 1792), p. 15.

Republican millennialists, mixing prophecy with politics, expanded this millennial vision to include the export of republican liberty, leading eventually to the creation of a universal republic. The scholarly Dr. Joseph Lathrop was among the political prophets, informing his West Springfield, Massachusetts, congregation of freedom's preordained future.

> The day is coming, when liberty and peace shall bless the human race. ... The rod of the oppressor will be broken, and the yoke will be removed from the shoulders of the oppressed. ... The whole earth will rest and be quiet: they will break forth into singing. ... Joy and gladness shall be found therein; thanksgiving and the voice of melody.[22]

American millennialists relied on this prophetic theory to explain the spread of revolutionary republicanism. According to prophecy, world revolution was not only desirable, it was inevitable. The French Revolution seemed an auspicious indication that the predicted universal republic was near at hand. Ministers began to announce the imminent arrival of the New Jerusalem, the "new heavens and a new earth," "the millennium state, or empire of holiness," "the general jubilee."[23] But their prophecy crossed over frequently into politics with predictions that the millennial state would provide not only personal but also "political salvation."[24] For twenty centuries anxious prophets had been searching the skies for the coming kingdom of heaven. With the French Revolution, millennialists could believe that heaven was being realized on earth. The events of the day, advised Maine's Reverend Samuel Deane, already presaged "no faint picture of the predicted millennial state."[25] Some began to prepare for its arrival. "We doubt not," declared William Jones, a wealthy Massachusetts trader, "that we are upon the eve of that long predicted period."[26] A few could see its outline already. "Methinks," concluded the influential Reverend Chandler Robbins, "I already see the dawn of that most auspicious day."[27]

[22] Joseph Lathrop, D.D., *The Happiness of a Free Government, and the Means of Preserving it: Illustrated in a Sermon* . . . (Springfield, Mass.: James R. Hutchinss, 1794), pp. 22–23.

[23] John McKnight, D.D., *God the Author of Promotion, A Sermon Preached in the New Presbyterian Church, New-York, on the 4th of July, 1794* . . . (New York: William Durrell, 1794), p. 24; Joseph Eckley, A.M., *A Sermon Preached at the Request of the Ancient and Honourable Artillery Company, June 4, 1792* . . . (Boston: Samuel Hall, 1792), p. 20; Chandler Robbins, D.D., *An Address, Delivered at Plymouth, on the 24th Day of January, 1793* . . . (Boston: Belknap and Hall, 1793), p. 17.

[24] Robbins, *An Address*, p. 17.

[25] Samuel Deane, D.D., *A Sermon, Preached Before His Honor Samuel Adams, Esq. . . . May 28th, 1794* . . . (Boston: Adams and Larkin, 1794), p. 31.

[26] William Jones, A.B., *An Oration, Pronounced at Concord, the Fourth of July, 1794* . . . (Concord, Mass.: Nathaniel Coverly, 1794), p. 19.

[27] Robbins, *An Address*, p. 7.

Millennial theory helped rationalize the excesses of revolution. By the early 1790s, proponents of progress were watching in horror as the French republic, the happy offspring of their revolutionary seed, became a raging brute that seemed dedicated to devouring all authority, convention, and religion. Paradoxically, however, among believers in the millennium such violence did not inspire despair. On the contrary, as the Revolution seemed to turn toward chaos, these believers began to see cause for celebration. Apocalyptic theory explains their reaction, for prophecy promised that before the consummation there would be one final battle in which the devil would be bound by the forces of the Lord. Providential catastrophes could appear in many manifestations, and revolutionary France, whether avenging angel or devil in disguise, might be exactly the providential force to announce the end of time. Thus, these millennialists were resigned to the conflict, whatever its duration or extent. "The world subsists by *revolutions*," explained one. "If the voice from heaven cry, 'REVOLUTION!' in vain would all the powers upon earth attempt to arrest the motions of these wheels."[28] Thus, while progressives cowered, millennialists cheered their revolutionary brothers. "The present aspect of the world is wonderful, and above description affecting!" confided Wall Street's Reverend Miller. "We behold nation rising up against nation, and kingdom against kingdom. . . . What designs the Governor of the Universe is carrying on, we know not. The Christian patriot, however, cannot help indulging in the confident hope, that all these things are designed to banish tyranny from the earth."[29]

Although progress had failed to predict the violence of the French Revolution, prophecy saw it as preordained. As events in France took their bloody course, progressives found themselves unable to justify the extent of the carnage. "Perhaps a revolution from the extremes of *Arbitrary Power*, to the fair midway region of temperate LIBERTY," suggested a troubled Elisha Lee, an up-and-coming Massachusetts lawyer, "without a vibration towards *Anarchy* and *Licentiousness* is impossible."[30] Millennialists, by contrast, saw good reason for the bloodshed. David Austin, the eccentric but immensely popular preacher-prophet, was typical when he described the French Revolution as the sword of righteousness leveled against the forces of evil. Americans could be proud that they had introduced the cleansing power of revolutionary war into the world. "Behold, then, this hero of America wielding the standard of civil and religious liberty over these United States!" Austin observed with his usual visionary ecstasy. "—Fol-

[28] *Prophetic Conjectures on the French Revolution, and Other Recent and Shortly Expected Events* . . . (Baltimore: John Hayes, 1794), p. 59.

[29] Miller, *A Sermon*, pp. 31–32.

[30] Elisha Lee, *An Oration Delivered at Lenox, on the 4th July, 1793* . . . (Stockbridge, Mass.: Loring Andrews, 1793), p. 12.

low him, in his strides, across the Atlantic! —See him, with his spear already in the heart of the beast! —See tyranny, civil and ecclesiastical, bleed-
ing at every pore!"[31]

Millennial theory stated that as violence became more extreme, peace became more imminent. Thus, some millennialists actually began to wish for
even more death and destruction, applauding the exportation of the revolution to other nations in Europe. Combining high-minded republicanism
with tough-minded millennialism, these thinkers felt assured that the ultimate end of universal freedom justified all the suffering. "It is indeed shock-
ing to think of the present slaughter amongst conflicting powers and parties," admitted one anonymous millennialist. "But prophecy holds out
consolation," he continued, "that when the judgment written shall be ac-
complished, and the present convulsions subside, —*the remnant shall give
glory to the God of heaven.*"[32]

In fact, millennialism made world revolution seem positively providential. With the extension of the French Revolution, ministers began to argue
in perplexing detail and with remarkable certainty that the prescribed
1,260 years of Antichristian rule were finally coming to an end. In 1793,
Samuel Hopkins, student of Jonathan Edwards and dean of American millennialists, could foresee the end in no more than 200 years, though neither,
he calculated, "this or the next generation are like to see it."[33] In 1794, as
the Revolution turned outward, the end seemed even closer to those like
Rutgers's President William Linn, who saw it approaching so rapidly that
the children alive at that time would experience its glorious arrival.[34] By
1795, with international war raging, millennialists were predicting that the
"*men of this generation*" would themselves witness the final scenes.[35] Many
predicted the coming end: "The present age is big with events;" the
"GRAND AERA" was "approaching with a speed rapid as the flight of
time;" the "seventh viol" (sic)—the final symbolic sign—would "e're long
be emptied."[36] Yet again prophecy seemed often indistinguishable from pol-

[31] David Austin, "The Downfall of Mystical Babylon; or, a Key to the Providence of God, in
the Political Operations of 1793-4," in *The Millennium, or the Thousand Years of Prosperity . . .
Shortly to Commence . . .* [ed. David Austin] (Elizabethtown, N.J.: Shepard Kollock, 1794),
pp. 392-93.

[32] *Prophetic Conjectures*, p. 58.

[33] Samuel Hopkins, D.D., *A Treatise on the Millennium . . .* (Boston: Isaiah Thomas and Ebe-
nezer T. Andrews, 1793), p. 150.

[34] See William Linn, D.D., *Discourses on the Signs of the Times* (New York: Thomas Greenleaf, 1794), pp. 26-27 and 166-71.

[35] John Watkins, *An Essay on the End of the World* (Worcester, Mass.: Isaiah Thomas, jun.,
1795), p. 35.

[36] Jones, *An Oration*, p. 19; Austin, "Downfall," in *The Millennium*, p. 425; George Blake,

itics. Predictions were meant to be read in a "figurative manner," the Reverend Joseph Eckley told a Boston audience. The coming consummation did not necessarily imply the literal end of the world. Instead, it symbolized the destruction of the corrupt monarchies that had long dominated the nations of the earth, "the final catastrophe of the tyrannical system."[37] American millennialists, exporters of freedom, welcomed world revolution. "The grand consummation is at hand," announced senior-class orator Samuel Worcester to an audience of his fellow Dartmouth students, "the conflagration of the political world."[38]

Isolationism

Yet in the new nation, intervention was never far removed from isolation. Although interventionists were eager to export the principles of revolution, their ideological forays were almost always exhortative and rhetorical. As soon as this moral intervention began to suggest military involvement, most retreated. The war between England and France was decisive in turning international revolutionaries into provincial seclusionists.[39] Members of both parties, frightened by the threat of European war—Republicans fearing the English, Federalists the French—began to pursue a policy of neutrality. "At a distance we hear the thunders roar, and see the lightnings play," declared one troubled observer; "who can tell how soon they may slash across our sky, and enkindle all the fire of war?"[40]

As President Washington announced his proclamation of neutrality, many millennialists, until this time ardent interventionists, added their assent, becoming suddenly and somewhat surprisingly isolationist. Millennial theory explains their dramatic reversal. The end of the world promised both chaos and salvation. With the frightening possibility of war, millennialists needed only to turn their attention from the threat of immediate conflict to the promise of ultimate peace. Americans had no need to worry, as young Worcester had told the assembled Dartmouth students; "aloof from the din of battle, and the ravage of war," they could "anticipate the day when war

An Oration, Pronounced July 4th, 1795, at . . . Boston . . . (Boston: Benjamin Edes, 1795), p. 28.

[37] Eckley, A Sermon, p. 8.

[38] Samuel Worcester, An Oration: Delivered, at the College Chapel, Hanover . . . (Hanover, N.H.: Durham and True, 1795), p. 9.

[39] On the role of the Anglo-French war, see Alexander DeConde, Entangling Alliance (Durham, N.C.: Duke University Press, 1958), p. 173.

[40] John B. Johnson, An Oration on Union, Delivered in the New Dutch Church . . . May, 1794 . . . (New York: John Buel, 1794), p. 19.

and tyranny, with all their horrors, shall cease from the earth, and when uninterrupted peace, benevolence, and happiness shall prevail."[41]

Millennialism helped ease the transition from intervention to isolation. Beyond describing events, millennial theory could interpret circumstances and inspire responses. At times of despair, for example, it offered hope. The chaos of the Old World might well foreshadow the demise of despotism; the peace and plenty of the New World seemed, by contrast, to portend the triumph of liberty. Americans could watch from afar "the sublime, the awful, and tremendous prospect of the conflict of armies and of battles, and of the wreck and fall of empires," observed the New York physician Dr. Phineas Hedges, adopting the well-worn verse from the book of Micah; "while the political atmosphere of Europe is dissolving with fervent heat, consuming and sweeping away the vile fabrics of despotism, we are sitting under our vines and fig-trees enjoying the sweet fruits of our former exertions."[42]

In fact, the distant conflict seemed to redound to their advantage. "The fruit, which the tempest is shaking from the vineyards of the nations," as the Reverend Elijah Kellog put it, was "falling into the lap of Columbia."[43] While progressive thinkers argued that a policy of isolation would profit them at home, their millennialist counterparts went one step further, arguing that isolation would be of benefit to the rest of the world as well. America was the model for other nations, a "miniature," as Dartmouth's Worcester suggested, "of what the world shall shortly be."[44] Instead of plunging rashly into war, Americans could best serve humanity by maintaining their perfect peace. Their chosen nation had been set aside to be the site of the coming millennial kingdom; it was surely, concluded one enthusiastic millennialist to a Rhode Island audience, "the *fifth Empire*: . . . in us, *all the nations of the earth shall be finally blessed*."[45]

Thus millennialists turned easily to isolationism. The chosen nation had the responsibility not only to extend its influence in the world but also to maintain itself at home. The United States had been blessed with riches. Others could go on contending for scarce resources; America would remain—"whatever may be the fate of other nations"—the land of abun-

[41] Worcester, *An Oration*, pp. 11–12.

[42] Phineas Hedges, M.D., *An Oration, Delivered Before the Republican Society, of Ulster County, and Other Citizens* . . . (Goshen, N.Y.: David M. Westcott, 1795), p. 14. The verse ("vine and fig-tree") is from Micah 4:4.

[43] Elijah Kellog, A.M., *An Oration, Pronounced at Portland, July 4, 1795* . . . (Newburyport, Mass.: Blunt and March, [1795]), p. 19.

[44] Worcester, *An Oration*, p. 8.

[45] Abraham Redwood Ellery, *An Oration, Delivered July 4th, A.D. 1796, in the Baptist Meeting-House, in Newport* . . . (Warren, R.I.: Nathaniel Phillips, 1796), p. 24.

dance.[46] As President Washington declared a Day of National Thanksgiving, millennialists began to emphasize this theme of peace and prosperity. The ancient vision of Isaiah once again became commonplace, as writers turned west to describe the unprecedented potential of their resource-rich continent: " 'The wilderness becomes a fruitful field, and the desert blossoms as the rose.' "[47] Some went so far as to extend the theme to the realm of marketplace economics, creating prospects of American lakes covered with sailing ships, canals and rivers teeming with vessels, harbors bulging with the produce of the world, and America, as one prophetic capitalist put it, "the emporium of the earth."[48] Progressives did not disagree; however, they stopped well short of arguing that the continent itself, blessed with providential resources, was the certain sign that the millennium would arrive in the New World. By contrast, millennialists pressed on eagerly: "This continent which we inhabit," rejoiced the Reverend Chauncey Lee in a New York Fourth of July oration, "presents to the contemplation of the astonished beholder, a theater for the noblest scenes of Time; and on which the last and finishing act of the World's grand drama will be displayed."[49]

Nevertheless, their isolationism was fearful and deeply defensive. After all, prophecy required that the coming kingdom could be brought about only through conflict. Thus, even at times of hope—indeed, especially at times of hope—this complex millennialism predisposed the prophets to look for the calamities that would usher in final success. A troubled Reverend Thomas Baldwin, pastor of Boston's Second Baptist Church, and a leader among American Baptists, used the occasion of the Thanksgiving to express their anxiety: "We know not how soon the present scene may be reversed, and the dark clouds of adversity overshadow our brightest prospects."[50]

The political prophets assumed that there would be threats to their domestic millennium. In particular they foresaw the danger of Constitutional dissolution arising from internal subversion. Federalist ideologues fed their fears by calling attention to the revolutionary sympathies of their Republican enemies, and claiming their complicity in initiating the Whiskey Rebellion. Some went so far as to intimate the existence of a Franco-Republi-

[46] Samuel Thacher, *An Oration, Pronounced July 4, 1796, at . . . Concord . . .* (Boston: Samuel Hall, 1796), p. 24.

[47] Thomas Barnard, D.D., *A Sermon, Delivered on the Day of National Thanksgiving, February 19, 1795* (Salem, Mass.: Thomas C. Cushing, 1795), p. 22. The verse is Isaiah 35:1.

[48] Jones, *An Oration*, p. 16.

[49] Chauncey Lee, A.M., *An Oration, Delivered at Lansingburgh, on the Fourth of July, A.D., 1797 . . .* (Lansingburgh, N.Y.: E. Moffit & Co., 1797), p. 13.

[50] Thomas Baldwin, A.M., *A Sermon Delivered February 19, 1795: Being the Day of National Thanksgiving . . .* (Boston: Manning & Loring, 1795), p. 19.

can plot to overthrow the Constitution.[51] Republicans countered with
allegations that Federalists had conspired in monarchical cabals with their
English allies.[52] With the controversy over Jay's Treaty, the United States
seemed to become another front for the conflict that raged three thousand
miles away. Unable to explain the swing from harmony to conflict, nonmil-
lennialists became disillusioned and fell into despair. It was surely only a
matter of time, a gloomy John Adams wrote to his wife, before "our country
must be deformed with divisions, contests, dissensions, and civil wars."[53]
But millennialists were neither surprised nor disheartened. Their theory
required that perfection be purchased with struggle. Hence, Americans
would be well advised, the Reverend Lathrop told his flock, "to mingle
prayers with our praises, and fears with our rejoicing."[54]

The millennialism of the 1790s explained both failure and success. It insisted on destruction, complete with "confusion, dismay, and carnage."[55]
At the same time, it promised deliverance, "a more improved and happy
state . . . before the final consummation of all things."[56] Some progressives
assumed a similar dualism. It was a law of nature, stated Oliver Fiske, a
recent Harvard graduate, that "excess should be followed by its opposite
extreme."[57] In contrast to their progressive counterparts, however, the millennialists were certain of ultimate vindication, for God had promised to
bring "good out of evil."[58] Thus, they seemed reconciled to the extremes of
desperation and hope that characterized this time of uncertainty. "Those
events which appear, at first, altogether threatening and sad," observed Salem's Reverend Thomas Barnard in a Massachusetts election sermon, "are

[51] See Smelser, "The Federalist Period," p. 410.

[52] See Howe, "Republican Thought," pp. 149–50.

[53] John Adams to Abigail Adams, 16 April 1796, in Letters, 2: 221. Though I am hesitant
to label John Adams a "progressive," John R. Howe, Jr. has made a persuasive case that while
Adams did not believe in human perfectibility, he definitely did believe in some idea of human
progress. See his The Changing Political Thought of John Adams (Princeton, N.J.: Princeton
University Press, 1966), pp. 39–40. His perspective is somewhat different, but Zoltan Haraszti seems to agree; see John Adams and the Prophets of Progress (Cambridge, Mass.: Harvard
University Press, 1952), p. 258.

[54] Joseph Lathrop, D.D., National Happiness, Illustrated in a Sermon, Delivered at West-
Springfield, on the Nineteenth of February, 1795. Being a Day of General Thanksgiving (Springfield, Mass.: J.W. Hooker and F. Stebbins, 1795), p. 19.

[55] G. J. Warner, Means for the Preservation of Public Liberty. An Oration . . . (New York:
Thomas Greenleaf and Naphtali Judah, 1797), p. 19.

[56] Chauncey Lee, An Oration, p. 15.

[57] Oliver Fiske, An Oration, Pronounced at Worcester . . . July 4, 1797 (Worcester, Mass.:
Isaiah Thomas, jun., 1797), p. 15.

[58] John Mellen, Jun., A Sermon, Delivered Before His Excellency the Governor . . . May 31,
1797 (Boston: Young & Minns, 1797), p. 29.

followed with agreeable consequences."[59] Americans had little to fear. The victories of their enemies were transitory. Their own defeats could only, as the Presbyterian preacher John Mason assured a New York audience, "confirm our faith," for the forces of darkness were "really, though ignorantly" working their own destruction.[60] They needed only to trust in their millennial Savior: "What, though Disorder spread from pole to pole, and mingle the nations in universal uproar?" asked a fearless Mason: ". . . *he* will bring order out of confusion, and light out of darkness."[61]

So it was that millennialists became armed isolationists. Progressive writers could frequently be found mourning the fate of the nation, warning that America would soon "break into parties," become "the dupes of foreign influence," or even "enter into destructive wars."[62] Millennialists did not disagree. Comforted by their two-edged theory, however, they found these threats reassuring. In effect, they were never so content as in times of trouble. "Impending calamity," explained the Reverend Mason, "should stimulate, and not dishearten, the disciples of Jesus. The walls of Jerusalem are commonly built in troublous times."[63]

The millennial prophets stressed preparation for possible conflict; their sermons were filled with exhortations to vigilance. "Let us gird our loins and stand clad in the armour of our defence," exclaimed New Hampshire's excited Reverend Simeon Williams in a Fourth of July sermon, "and our banner will be terrifying to every invading foe."[64] None seemed to suggest that preparation might lead to conflict. On the contrary, as Williams explained in an argument that has echoed down through the history of American foreign policy, their efforts were not aggressive but defensive: "preparation for danger will never hasten it upon us."[65] In short, these isolationists sought to create a fortress nation. Millennial theory held that attack was inevitable. When it came, they could look forward fearlessly to defending their land. After all, as Mason informed his listeners in another still-echoing phrase, "With the Lord of Hosts on our side, whom or what shall we fear?"[66] Besides, war was only the preparation for peace, announcing the

[59] Barnard, *A Sermon*, p. 17.

[60] John M. Mason, A.M., *Hope for the Heathen: A Sermon, Preached in the Old Presbyterian Church . . . November 7, 1797* (New York: T. & J. Swords, 1797), p. 27. See also Davidson, "Searching for the Millennium," pp. 258–59.

[61] Ibid., p. 28.

[62] John Taylor, A.M., *An Oration, Delivered on the Anniversary of Independence, at Deerfield . . .* (Greenfield, Mass.: Thomas Dickman, 1796), p. 20.

[63] Mason, *Hope for the Heathen*, p. 36.

[64] Simeon Finley Williams, A.M., *An Oration, Delivered on the Fourth of July 1796 . . . at Meredith Bridge* (Dover, N.H.: Samuel Bragg, Jun., 1796), p. 21.

[65] Ibid., p. 23.

[66] Mason, *Hope for the Heathen*, p. 38.

time when, as the Reverend Williams recited the familiar refrain from Isaiah, "swords shall be beaten into ploughshares, spears into pruning hooks, nation shall not lift up the sword against nation, nor learn war any more."[67]

Xenophobia

At least in the 1790s, isolation seemed to lead logically to xenophobia. The ideology of self-protection required enemies.[68] With the turbulent events at the end of the decade—the xyz Affair, the rebellions in the West, the party warfare and partisan plots—American republicans seemed to find enemies everywhere, "foes from without," as one put it, "and traitors within."[69] Supporters of the new nation began to exhibit an irrational blend of paranoid fear and boastful belligerence. Federalists again led the way with the charge that secret societies led by the international "Order of the Illuminati" were conspiring to overthrow the government from within.[70] Frantic Federalist ministers went to their pulpits to speak with extraordinary passion of the imagined threat. Republicans responded in kind with their own charges of conspiracy and cabal. Many of those who participated were partisan ideologues rather than millennial prophets. But the partisans were often faint hearted, begging their fellow party loyalists to pull back from the brink, warning solemnly of "the most direful of calamities, a *Civil War*."[71]

Far different were the millennialists who, certain that the end was drawing near, seemed prepared to meet their fate. Millennial theory could comfort and reconcile, but it could also exhort and incite. Its logic was compelling. Salvation came only through crisis; it required violent conflict, demanded the constant threat of enemies, and insisted on readiness. Millennialists found themselves, many almost unwillingly, reiterating the importance of this element of conflict. The Scriptures promised that the clash of kingdoms would precede the end of time. Hence, they could only conclude that their enemies were preparing to begin the final battle. All the signs,

[67] Williams, *An Oration*, p. 22. The verse is Micah 4:3.

[68] See Alexander DeConde, *The Quasi-War* (New York: Charles Scribner's Sons, 1966), pp. 3–108.

[69] Samuel Rockwell, *An Oration, Delivered at the Celebration of American Independence, at Salisbury, Fourth July, Ninety-Seven* (Litchfield, Conn.: T. Collier, [1798]), p. 5.

[70] See Timothy Dwight, D.D., *The Duty of Americans, at the Present Crisis, Illustrated in a Discourse, Preached on the Fourth of July, 1798* . . . (New Haven, Conn.: Thomas and Samuel Green, 1798), p. 31; and Jedidiah Morse, D.D., *A Sermon, Exhibiting the Present Dangers, and Consequent Duties of the Citizens of the United States of America. Delivered at Charlestown, April 25, 1799* . . . (Charlestown, Mass.: Samuel Etheridge, 1799).

[71] Jabez Parkhurst, *An Oration, Delivered on the Fourth of July, 1798 in the Presbyterian Church, at Newark* (Newark, N.J.: Bennington and Dodge, 1798), p. 12.

the redoubtable Timothy Dwight assured his many readers, had been "marked out in prophecy, exhibited as parts of one closely united system, and [were] to be expected at the present time; they shew that this affecting declaration is even now fulfilling in a surprising manner, and that the advent of Christ is at least at our doors."[72]

The millennialists became captives of their metaphor. Beyond explanation, beyond interpretation, their millennial faith seemed to exhort them to action. Accordingly they found themselves demanding—even inciting—the disorder that would bring on ultimate victory. As prophecies became more irrational, policies became more extreme. Federalists lobbied for passage of the Alien and Sedition Acts, called for the creation of a Provisional Army to put down their Republican opponents, and insisted on full pursuit of the "Quasi-War" with France. Republicans replied with calls for resistance and secession. Debate took place in an atmosphere of near hysteria.[73] Ideology can account for the content of the conflict, but prophecy provided much of its frenzy.[74] Among Democratic-Republicans, millennialists like the fiery Austin announced that the last days were closer than ever, that the sixth trumpet had already sounded, and that the moment for the final battle was "at hand."[75] Federalist millennialists like the Reverend David Osgood, point man for New England's Federalist clergy in the attack on France, concurred that the end was near: "Not in France only," Osgood announced, "but in various other countries, is the devil let loose."[76] The Antichrist seemed to be preparing his attack: "the last vials of divine wrath," Osgood declared, "are pouring forth upon a guilty world."[77] The millennialist prophets exhorted their fellow citizens to prepare themselves for the fight. The ardent Federalist Elijah Parish was only one of many who called for total war against the powers of evil, meaning, in his case, France and the Republicans. "Go then, be the soldiers of God," Parish told his Massachusetts congregation. "Like David assaulting the giant of Gath, go in the name of the God of battles. Go and conquer; then shall there be a new song in heaven—'BABYLON is fallen, is fallen.' "[78]

Preparing their audiences for this cosmological conflict, the political

[72] Dwight, *The Duty of Americans*, p. 31.

[73] See Smelser, "The Federalist Period," pp. 411–19.

[74] See Howe, "Republican Thought," p. 148; and James M. Banner, Jr., *To the Hartford Convention* (New York: Alfred A. Knopf, 1970), pp. 44–45.

[75] [David Austin], *The First Vibration of the Jubilee Trump!* (Elizabethtown, N.J.: [n.p., 1799]), p. 3.

[76] David Osgood, *THE DEVIL LET LOOSE . . . Illustrated in a Discourse Delivered on the Day of the National Fast, April 25, 1799* (Boston: Samuel Hall, 1799), p. 13.

[77] Ibid., p. 14.

[78] Elijah Parish, A.M., *An Oration; Delivered at Byfield, July 4, 1799* (Newburyport, Mass.: Angier March, [1799]), p. 18.

prophets seemed unafraid of the actual consequences of war or insurrection. While President Adams declared a Day of National Fast, and more moderate ministers led their flocks in earnest prayer, the prophets, relying on the twin themes of doom and redemption, were pointing to the future with what one called the "most unreserved confidence."[79] The coming conflicts, they argued, would be nothing less than "the fulfillment of ancient predictions."[80] War and revolution might well wreak devastation, but out of the rubble would arise, "like a phoenix," a new, more righteous world.[81] In effect, the approaching struggles would be the first of what would become a long line of American wars to end all wars. In the final reckoning the armies of righteousness would triumph, while the legions of evil, which had "so disturbed and distressed the world," would "vanish like chaff before the wind."[82] The millennialists assured their listeners that heaven had intended from the start for America to witness the millennium. This certain promise, a confident Dwight suggested, "shed the dawn of hope and comfort over this melancholy period."[83] With the growing threat of conflict, the thousand years of peace seemed almost upon them. "The sorrows of present scenes—the expectation of many, and the testimony of Holy Writ all unite in teaching that the Great Day is at hand," announced Austin. "The long predicted jubilee trump is about to sound."[84]

Millennial theory demanded the inevitability of destruction. France had no intention of attacking the United States. Yet millennialists pictured the French as a taloned bird of prey, poised and ready to sweep down upon its helpless victim. Ministers encouraged their congregations to pray to God, confess their sins, and humiliate themselves, lest God "suffer even this wicked nation [France] to scourge, if not wholly to destroy us."[85] Orators identified Bonaparte as the embodiment of the Antichrist, denounced French actions as examples of the "wiles of the Devil," and described how the revolutionary armies had "waged war with heaven as well as with earth."[86] The United States was not in danger of invasion or insurrection.

[79] John Wells, Esq., *An Oration, Delivered on the Fourth of July, 1798, at St. Paul's Church, Before the Young Men of the City of New-York* . . . (New York: McLean & Lang, 1798), p. 21.

[80] Mellen, *A Sermon*, p. 28.

[81] Caleb Page Fessenden, *An Oration, Delivered at Conway . . . on the Fourth day of July, 1798* . . . (Freyburg, Me.: [Ezekiel Russell], 1798), p. 16.

[82] Jeremy Belknap, D.D., *A Sermon, Delivered on the 9th of May, 1798, the Day of the National Fast* . . . (Boston: Samuel Hall, 1798), p. 26.

[83] Dwight, *The Duty of Americans*, p. 29.

[84] David Austin, Jun., *The Millennial Door Thrown Open; or the Trump of the Latter Day Glory* . . . (East-Windsor, Conn.: Luther Pratt, 1799), p. 24.

[85] Eliab Stone, A.M., *A Discourse, Delivered at Reading, on the Day of the National Fast, April 25, 1799* (Boston: Manning & Loring, 1799), p. 29.

[86] Simeon Doggett, Jun., *An Oration, Delivered at Taunton, on the Fourth of July, 1799* (New

But frenzied millennialists of all kinds, certain of their cosmological enemies, drew fantastic pictures of imminent conflict. New Hampshire's
preacher-legislator Noah Worcester spoke of the threat of "assassination and
massacre."[87] Thomas Grant of New Jersey described burning villages, des-
olated farms, violated wives, and murdered children.[88] Hartford's William
Brown pictured Haitian-style slave uprisings, with "white-men, butchered
by their infuriate slaves, the shrieks of mothers, and of virgins, a prey to
more than demonic lust and barbarity, and the cries of infants."[89] By the
close of the century, millennialists had come face to face with the ultimate
implication of their theory: they found themselves demanding their own
Armageddon. At that very moment, stated a fearful Reverend Daniel Humphreys, God was pouring out his wrath. The political world would soon be
destroyed. "Even so," prayed the resigned Humphreys, "come Lord Jesus."[90]

The Prophets of Progress

At the close of the 1790s, Americans found themselves surrounded by
threats of invasion and insurrection. Few if any seemed to know how they
had come to such a pass. But at least a few thinkers began to search for the
causes of the crisis, and to lay blame for the contradictory and extreme policies of the time. In part, their criticism was aimed at the partisan ideologues
who had led them down what one called "the dark abyss of visionary speculation."[91] But much was leveled against the millennialists as well. Skeptics
pointed out that their end-of-the-world predictions had not transformed the
new nation into the New Jerusalem. Such prophecies had consisted of "one
fine and glittering notion after another."[92] The prophets had foreseen "new
Edens," pictured "modern *Paradises*," predicted the "golden age."[93] Their

---

Bedford, Mass.: John Spooner, 1799), p. 20; Abel Fiske, A.M., *A Discourse, Delivered at Wil-
ton, November 15, 1798* . . . (Amherst, N.H.: Samuel Preston, 1799), p. 23.

[87] Noah Worcester, A.M., *An Election Sermon, Delivered at CONCORD, June 4, 1800* . . .
(Concord, N.H.: Elijah Russell, [1800]), p. 26.

[88] Thomas Grant, A.M., *A Sermon, Delivered at Felmington, on the 4th of July, 1799* (Tren-
ton, N.J.: G. Craft, 1799), p. 15.

[89] William Brown, *An Oration, Spoken at Hartford . . . July 4th, A.D., 1799* (Hartford, Conn.:
Hudson and Goodwin, 1799), p. 20.

[90] Daniel Humphreys, *A Plain Attempt to Hold up to View the Ancient Gospel* . . . (Portsmouth,
N.H.: Republican Press, 1800), p. 35.

[91] Israel B. Woodward, A.M., *American Liberty and Independence: A Discourse, Delivered at
Watertown, on the Fourth of July, 1798* (Litchfield, Conn.: T. Collier, [1798]), p. 15.

[92] Samuel Mitchell, *An Address to the Citizens of New-York* . . . (New York: George F. Hopkins, 1800), p. 9.

[93] Ibid.; Edward Bangs, Esq., *An Oration on the Anniversary of American Independence, Pronounced at Worcester* (Worcester, Mass.: Isaiah Thomas, Jun., 1800), p. 5.

promises, however, had proved "theoretic, speculative, and delusive," as the
tough-minded David Daggett put it in a savagely witty oration entitled
Sun-Beams May Be Extracted From Cucumbers, But the Process Is Tedious.[94]
By the close of the century, critics had come to contend that, in their search
for appropriate political theories, they had looked too often to what one
called "the precarious credit of political prophecies."[95]

Millennial prophecy began to be seriously challenged by the idea of pragmatic reform. A new cohort of progressive nationalists—doctors, lawyers,
merchants, even a few ministers—began to suggest that politics be based
on more than the promise of heavenly perfection. The American people
might well assume that God had led them to their present state, but Providence alone would not suffice to lead them in the future. Americans, one of
these new-style nationalists advised, must " 'work out our own salvation.' "[96] More pragmatic than earlier progressives, they demanded plan-
ning and the expedient use of power, informing their audiences that the
future demanded what one called "proper management."[97] Progress was
not inevitable: prosperity was only "considerably certain," according to the
youthful Reverend Samuel Austin of Worcester, Massachusetts, or "at least
probable."[98] Nevertheless, prophetic predictions were not necessary for success. Instead, these pragmatists relied on "prosperous enterprise, successful
industry, and a long course of fortunate events."[99] In the future, Americans
might best look to political power to take the place of predestination. "Our
own happiness," concluded David Ogden, addressing a Fourth of July
gathering as a representative of the Association of Young Men of Newark,
"is in our own hands."[100]

The idea of progress seemed inimical to millennial theory. Yet the conflict was more apparent than real, for, surprisingly, these pragmatic progressives held visions of the future every bit as grand as any millennial
prophecies. In the New World, remarked one, even a "short life" was "of

[94] David Daggett, *Sun-Beams May Be Extracted From Cucumbers, But the Process Is Tedious.*
An Oration . . . (New Haven, Conn.: Thomas Green and Son, 1799), p. 18.

[95] James Gould, *An Oration, Pronounced at Litchfield* . . . (Litchfield, Conn.: T. Collier,
[1798]), p. 12.

[96] Zechariah Lewis, *An Oration, On the Apparent, and the Real Political Situation of the*
United States . . . (New Haven, Conn.: Thomas Green and Son, 1799), p. 25.

[97] Thomas Andros, *An Oration, Delivered at Dighton, (Massachusetts), July 4, 1799* . . .
(Newbedford, Mass.: John Spooner, 1799), p. 13.

[98] Samuel Austin, A.M., *An Oration, Pronounced at Worcester, on the Fourth of July, 1798*
. . . (Worcester, Mass.: Leonard Worcester, 1798), p. 11.

[99] George Sullivan, Esquire, *An Oration, Pronounced at Exeter on the Fourth Day of July,*
1800 . . . (Exeter, N.H.: H. Ranlet, 1800), p. 11.

[100] David B. Ogden, Esquire, *An Oration, Delivered on the Fourth of July, 1798* . . . (Newark,
N.J.: Jacob Halsey & Co., 1798), p. 9.

more worth than Methuselah's term of years."[101] Within the space of only a decade, a sleepy provincial colony had been converted into a rising world power. The future promised even more extraordinary advancement. Progress, ventured another, might "almost exceed the bounds of calculation."[102] In fact, progressive reform provided its own version of prophecy. "We have no reason to pronounce visionary," announced the Worcester lawyer Edward Bangs, "the hope and faith of pious men who pray for a millennial state."[103] Americans did not need to abandon the millennium. Instead they could set to work creating it themselves. The New Jerusalem, offered the Reverend Israel Woodward, would be "ushered in by human means."[104]

The new progressives replaced faith in prophecy with an even more ardent faith in progress. Millennial ideas seemed finally to fade. The spirit of the apocalypse was banished to the realm of radical religion, where hot-blooded preachers like David Austin could persist in declaring that the end of the world had arrived at last, and that the "New Jerusalem-day," as he announced again and again, was "at the door."[105] Similarly, the vision of paradise was consigned to the domain of liberal theology, where cooler heads like Jeremy Belknap could urge their flocks to work toward perfection "by slow degrees," cultivating "in our own minds and conduct" the moral virtues that would prepare the way "for the universal reign of the Prince of peace."[106] But much of the old millennialism was absorbed into this new form of progressive nationalism. Throughout the final decade, millennialists had spoken of the end of the century as the time that would announce the end of the world. With the new century, they were forced to admit that the end had not yet come, and that the millennium, as the chastened New Hampshireman Robert Fowle conceded to a Fourth of July audience, "may be more distant than our wishes may lead us to expect."[107] Yet as the certainty of a heavenly millennium retreated, the possibility of an earthly one seemed closer than ever. To these progressive nationalists, the perfect future state would be the new American nation, "an empire," as one prophet of reform phrased it, "shining with celestial splendour."[108]

[101] Thurston Whiting, *An Oration, Delivered in the Baptist Meeting House, in Thomaston, July 4th, 1798* . . . (Hallowell, Me.: Howard S. Robinson, [1798]), p. 18.

[102] Andros, *An Oration*, p. 10.

[103] Bangs, *An Oration*, p. 15.

[104] Woodward, *A Discourse*, p. 26.

[105] [David Austin], *The Dawn of Day, Introductory to the Rising Sun* . . . (New Haven, Conn.: Reed and Morse, 1800), p. 18.

[106] Belknap, *A Sermon*, pp. 27; 29.

[107] Robert Fowle, *An Oration, Delivered at Plymouth, in New-Hampshire* . . . (Concord, N.H.: Geo. Hough, 1800), p. 14.

[108] M. L. Davis, *An Oration, Delivered in St. Paul's Church, on the Fourth of July, 1800* . . . (New York: W. A. Davis, 1800), p. 21.

The close of the century marked the end of an era. With the election of Jefferson, and the Federalist acceptance, however reluctant, of the role of a loyal opposition, a generation of domestic conflict had come to an end. At the same time, with Britain and France pausing for a while in their protracted struggle, the threat of international war seemed to fade from the scene. At least for the moment, politics appeared somehow more placid, or at least more predictable. For the first time, Americans began to consider the founding to be over, to be ancient history—a heroic age that had already begun to be elevated, as symbolized by the death of Washington in late 1799, into the realm of legend and political mythology.

Simultaneously, the coming of the new century was greeted as the dawn of another age. Looking ahead, in some sense for the first time, progressives could boast that they had created a new way of thinking about their future. Simultaneously, they had created a new way of thinking about their politics, because with the transformation of the old prophetic religion into a newfound faith in progress, they had moved one more step away from classical republicanism, and added yet another aspect to what would become modern liberalism. With this, the transition to modern political thought seemed all but complete, and there appeared to be something new under the sun.

Nevertheless, the transition was not total. Classical republicanism had been transformed but not destroyed. Many of its most significant characteristics—its concern with corruption, its conspiratorial view of the world, even its millennial vision of the future—all remained very much alive, and would remain very much a part of modern liberalism. Indeed, as the young John Quincy Adams had announced already, the commitment to these classical themes lay deep within the American soul. Just how deep, the next two hundred years would tell.

EPILOGUE

WITH THE ELECTION of Thomas Jefferson, America had become a modern nation. The new President stood as a symbol of the new order. In his First Inaugural, he would put forth the basic principles of modern liberalism, including a commitment to commerce, to continental expansion, and above all to compromise—a pragmatic nonpartisanship in which all were Federalists, all were Republicans, and all could agree on the potential for progress in both the public and the private realms. Coming to office at a time of at least temporary peace abroad and moving rapidly to secure the Louisiana Purchase, Jefferson could point ahead confidently to growing power in the world and almost limitless prosperity at home. With this ever-expanding future in mind, he announced the arrival of a new American era, what he would call "the revolution of 1800."[1]

Yet for all its its potential, America in 1800 remained in many ways an eighteenth-century republic. Again Jefferson was symbolic, for despite his determination to usher in a century of progress, he remained deeply distrustful of both public power and an expanding private economy. Once in office, his administration set itself successfully to the task of reducing taxes and—unlikely as it may seem today—paying off the national debt. In this sense, the "revolution of 1800" can also be considered as a return to the classical republican tradition, a reversion to earlier principles, or, as at least some unreconstructed republicans saw it at the time, a revival of the spirit of 1776.[2]

America in 1800 was both classical republic and modern nation. As Merrill Peterson has shown, Jefferson himself epitomized the transition: he was the eighteenth-century philosopher who became the nineteenth-century pragmatist, the agrarian turned capitalist, localist turned nationalist, small-republic republican turned continental expansionist. Nevertheless, for Jefferson these transformations were problematic, and the result was an often paradoxical personality.[3] For America as well, the transition was troubling,

---

[1] For background, see Banning, *The Jeffersonian Persuasion*, pp. 273–302.

[2] See Norman K. Risjord, *The Old Republicans* (New York: Columbia University Press, 1965), pp. 11–71.

[3] See Merrill D. Peterson, *The Jefferson Image in the American Mind* (New York: Oxford University Press, 1960).

and the end product was an uneasy accommodation between the old and the new, in which the ideal of the classical republic and the reality of the modern liberal nation would become hopelessly intertwined, creating a tangled web that would bind and hold Americans captive for the next two hundred years.[4]

For decades, it has been taken for granted that the coming of the new century marked the beginning of America's modern age. In large part, the assumption has been based on the premise that in the nineteenth century progress was pervasive. Among American historians, few interpretations have been accepted so easily or widely. In *The Idea of Progress in America*, Arthur Ekirch argued that at least by 1815 progress had become "the most popular American philosophy."[5] Although he traced its origins back even further, Rutherford Delmage agreed, contending that by 1800, progress had already begun to provide the "dominant note in American thought."[6] Rush Welter continued the case, arguing that the idea of progress that presided over the nineteenth century was especially powerful in that it pictured the future as a continuation of the present, allowing not only constant development but also constant stability.[7] No less than Charles Beard, writing in his 1932 introduction to J. B. Bury's *The Idea of Progress*, extended the theme even further, suggesting that no idea had been "more significant or likely to exert more influence in the future."[8] In any case, progress was seen as a first principle of American politics, for the nineteenth century and well beyond. "The United States" Welter summed up, "both *had* progressed and *was* progress; the almost universal experience of its inhabitants testified to the fact."[9]

However, the case for progress has never been so simple. Beginning with Stow Persons, continuing with Bailyn and Wood, and culminating in the writings of John Murrin and Rowland Berthoff, postprogressive scholars have convincingly demonstrated that decline and degeneration have been every bit as prevalent as progress in modern American politics.[10] Murrin

[4] See Appleby, "What Is Still American in the Political Thought of Thomas Jefferson?" pp. 288–309.

[5] Arthur K. Ekirch, Jr., *The Idea of Progress in America, 1815–1860* (New York: Peter Smith, 1951), p. 267.

[6] Rutherford E. Delmage, "The American Idea of Progress, 1750–1800," *Proceedings of the American Philosophical Society*, 91, 4 (October 1947): 313.

[7] See Rush Welter, "The Idea of Progress in America: An Essay on Ideas and Method," *Journal of the History of Ideas*, 16, 3 (June 1955): 401–15.

[8] Charles A. Beard, Introduction to *The Idea of Progress* by J. B. Bury (1932; reprint, New York: Dover Publications, 1955), p. xi.

[9] See Welter, "The Idea of Progress," p. 402.

[10] See Persons, "Cyclical Theory," pp. 147–61; Bailyn, *Ideological Origins*, pp. 55–93;

and Berthoff in particular have traced the classical republican idea of corruption through the nineteenth and well into the twentieth century, finding fears of aristocracy, conspiracy, and entrenched power that run from Federalist fears of "King Andrew" to Abolitionist denunciations of the "Slave Power Conspiracy" to recent concern about the creation of an "Imperial Presidency."[11] "Corruption," Berthoff concluded, "has been the lament of Americans from Shays's Rebellion down to Watergate."[12]

The result of this reinterpretation has been confusion, along with sometimes troubled attempts to come to terms with the complexity of modern American political thought. In describing the continuing persistence of both progressive and nonprogressive strains, some writers have relied on tried-and-true descriptions of "optimists" and "pessimists."[13] Others have created whole new categories, including parties of "hope," "memory," and the "eternal present."[14] Still others have found themselves in an increasingly futile rear-guard action, attempting to isolate that crucial moment at which progress took the place of corruption, drawing lines like frustrated millennialists, first at 1800, then 1812, then the Civil War, Reconstruction, and beyond.[15] Recently, Pocock has suggested the futility of this enterprise, contending that progress never supplanted classical corruption, and that Wood's "end of classical politics" must be seen as the "end of one guiding thread in a complex tissue, not as a disappearance of the whole web."[16]

Thus, some have begun to chart the continuing influence of the classical tradition. In his essay "Independence and Attachment: Virtue and Interest," Berthoff made a persuasive case that the coexistence of a classical republican ideal and a modern liberal reality has created an increasingly unrealistic politics.[17] In other words, as America expanded into the modern world, it carried along the conceptual baggage of the classical past, allowing ruthless robber barons to be seen as struggling entrepreneurs, multinational corporations as successful versions of the neighborhood store, and large-scale agricultural operations as new versions of the family farm. Berthoff's argument, while impressive, is incomplete. For the republican tradition, far from merely nostalgic, has also been a continuing source of inspiration for those reformers and radicals who have resisted the seemingly inexorable

---

Wood, *Creation*, pp. 91–124; Murrin, "The Great Inversion," esp. pp. 404–30; and Berthoff, "Independence and Attachment," pp. 99–124.

[11] See Murrin, "The Great Inversion," pp. 415–30; and Berthoff, "Independence and Attachment," pp. 106–24.

[12] Berthoff, "Independence and Attachment," p. 99.

[13] See Appleby, "What is Still American in the Thought of Thomas Jefferson?" pp. 308–09.

[14] See Wilson, "The Concept of Time and the Political Dialogue in the United States," p. 15.

[15] See Pocock, *Machiavellian Moment*, pp. 523–26.

[16] Ibid., p. 526.

[17] Berthoff, "Independence and Attachment," p. 106.

march of corporate and public power.[18] In each case, the resulting politics has been problematic and unique, with classical republican and modern liberal influences combining in continuously changing patterns, creating an effect that sometimes seems nothing less than kaleidescopic.

Indeed, the most significant fact about modern American political thought may well be that it is not entirely modern. Put somewhat differently, one of the most consistent characteristics of American political thought has been the ability to maintain, in the face of modernity, a commitment to classical principles. As Louis Hartz himself admitted more than thirty years ago, America's most enduring secret has been this ability to bring together the attributes of two ages, combining, in his terms, "rock-ribbed tradition with high inventiveness, ancestor worship with ardent optimism."[19]

Typical of this anomalous amalgamation is the persistence of the covenant idea that lies at the heart of republican thought. In spite of increasing secularity, and in the face of sweeping social and technological change, Americans have continued to think of their republic as a chosen nation with a peculiar destiny to do great things. The descriptions are different, but America remains the "New Israel," the modern chosen nation, providing a model for the rest of the world to follow. It also retains a special relationship with the continent, its "errand into the wilderness," requiring citizens to carry out their "manifest destiny" to subdue the land, extend their commerce, and secure their Christian capitalist version of civilization, not only to the North American continent but to the Western Hemisphere and beyond.[20] The powerful symbol of the American Zion persists as well, as Americans continue to think of their country as the new Promised Land, not only a refuge but a place for people to begin their lives again, as witnessed by generations of Germans, Irish, and East Europeans in the last century, and Southeast Asians, Latin Americans, Africans, and others in the present one.[21]

This special status has been regularly reaffirmed, with patriots persistently placing God "on our side," be it at the Battle of New Orleans, Gettysburg, Verdun, or Khe San. Moreover, as Robert Bellah has shown, the presumption has persisted that what is good for America is good for the world, or at least, since the time of John Foster Dulles, for the "free

[18] See Michael Kammen, *A Season of Youth* (New York: Oxford University Press, 1978), pp. 15–21.

[19] Louis Hartz, "American Political Thought and the American Revolution," *American Political Science Review*, 46, 2 (June 1952): 331.

[20] See Weinberg, *Manifest Destiny*, p. 17.

[21] See Robert N. Bellah, *The Broken Covenant* (New York: The Seabury Press, 1975), pp. 87–111.

world."[22] The record has by no means been spotless, for in carrying out their mission Americans have been energetic, openhanded, and idealistic, but they have also been overbearing, domineering, and sometimes recklessly destructive. All too often they have done damage, interfering in the affairs of others, doing harm to the land and nature's most fragile features, reviling and persecuting those of different backgrounds or views, at home and abroad. Throughout, the troubling combination of self-confidence and self-doubt that animated early Americans has been present for later ones as well, and they have borne the burden of world power uneasily, constantly conscious both of their power to do right and of their capacity to act wrongly. Nevertheless, if only in their technological might, their unthinkable ability to bring about universal nuclear destruction, Americans retain their chosen status.[23]

Similarly, the classical republican conception of change has proved exceedingly persistent. Faith in progress notwithstanding, the belief in corruption has not disappeared. From early Federalist fears of the Bavarian Illuminati, to Prohibitionist denunciations of "Rum, Romanism, and Rebellion," to Senator McCarthy's campaign against Communism and the recent Christian conservative assault on "secular humanists," Americans have continued to seek out subversive forces, and to scourge them.[24]

At the same time, concern about corruption has been manifested in the continuing preoccupation with public power. Here examples can be found across the politicial spectrum, with conservatives from Fisher Ames to Howard Jarvis pitting themselves against the bureaucrats of "big government," while progressives from William Leggett to William Jennings Bryan to Walter Reuther and William Wimpisinger condemn the bosses of "big business."[25] So pervasive has been the concern with corruption that government itself has sought to limit its own prerogatives. Thus, just as Jefferson could retire the national debt and Jackson could dismantle the National Bank, so Ronald Reagan can call for the end to an overblown federal bureaucracy, and contemporary "neoliberals" can denounce deficits and the evils of Keynesian economics.

Yet the cries of corruption have been but counterpoints to an ever-expanding economy and an incessantly growing government. In truth, Americans have been ambivalent about change, neither nostalgic traditionalists seeking to revive a long lost republican society nor eager innovators in search of a liberal utopia, but a hybrid breed attempting to find some reformulated reconciliation of traditional values and modern pragmatic tech-

[22] See ibid., pp. 36–60.
[23] See ibid., pp. 162–63.
[24] See Wood, "Conspiracy and the Paranoid Style," pp. 401–06.
[25] See Berthoff, "Independence and Attachment," pp. 100–101.

niques. They have marched into the future fearfully, and always with an eye to the past.[26]

By extension, the republican predilection for periodic reform has remained intact. As Berthoff has shown so well, Americans prefer to assume that bad times will be followed by good, and that corruption can be contained, if not cured, by periodic purges.[27] In essence, for every Adams there is a Jefferson; Jay Gould and Boss Tweed give way to Lincoln Steffens and Jane Addams; Hoover is replaced by Roosevelt. Americans prefer to "throw the rascals out," removing personalities rather than reforming institutions. In recent years, Lyndon Johnson has borne the burden of Vietnam, Nixon paid the price for Watergate, and Jimmy Carter reaped a harvest of rebuke in the wake of the Iranian hostage crisis. In sum, the politicians change, and sometimes the policies, but the political order remains the same.

Simultaneously, as Murrin has contended, Americans have preferred to direct their reform at the society rather than the polity.[28] From John F. Kennedy's Inaugural incantation ("ask not what your country can do for you—ask what you can do for your country") to Jimmy Carter's fireside condemnation of a "narcissistic" nation, America's leaders have called on their fellow citizens to replace self-interest with self-sacrificing civic virtue. Nevertheless, and in spite of their suspicion of "special interests," citizens have been reluctant to shoulder the sacrifices required of a virtuous citzenry, let alone face losing their tax shelters, low-interest loans, or social-security payments. Hence, the calls for sacrifice seem to be both more frequent and more hollow.

Above all, reform has been irregular, and as a result all too often ineffective.[29] To take only one example, from Albert Gallatin in 1807, who denounced the military contractors, the jobbers, and the speculators, to Dwight D. Eisenhower in his farewell warning about the creation of a military-industrial complex, critics have sought with little success to control the power of that most insidious of republican enemies, an unchecked military machine. The situtation is symptomatic, for Americans have been reluctant reformers: rather than act, they have preferred to react, and their reform politics all too often has lurched along from crisis to crisis.

In part, their complacency has been encouraged by the existence of the American continent. In some sense, Americans have had no choice but to be complacent, for the vast open spaces of the West have provided an all too enticing escape from the complexity of the modern world. Moreover, as

[26] This is the argument of Robert H. Wiebe, *The Search for Order, 1877–1920* (New York: Hill and Wang, 1967).

[27] See Berthoff, "Independence and Attachment," p. 119.

[28] See Murrin, "The Great Inversion," pp. 429–30.

[29] See Berthoff, "Independence and Attachment," pp. 100–101.

Henry Nash Smith has shown, the mythic power of the open land has remained even long after the frontier has been closed.[30] As a result, Americans have sought their utopias in the West, in Daniel Boone's Kentucky, or Lewis and Clark's Louisiana, or William Randolph Hearst's California. Expanding relentlessly westward, they have often blithely turned their backs on the problems of advanced civilization, on the crowded sweatshops and the unsafe factories, on environmental pollution, and on the inequalities and the potential for class conflict that are among the products of an advanced industrial economy. Instead, they go West, or at least South and West, moving from Snow Belt to Sun Belt, and begin all over again.

In the move westward, agrarian republicanism has been continuously compromised, for advanced civilization, with its land speculators, its real-estate interests, and its condominium developers has seemed only a short step behind the first settlers. Nevertheless, the myth of agrarian innocence remains, not only in those corporate farmers who present themselves as hardy, independent yeomen, but also in self-styled Western heroes, the "Lone Rangers" and "Marlboro men," along with the Sam Spades and Philip Marlowes who have given a distinctive Western cast to popular culture. Indeed, the romance of the West has had political manifestations as well, with virile "Westerners" from Teddy Roosevelt to Ronald Reagan offering simple solutions to what are often exceedingly complex problems.[31]

Nevertheless, American expansionism has required extraordinary human sacrifice, lives lost not only at home, in the conflicts over "Indian removal" and in the Civil War, but also abroad, in the Spanish-American War, in Vietnam, in the Middle East, and in central America. The cost of empire has been high, and many have been reluctant to pay the price. The young Abraham Lincoln, denouncing the Mexican War as a war of Slave Power imperialism, was only the first in what has come to seem like a continuous line of placard-carrying protesters. Nor have the protests been futile, for unlike their Soviet counterparts on the other side of the world, Americans have been reticent imperialists.[32] If nothing else, the heritage of classical republicanism, the ideal of the small, self-contained republic, leaves them exceedingly ambivalent about national expansion, and about empire.

In its own way, American Constitutional history further reflects this ambivalence. On the one hand, the Constitution has proved to be a dynamic document, capable of responding remarkably well to the changes of two centuries. From Chief Justice Marshall on, judges have asserted the right of the federal courts not only to interpret the Constitution but also to estab-

---

[30] Smith, *Virgin Land*, pp. 250–60.

[31] See Richard Slotkin, "Nostalgia and Progress: Theodore Roosevelt's Myth of the Frontier," *American Quarterly*, 33, 5 (Winter 1981): 608–37.

[32] See Weinberg, *Manifest Destiny*, pp. 451–85.

lish the meaning and limits of Constitutional power. To an extraordinary degree, this judicial interpretation has increased the power of the federal government at the expense of the states. Simultaneously, the courts have expanded the rights of citizens, and extended the liberties guaranteed under the First Amendment.[33]

On the other hand, the Constitution itself continues to echo Antifederalist calls for strict limits on all forms of power, including judicial power. Hence, the courts have moved cautiously, reluctantly recognizing the sensibilities of the other coequal branches.[34] The words of Andrew Jackson ("John Marshall has made his decision; now let him enforce it!") are deeply etched in judicial memory. In addition, for every *McCulloch v. Maryland*, extending the power of the federal government, there are scores of lesser cases assuring the rights of the states. In the protection of personal liberties as well, the courts have exercised caution, for as the postwar Warren Court found out, decisions to improve the lot of minorities or assure the rights of prisoners are by no means altogether popular. In any case, the Constitution's legacy has been highly problematic, resulting in continuing judicial conflict, a constant tension between activism and restraint.

This ambivalent legal legacy suggests an even more profound set of political problems. However expedient, the compromises that allowed for the creation of the Constitution have provided few solutions to the problems presented by an enduring republican legacy of sectionalism and states' rights.[35] From the Hartford Convention to the Nullification Crisis to the Civil War itself, liberty and union have been at odds. Jefferson himself would capture the divided loyalties inherent in the federal system by referring throughout his lifetime to both the United States and the state of Virginia as "my country." Furthermore, the Civil War did not put an end to the specter of sectional conflict, for from that time sectionalism has tended to be channeled into partisanship, with post-Reconstruction political parties aligning along regional lines, pitting most often the West and the South (whether Bryan Democracts or Reagan Republicans) against the upper Midwest and the Northeast (Harding and Coolidge; Al Smith and FDR).[36]

Perhaps even more deeply rooted, and ultimately more influential has

33 See Robert G. McCloskey, *The American Supreme Court* (Chicago: University of Chicago Press, 1960), pp. 180–219.

34 See ibid., pp. 220–31.

35 See Richard Franklin Bensel, *Sectionalism and American Political Development, 1880–1980* (Madison, Wis.: University of Wisconsin Press, 1984). For background, see Joseph L. Davis, *Sectionalism in American Politics, 1774–1787* (Madison, Wis.: University of Wisconsin Press, 1977).

36 See James L. Sundquist, *Dynamics of the Party System*, rev. ed. (Washington, D.C.: The Brookings Institution, 1983), pp. 412–49.

been the legacy of localism, the time-honored republican predisposition to look to one's city or neighborhood, to one's family and friends to find political purpose. The recent efflorescence of local politics, the gathering of citizens to protect their neighborhoods, whether from criminals or chemical dump sites, has been symptomatic of this recurring republican strain.[37] Yet at the same time, with increasing economic and technological interdependence, citizens have come to realize that the boundaries between the local community and the larger nation are disappearing. Corner diners give way to fast-food chains, and farmer's gardens sprout satellite dishes. Under the circumstances, local ties seem tenuous at best, and local politics are often defensive and sometimes—in antibusing campaigns or antihomosexual crusades—restrictive and repressive.

Amid these changes, Americans have remained confused about the meaning of their citizenship. In part, their confusion lies with a Constitutional tradition that requires them to be private rather than public citizens. Here they have succeeded only too well, throwing their endless energies into an economic system that has been a miracle of the modern world. At the same time, the Revolutionary tradition has survived in at least a generational pattern of protest, in which citizens have emerged into the public sphere at times of crisis, and then retreated.[38] To some extent, this public role has been highly suspect, requiring William Lloyd Garrison to burn the Constitution itself, or the socialists of the early twentieth century to look to Marxism or Russian anarchism for inspiration and legitimation, or for the student protesters of the 1960s to denounce the "establishment" and distrust everyone over thirty.

Even more problematic, however, has been the pervasiveness of privatism, the tendency for Americans to look to the marketplace and to themselves.[39] Today's "culture of narcissism," with its narrow consumerism, its preoccupation with fashion, and its fascination with the rich and famous is only the most recent manifestation of a political culture that from Benjamin Franklin to Dale Carnegie has been first and foremost interested in the rights to pursue self-improvement and personal success, and only secondarily, and sometimes not at all, in the responsibilities that make those privileges possible.[40]

Ultimately, the most effective elixir to this self-interested society has been

[37] See Wilson Carey McWilliams, "Politics," *American Quarterly*, 35, 1 & 2 (Spring/Summer 1983): 19–38.

[38] See Michael Paul Rogin, *Fathers and Children* (New York: Alfred A. Knopf, 1975), pp. 3–15.

[39] See Christopher Lasch, *The Culture of Narcissism* (New York: W. W. Norton, 1978).

[40] See John G. Cawelti, *Apostles of the Self-Made Man* (Chicago: University of Chicago Press, 1965).

millennialism. With its promise of destruction followed by reconstruction, the millennial theme has provided a periodic purgative to a people not entirely in control of themselves, or of their world. From Timothy Dwight to Julia Ward Howe to Woodrow Wilson, millennialists have looked for the Second Coming, or at least for the end of one era and the beginning of another and better one.[41] Often their prophecies have been tied to the devastation of war ("Mine eyes have seen the glory of the coming of the Lord," wrote Howe in the "Battle Hymn of the Republic.")[42] Just as often, their predictions have been of peace and prosperity, for as Tuveson has shown, millennialism and utopianism have been closely connected, and the thousand years of peace have through time come to be seen as a thousand years of postindustrial prosperity.[43]

Almost always the millennium has been a universal vision, in which Americans have reached out to liberate and save the world. Its outlines can be seen in the Marshall Plan and the Vietnam War, in human rights campaigns and anticommunist crusades. Perhaps more surprising, the same millennial mission, turned inward, is present in the charismatic sectarianism of the followers of the Yogi Bhajan, the Majaraj Ji, or, in a much more deadly fashion, Jim Jones.[44] In a more diffuse but even deeper sense, however, Americans of all faiths and persuasions continue to be touched by millennial theory, by their fears of economic collapse and atomic destruction, and in their hopes for a world without scarcity and without war.

In recent times, Americans have seemed to be more at ease with modernity. Emerging from World War II with Nazism in ruins and the New World relatively unscathed, they embarked on an era of prosperity unparalleled in the history of the world. The result was what has been called the American Era, a seemingly innocent interlude in which, the Cold War notwithstanding, this people of plenty lived lives of excess and generosity, secure in the illusion of limitless progress.[45]

By the mid-1970s, however, the lure of the modern had begun to fade. Trapped in a terrible and senseless war in Asia, buffeted economically as a result of our policies in the Middle East, witnessing the continuing spectacle of political scandals that eventually would reach the presidency itself, citizens began to realize that they had come to the end of an era. For the first time since World War II, America appeared to be weak in the world, what Richard Nixon called a "pitiful helpless giant." Perhaps even more disconcerting was the rediscovery of scarcity, the reluctant recognition,

[41] See Tuveson, *Redeemer Nation*, pp. vii–xi.

[42] See ibid., pp. 187–214.

[43] See ibid., pp. 91–136.

[44] See Bellah, *The Broken Covenant*, p. 154.

[45] See Potter, *People of Plenty*, pp. 78–90.

often in one of the long lines that motorists were forced to form in search of gasoline, that the pie could expand no more. Jeremiads became popular, and for the first time in twenty-five years, as Wilson Carey McWilliams has suggested, people became predisposed to expect things to get even worse.[46]

The response to this transition has been predictable. On the one hand, progressives have tended to retool the engine of progress, looking for solutions in administrative reorganization or state-of-the-art techology. On the other hand, traditionalist conservatives have looked back nostalgically to a time when the churches were filled, when families were strong, and when women kept to the home. Interestingly, with his curious combination of supply-side economics and profamily moralizing, Ronald Reagan, calling forth the ghosts of FDR and Coolidge alike, has been able to draw on both of these strains at once.[47] Yet the response has not been satisfactory, for many continue to consider the American dream to be increasingly illusory. While politicians seek desperately to keep the dream alive, reinspiring the doubters with technological promises and nostalgic memories, the doubts remain.[48]

So as Americans look ahead in search of a political theory for these post-progressive times, they may find themselves looking backward as well. Ironically, by reaching back two hundred years, they might well discover a model for the future. For in the Americans of the Constitutional age, they will find a people who did not rely on progress to save them, but who put their faith in the capacity of citizens to act for themselves. With their example in mind, Americans of today can look ahead less with hope than with confidence. The future is ours, if we act as they did, with audacity and prudence, and in the fullness of time.

[46] See McWilliams, "Politics," esp. p. 29.

[47] See Sheldon Wolin, "Reagan Country," *New York Review of Books*, 27, 20 (18 December 1980): 9–12.

[48] See McWilliams, "Politics," pp. 28–38.

BIBLIOGRAPHY

Note: Complete citations for all orations, pamphlets, and sermons can be found in American Bibliography, *14 vols. Edited by Charles Evans. Chicago: Private printing, 1903–1955.*

Adair, Douglass. *Fame and the Founding Fathers: Essays by Douglass Adair.* Edited by Trevor Colbourn. New York: W. W. Norton, 1974.
———. "The Intellectual Origins of Jeffersonian Democracy: Republicanism, the Class Struggle, and the Virtuous Farmer." Ph.D. diss., Yale University, 1943.
Adams, Abigail, John Adams, and Thomas Jefferson. *The Adams-Jefferson Letters: The Complete Correspondence Between Thomas Jefferson and Abigail and John Adams.* 2 vol. Edited by Lester J. Cappon. Chapel Hill, N.C.: University of North Carolina Press, 1959.
Adams, John. *Letters of John Adams, Addressed to His Wife.* 2 vol. Edited by Charles Francis Adams. Boston: Little, Brown, 1841.
———. *The Works of John Adams.* 10 vol. Edited by Charles Francis Adams. Boston, Mass.: Little, Brown, 1851–1865.
Adams, John, and Benjamin Rush. *The Spur of Fame: Dialogues of John Adams and Benjamin Rush, 1805–1813.* Edited by John A. Schutz and Douglass Adair. San Marino, Calif.: The Huntington Library, 1966.
Adams, John Quincy. *The Diary of John Quincy Adams.* Edited by Robert J. Taylor. Cambridge, Mass.: Harvard University Press, 1981.
Adams, Samuel. *The Writings of Samuel Adams.* 3 vol. Edited by Harry Alonzo Cushing. New York: G. P. Putnam's Sons, 1904–1908.
The American Puritans: Their Prose and Poetry. Edited by Perry Miller. Garden City, N.Y.: Anchor Books, 1956.
The American Museum: or Repository of Ancient and Modern Fugitive Pieces, &c. Prose and Poetical, 2nd ed. Philadelphia: Matthew Carey, 1789.
Ames, Fisher. *Works of Fisher Ames.* 2 vol. Edited by Seth Ames. Boston: Little, Brown and Company, 1854.
Appleby, Joyce. *Capitalism and a New Social Order: The Republican Vision of the 1790s.* New York: New York University Press, 1984.
———. "Republicanism in Old and New Contexts." *The William and Mary Quarterly,* 3rd ser., 43, 1 (January 1986): 20–34.
———. "The Social Origins of American Revolutionary Ideology." *Journal of American History,* 64, 4 (March 1978): 935–58.
———. "What is Still American in the Political Philosophy of Thomas Jefferson?" *The William and Mary Quarterly,* 3rd ser., 39, 2 (April 1982): 287–309.

Arendt, Hannah. *The Human Condition*. Chicago: University of Chicago Press, 1958.

———. *On Revolution*. New York: The Viking Press, 1963. Reprint. 1965.

Bailyn, Bernard. *The Ideological Origins of the American Revolution*. Cambridge, Mass.: Harvard University Press, 1967. Reprint. 1973.

Banner, James M., Jr. *To the Hartford Convention*. New York: Alfred A. Knopf, 1970.

Banning, Lance, "Jeffersonian Ideology Revisited: Liberal and Classical Ideas in the New American Republic." *The William and Mary Quarterly*, 3rd ser., 43, 1 (January 1986): 3–19.

———. *The Jeffersonian Persuasion: Evolution of a Party Ideology*. Ithaca, N.Y.: Cornell University Press, 1978.

———. "Republican Ideology and the Triumph of the Constitution, 1789 to 1798." *The William and Mary Quarterly*, 3rd ser., 31, 2 (April 1974): 167–88.

Barlow, Joel. *The Vision of Columbus; A Poem in Nine Books*, 2nd ed. Hartford, Conn.: Hudson & Goodwin, 1787.

Beard, Charles A. *Economic Origins of Jeffersonian Democracy*. New York: Macmillan, 1915.

Bellah, Robert. *The Broken Covenant: American Civil Religion in Time of Trial*. New York: The Seabury Press, 1975.

Bensel, Richard Franklin. *Sectionalism and American Political Development, 1880–1980*. Madison, Wis.: The University of Wisconsin Press, 1984.

Bercovitch, Sacvan. *The American Jeremiad*. Madison, Wis.: University of Wisconsin Press, 1978.

Berens, John F. *Providence and Patriotism in Early America, 1640–1815*. Charlottesville, Va.: University Press of Virginia, 1978.

Berger, Peter L., and Thomas Luckmann. *The Social Construction of Reality: A Treatise in the Sociology of Knowledge*. Garden City, N.Y.: Doubleday, 1964.

Berkhofer, Robert F., Jr. "Jefferson, the Ordinance of 1784, and the Origins of the American Territorial System." *The William and Mary Quarterly*, 3rd ser., 29, 1 (January 1972): 231–62.

Berthoff, Rowland. "Independence and Attachment, Virtue and Interest: From Republican Citizen to Free Enterpriser, 1789–1837." In *Uprooted Americans: Essays to Honor Oscar Handlin*, edited by Richard L. Bushman, Neil Harris, David Rothman, Barbara Miller Solomon, and Stephen Thernstrom. Boston: Little, Brown and Company, 1979.

Berthoff, Rowland, and John Murrin. "Feudalism, Communalism, and the Yeoman Freeholder: The American Revolution Considered as a Social Accident." In *Essays on the American Revolution*, edited by Stephen G. Kurtz and James H. Hutson. Chapel Hill, N.C.: University of North Carolina Press, 1973.

Bissell, Benjamin. *The American Indian in English Literature of the Eighteenth Century*. New Haven, Conn.: Yale University Press, 1925.

Boorstin, Daniel J. *The Genius of American Politics*. Chicago: University of Chicago Press, 1953.

Bourne, E. G. "The Use of History Made by the Framers of the Constitution." *Annual Report of the American Historical Association*, 1896, vol. 1, 223–30.

Brown, Ira V. "Watchers for the Second Coming: The Millenarian Tradition in America." *The Mississippi Valley Historical Review*, 39, 3 (December 1952): 441–58.

Buel, Richard, Jr. *Securing the Revolution: Ideology in American Politics, 1789–1815*. Ithaca, N.Y.: Cornell University Press, 1972.

Bury, J. B. *The Idea of Progress: An Inquiry into its Origins and Growth*. 1932. Reprint. New York: Dover Publishers, 1955.

Cawelti, John G. *Apostles of the Self-Made Man: Changing Concepts of Success in America*. Chicago: University of Chicago Press, 1965.

Chambers, William N. *The First Party System: Federalists and Republicans*. New York: Wiley, 1972.

———. *Political Parties in a New Nation*. New York: Oxford University Press, 1980.

Cohen, Lester H. *The Revolutionary Histories: Contemporary Narratives of the American Revolution*. Ithaca, N.Y.: Cornell University Press, 1980.

Cohn, Norman. *The Pursuit of the Millennium: Revolutionary Millenarians and Mystical Anarchists of the Middle Ages*. Rev. ed. 1970. Reprint. New York: Oxford University Press, 1976.

Colbourn, H. Trevor. *The Lamp of Experience: Whig History and the Intellectual Origins of the American Revolution*. Chapel Hill, N.C.: University of North Carolina Press, 1965.

———. "Thomas Jefferson's Use of the Past." *The William and Mary Quarterly*, 3rd ser., 15, 1 (January 1958): 56–70.

Collingwood, R. G. *The Idea of History*. London: Clarendon Press, 1946.

The Complete Anti-Federalist. Edited by Herbert J. Storing. Chicago: University of Chicago Press, 1981.

Coxe, Tench. *A View of the United States of America, In a Series of Papers, Written at Various Times Between the Years 1787 and 1794*. Philadelphia: William Hall, 1794.

Craven, Wesley Frank. *The Legend of the Founding Fathers*. Ithaca, N.Y.: Cornell University Press, 1956.

[Crèvecoeur], J. Hector St. John. *Letters From An American Farmer. . . .* London: Thomas Davies and Lockyer Davis, 1782.

Cunningham, Noble E. *The Jeffersonian Republicans: The Formation of Party Organization, 1789–1801*. Chapel Hill, N.C.: University of North Carolina Press, 1957.

———. *The Jeffersonian Republicans in Power: Party Operations, 1801–1809*. Chapel Hill, N.C.: University of North Carolina Press, 1963.

Dahl, Robert A. *A Preface to Democratic Theory*. Chicago: University of Chicago Press, 1956.

Dauer, Manning J. *The Adams Federalists*. Baltimore: Johns Hopkins Press, 1953.

Davidson, James West. *The Logic of Millennial Thought: Eighteenth Century New England*. New Haven, Conn.: Yale University Press, 1977.

Davidson, James West. "Searching for the Millennium: Problems for the 1790's and the 1970's." *The New England Quarterly*, 45, 2 (June 1972): 241–61.

Davis, Joseph L. *Sectionalism in American Politics, 1774–1787*. Madison, Wis.: The University of Wisconsin Press, 1977.

DeConde, Alexander. *Entangling Alliance: Politics and Diplomacy under George Washington*. Durham, N.C.: Duke University Press, 1958.

————. *The Quasi-War: The Politics and Diplomacy of the Undeclared War with France, 1797–1801*. New York: Charles Scribner's Sons, 1966.

Delmage, Rutherford E. "The American Idea of Progress, 1750–1800." *Proceedings of the American Philosophical Society*, 91, 4 (October 1947): 307–14.

Diamond, Martin. "The American Idea of Equality." *The Review of Politics*, 38, 3 (July 1971): 313–31.

————. "The Declaration and the Constitution." *The Public Interest*, 41, 3 (Fall 1975): 39–55.

————. "Democracy and *The Federalist*: A Reconstruction of the Framers' Intent." *American Political Science Review*, 53, 1 (March 1959): 53–68.

————. "The Separation of Powers and the Mixed Regime." *Publius*, 8, 3 (Summer 1978): 33–43.

————. "What the Framers Meant by Federalism." In *A Nation of States*, edited by Robert A. Goldwin. Chicago: Rand McNally, 1961.

Dickinson, John. *The Political Writings of John Dickinson, Esquire. . . .* 2 vol. Wilmington, Del.: Bosnal and Niles, 1801.

Diggins, John P. *The Lost Soul of American Politics*. New York: Basic Books, 1984.

East, Robert A. "The Massachusetts Conservatives in the Critical Period." In *The Era of the American Revolution*, edited by Richard B. Morris. New York: Columbia University Press, 1939.

Eisenstein, Elizabeth L. "Clio and Chronos: Some Aspects of History-Book Time." In *History and the Concept of Time*. Middletown, Conn.: Wesleyan University Press, 1966.

Ekirch, Arthur K., Jr. *The Idea of Progress in America, 1815–1860*. New York: Peter Smith, 1951.

Elkins, Stanley, and Eric McKitrick. "The Founding Fathers: Young Men of the Revolution." *Political Science Quarterly*, 76, 2 (June 1961): 181–216.

Elliott, Jonathon, ed. *The Debates in the Several State Conventions on the Adoption of the Federal Constitution. . . .* 5 vol. 2nd ed. Philadelphia: J. B. Lippincott, 1861–63.

Fairchild, Hoxie Neale, *The Noble Savage: A Study in Romantic Naturalism*. New York: Columbia University Press, 1928.

Farrand, Max. *The Fathers of the Constitution*. New Haven, Conn.: Yale University Press, 1921.

————. *The Framing of the Constitution of the United States*. New Haven, Conn.: Yale University Press, 1913.

Farrand, Max, ed. *The Records of the Federal Convention of 1787*. 3 vol. New Haven, Conn.: Yale University Press, 1911.

Ferguson, E. James. "The Nationalists of 1781–1783 and the Economic Interpretation of the Constitution." *Journal of American History*, 56, 2 (September 1969): 241–61.

———. "Political Economy, Public Liberty, and the Formation of the Constitution." *The William and Mary Quarterly*, 3rd ser., 40, 3 (July 1983), 389–412.

———. *The Power of the Purse: A History of American Public Finance, 1776–1790*. Chapel Hill, N.C.: University of North Carolina Press, 1961.

Fink, Zera S. *The Classical Republicans: An Essay in the Recovery of a Pattern of Thought in Seventeenth-Century England*. 2nd ed. Evanston, Ill.: Northwestern University Press, 1962.

Finley, M. I. "Myth, Memory, and History." *History and Theory*, 4 (1964): 281–302.

Fischer, David Hackett. *The Revolution of American Conservatism: The Federalist Party in the Era of Jeffersonian Democracy*. New York: Harper & Row, 1965.

Fiske, John. *The Critical Period of American History, 1783–1789*. Boston: Houghton, Mifflin, 1888.

Ford, Henry Jones. *The Rise and Growth of American Politics*. New York: Macmillan, 1898.

Ford, Paul Leicester, ed. *Essays on the Constitution of the United States*. New York: Burt Franklin, 1892.

———. *Pamphlets on the Constitution of the United States*. Brooklyn, N.Y.: n.p., 1888.

Foucault, Michel. *The Archaeology of Knowledge*. New York: Pantheon Books, 1972.

Franklin, Benjamin. *A Dissertation on Liberty and Necessity, Pleasure and Pain*. London: n.p., 1725.

———. *The Papers of Benjamin Franklin*. Edited by Leonard W. Larabee. New Haven, Conn.: Yale University Press, 1959–.

———. *The Writings of Benjamin Franklin*. 10 vol. Edited by Albert Henry Smyth. New York: Macmillan, 1905–1907.

Gallie, W. B. "Essentially Contested Concepts." *Proceedings of the Aristotelian Society*, 56 (1955–56): 167–98.

Geertz, Clifford. "Ideology as a Cultural System." In *Ideology and Discontent*, edited by David Apter. New York: Free Press of Glencoe, 1964.

Goldwin Robert A., and William A. Schambra, eds. *How Democratic Is The Constitution?* Washington, D.C.: American Enterprise Institute, 1980.

Goodman, Paul. *The Democratic-Republicans of Massachusetts: Politics in a Young Republic*. Cambridge, Mass.: Harvard University Press, 1964.

Gray, John. "On the Contestability of Social and Political Concepts." *Political Theory*, 5, 3 (August 1977): 331–48.

Gruman, Gerald J. " 'Balance' and 'Excess' as Gibbon's Explanation for the Decline and Fall." *History and Theory*, 1 (1961): 75–86.

Gummere, Richard M. *The American Colonial Mind and the Classical Tradition: Essays in Comparative Culture*. Cambridge, Mass.: Harvard University Press, 1963.

Gummere, Richard M. "The Heritage of the Classics in Colonial North America: An Essay on the Greco-Roman Tradition." *Proceedings of the American Philosophical Society*, 99, 2 (April 1955): 68–78.

Gwyn, W. B. *The Meaning of Separation of Powers*. New Orleans: Tulane University, 1965.

Haller, William. *The Elect Nation: The Meaning and Relevance of Foxe's Book of Martyrs*. New York: Harper & Row, 1963.

Hamilton, Alexander. *The Papers of Alexander Hamilton*. Edited by Harold C. Syrett. New York: Columbia University Press, 1961–.

———. *The Works of Alexander Hamilton*. 2nd ed. 12 vol. Edited by Henry Cabot Lodge. New York: G. P. Putnam's Sons, 1903–1904.

Hampsher-Monk, Iain. "Political Languages in Time: The Work of J.G.A. Pocock." *British Journal of Political Science*, 14, 1 (January 1984): 89–116.

Hanson, Russell. *The Democratic Imagination in America: Conversations with Our Past*. Princeton, N.J.: Princeton University Press, 1985.

Haraszti, Zoltan. *John Adams and the Prophets of Progress*. Cambridge, Mass.: Harvard University Press, 1952.

Harris, Victor. *All Coherence Gone*. Chicago: University of Chicago Press, 1949.

Hartz, Louis. "American Political Thought and the American Revolution." *American Political Science Review*, 46, 2 (June 1952): 321–42.

———. *The Liberal Tradition in America*. New York: Harcourt, Brace, & World, 1955.

Hatch, Nathan O. "The Origins of Civil Millennialism in America: New England's Clergymen, War with France, and the Revolution." *The William and Mary Quarterly*, 3rd ser., 31, 3 (July 1974): 407–30.

———. *The Sacred Cause of Liberty: Republican Thought and the Millennium in Revolutionary New England*. New Haven, Conn.: Yale University Press, 1977.

Heimert, Alan. *Religion and the American Mind*. Cambridge, Mass.: Harvard University Press, 1966.

Higginson, Stephen. "Letters of Stephen Higginson, 1783–1804." Edited by J. Franklin Jameson, Talcott Williams, Frederick Jackson Turner, and William P. Nent. *Annual Report of the American Historical Association*, 1896, vol. 1, 704–841.

Hildreth, Richard. *The History of the United States of America*. 6 vol. New York: Harper & Brothers, 1856.

Hill, Christopher. *Antichrist in Seventeenth-Century England*. London: Oxford University Press, 1971.

Hindle, Brooke. *The Pursuit of Science in the Revolutionary America, 1735–1789*. Chapel Hill, N.C.: University of North Carolina Press, 1956.

Hitchcock, Enos. *The Farmer's Friend, or the History of Mr. Charles Worthy. . . .* Boston: I. Thomas and E. T. Andrews, 1793.

Hoffer, Peter C. "The Constitutional Crisis and the Rise of a Nationalistic View of History in America, 1786–1788." *New York History*, 52, 3 (July 1971): 305–23.

Hofstadter, Richard. *The American Political Tradition and the Men Who Made It*. New York: Vintage Books, 1948.

————. *The Idea of a Party System: The Rise of Legitimate Opposition in the United States, 1780–1841.* Berkeley, Calif.: University of California Press, 1969.

Home, Henry, Lord Kames. *Sketches of the History of Man.* 2nd. ed. Edinburgh: W. Creech, 1788/London: W. Strahan and T. Cadell, 1788.

Howe, John R., Jr. *The Changing Political Thought of John Adams.* Princeton, N.J.: Princeton University Press, 1966.

————. "Republican Thought and the Political Violence of the 1790s." *American Quarterly*, 19, 2 (Summer 1967): 147–65.

Huizinga, J. *The Waning of the Middle Ages.* 1924. Reprint. Garden City, N.Y.: Doubleday, 1954.

Hume, David. *Essays: Moral, Political, and Literary.* Edited by T. H. Green and T. H. Grose. New York: Longmans, Green, 1898.

Humphreys, David. *The Miscellaneous Works of David Humphreys.* New York: T. & J. Swords, 1804.

Humphreys, David, Joel Barlow, John Trumbull, and Dr. Lemuel Hopkins. *The Anarchiad: A New England Poem.* Edited by Luther G. Riggs. New Haven, Conn.: Thomas H. Pease, 1861.

Hutson, James H. "Country, Court, and Constitution: Antifederalism and the Historians." *The William and Mary Quarterly*, 3rd ser., 38, 2 (July 1981): 337–68.

Jay, John. *The Correspondence and Public Papers of John Jay.* 4 vol. Edited by Henry P. Johnston. New York: G. P. Putnam's Sons, 1890–93.

Jefferson, Thomas. *The Papers of Thomas Jefferson.* Edited by Julian P. Boyd. Princeton, N.J.: Princeton University Press, 1950–.

————. *The Writings of Thomas Jefferson.* 10 vol. Edited by Paul Leicester Ford. New York: The Knickerbocker Press, 1892–99.

Jensen, Merrill. "The Idea of a National Government During the American Revolution." *Political Science Quarterly*, 53, 3 (September 1943): 356–79.

————. *The New Nation: A History of the United States During the Confederation, 1781–1789.* New York: Vintage Books, 1950.

Jones, Richard Foster. *Ancients and Moderns: A Study of the Rise of the Scientific Movement in Seventeenth-Century England.* St. Louis, Mo.: Washington University Studies, 1936.

Kammen, Michael. *A Season of Youth: The American Revolution and the Historical Imagination.* New York: Oxford University Press, 1978.

Kasson, John F. *Civilizing the Machine: Technology and Republican Values in America, 1776–1900.* Harmondsworth: Penguin Books, 1977.

Kenyon, Cecelia M. "Men of Little Faith: The Anti-federalists on the Nature of Representative Government." *The William and Mary Quarterly*, 3rd ser., 12, 1 (January 1955): 3–43.

Kerber, Linda K. *Federalists in Dissent: Imagery and Ideology in Jeffersonian America.* Ithaca, N.Y.: Cornell University Press, 1970.

Kinloch, Francis, "Letters of Francis Kinloch to Thomas Boone, 1782–1788," edited by Felix Gilbert. *The Journal of Southern History*, 8, 1 (February 1942): 87–105.

Krammick, Isaac. *Bolingbroke and His Circle: The Politics of Nostalgia in the Age of Walpole*. Cambridge, Mass: Harvard University Press, 1968.

———. "Republican Revisionism Revisited." *American Historical Review*, 87, 3 (June 1982): 629–64.

Kuhn, Thomas. *The Structure of Scientific Revolutions*. 2nd ed. Chicago: University of Chicago Press, 1970.

Lamont, William M. *Richard Baxter and the Millennium*. London: Croom Helm, 1979.

Lasch, Christopher. *The Culture of Narcissism: American Life in an Age of Diminishing Expectations*. New York: W. W. Norton, 1978.

Lee, Richard Henry, *The Letters of Richard Henry Lee*. 2 vol. Edited by James Curtis Ballagh. New York: The Macmillan Company, 1911–14.

Lerner, Ralph. "Commerce and Character: The Anglo-American as a New-Model Man." *The William and Mary Quarterly*, 3rd ser., 36, 1 (January 1979): 3–26.

Lewis, John D., ed. *Anti-Federalist versus Federalist*. San Francisco, Calif.: Chandler Publishing Company, 1967.

Lewis, R.W.B. *The American Adam: Innocence, Tragedy, and Tradition in the Nineteenth Century*. Chicago: University of Chicago Press, 1955.

Lincoln, Abraham, *The Collected Works of Abraham Lincoln*. Edited by Roy P. Basler. New Brunswick, N.J.: Rutgers University Press, 1953–.

Lipset, Seymour Martin. *The First New Nation*. New York: Basic Books, 1963.

Lovejoy, Arthur O., and George Boas. *Primitivism and Related Ideas in Antiquity*. Baltimore: Johns Hopkins Press, 1935.

Lutz, Donald S. "Bernard Bailyn, Gordon S. Wood, and Whig Political Theory." *The Political Science Reviewer*, 7 (Fall 1977): 111–44.

———. *Popular Consent and Popular Control: Whig Theory in the Early State Constitutions*. Baton Rouge, La.: Louisiana State University Press, 1980.

———. "The Relative Influence of European Writers on Late Eighteenth-Century American Political Thought." *American Political Science Review*, 78, 1 (March 1984): 189–97.

McCloskey, Robert G. *The American Supreme Court*. Chicago: University of Chicago Press, 1960.

McCoy, Drew R. "Benjamin Franklin's Vision of a Republican Political Economy for America." *The William and Mary Quarterly*, 3rd ser., 35, 4 (October 1978): 605–28.

———. *The Elusive Republic: Political Economy in Jeffersonian America*. Chapel Hill, N.C.: University of North Carolina Press, 1980.

McDonald, Forrest. *E Pluribus Unum: The Formation of the American Republic, 1776–1790*. Indianapolis, Ind.: Liberty Press, 1965.

———. *Novus Ordo Seclorum: The Intellectual Origins of the Constitution*. Lawrence, Kan.: University of Kansas Press, 1985.

Maclear, J. F. "New England and the Fifth Monarchy: The Quest for the Millennium in Early American Puritanism." *The William and Mary Quarterly*, 3rd ser., 32, 2 (April 1975): 223–60.

————. "The Republic and the Millennium." In *The Religion of the Republic*, edited by Elwyn A. Smith. Philadelphia: Fortress Press, 1971.

McLoughlin, William G. "The Role of Religion in the Revolution." In *Essays on the American Revolution*, edited by Stephen G. Kurtz and James H. Hutson. Chapel Hill, N.C.: University of North Carolina Press, 1973.

McWilliams, Wilson Carey. "Politics." *American Quarterly*, 35, 1 & 2 (Spring/Summer 1983): 19–38.

Madison, James. *The Papers of James Madison*. Edited by Robert A. Rutland. Chicago: University of Chicago Press, 1962–.

Madison, James, Alexander Hamilton, and John Jay. *The Federalist Papers*. Edited by Clinton Rossiter. New York: Mentor Books, 1961.

Maier, Pauline. *The Old Revolutionaries: Political Lives in the Age of John Adams*. New York: Alfred A. Knopf, 1980.

————. "Popular Uprisings and Civil Authority in Eighteenth-Century America." *The William and Mary Quarterly*, 3rd ser., 26, 1 (January 1970): 3–35.

Main, Jackson Turner. *The Antifederalists: Critics of the Constitution, 1781–1788*. Chapel Hill, N.C.: University of North Carolina Press, 1961.

————. Review of *The Creation of the American Republic, 1776–1787*, by Gordon S. Wood, *The William and Mary Quarterly*, 3rd ser., 26, 4 (October 1969): 604–607.

Manuel, Frank E. *The Eighteenth Century Confronts the Gods*. Cambridge, Mass.: Harvard University Press, 1959.

————. *Isaac Newton: Historian*. Cambridge, Mass.: Belknap Press of Harvard University Press, 1963.

Marx, Leo. *The Machine in the Graden: Technology and the Pastoral Ideal in America*. New York: Oxford University Press, 1964.

May, Henry F. *The Englightenment in America*. New York: Oxford University Press, 1976.

Meek, Ronald L. *Social Science and the Ignoble Savage*. Cambridge: Cambridge University Press, 1976.

Middlekauff, Robert. *The Mathers: Three Generations of Puritan Intellectuals, 1596–1728*. New York: Oxford University Press, 1971.

Miller, John C. *The Federalist Era, 1789–1801*. New York: Harper & Row, 1960.

Miller, Perry. *Errand Into the Wilderness*. Cambridge, Mass.: Belknap Press, 1956. Reprint. New York: Harper & Row, 1964.

————. *The New England Mind: From Colony to Province*. Boston: Beacon Press, 1953.

————. *The New England Mind: The Seventeenth Century*. New York: Macmillan, 1939.

Minot, George Richards. *The History of the Insurrections, in Massachusetts. . . .* Worcester, Mass.: Isaiah Thomas, 1788.

Momigliano, Arnaldo. "Time in Ancient Historiography." In *History and the Concept of Time*. Middletown, Conn.: Wesleyan University Press, 1966.

Montesquieu. *The Spirit of the Laws*. Edited by David Wallace Carrithers. Berkeley, Calif.: University of California Press, 1977.

Moorhead, James H. *American Apocalypse: Yankee Protestantism and the Civil War*, *1860–1869*. New Haven, Conn.: Yale University Press, 1978.

Morgan, Edmund S. "The Puritan Ethic and the American Revolution." *The William and Mary Quarterly*, 3rd ser., 24, 1 (January 1967): 3–43.

Morris, Richard B. "The Confederation Period and the American Historian." *The William and Mary Quarterly*, 3rd ser., 13, 2 (April 1956): 139–56.

Mullett, Charles F. "Classical Influences on the American Revolution." *The Classical Journal*, 35, 2 (November 1939): 92–108.

Murrin, John. "The Great Inversion, or Court versus Country: A Comparison of the Revolution Settlements in England (1688–1721) and America (1776–1816)." In *Three British Revolutions*. Edited by J.G.A. Pocock. Princeton, N.J.: Princeton University Press, 1980.

Myers, Marvin. *The Jacksonian Persuasion: Politics and Belief*. Stanford, Calif.: Stanford University Press, 1957.

Onuf, Peter S. *The Origins of the Federal Republic: Jurisdictional Controversies in the United States*, *1775–1787*. Philadelphia: University of Pennsylvania Press, 1983.

Pearce, Roy Harvey. *Savagism and Civilization: A Study of the Indian and the American Mind*. Baltimore: Johns Hopkins Press, 1953.

Persons, Stow. "The Cyclical Theory of History in Eighteenth Century America." *American Quarterly*, 6, 2 (Summer 1954): 147–63.

Peterson, Merrill D. *The Jefferson Image in the American Mind*. New York: Oxford University Press, 1960.

Pocock, J.G.A. "Cambridge Paradigms and Scotch Philosophers: A Study of the Relations Between the Civic Humanist and the Civil Jurisprudential Interpretation of Eighteenth-Century Social Thought." In *Wealth and Virtue: The Shaping of Political Economy in the Scottish Enlightenment*, edited by Istvan Hont and Michael Ignatieff. Cambridge: Cambridge University Press, 1983.

———. "The History of Political Thought: A Methodological Enquiry." In *Philosophy, Politics and Society*. 2nd ser. Edited by Peter Laslett and W. C. Runciman. Oxford: Basil Blackwell, 1962.

———. *The Machiavellian Moment: Florentine Political Thought and the Atlantic Tradition*. Princeton, N.J.: Princeton University Press, 1975.

———. "Political Ideas as Historical Events: Political Philosophers as Historical Actors." In *Political Theory and Political Education*, edited by Melvin Richter. Princeton, N.J.: Princeton University Press, 1980.

———. *Politics, Language, and Time: Essays on Political Thought and History*. New York: Atheneum, 1971.

———. "Reconstructing the Traditions: Quentin Skinner's Historian's History of Political Thought." *Canadian Journal of Political and Social Theory*, 3, 3 (Fall 1979): 95–112.

———. "Verbalizing as a Political Act: Towards a Politics of Speech." *Political Theory*, 1, 1 (February 1973): 27–45.

———. "Virtue and Commerce in the Eighteenth Century." *Journal of Interdisciplinary History*, 3, 2 (Summer 1972): 119–34.

Pole, J. R. *Political Representation in England and the Origins of the American Republic.* London: Macmillan, 1966.

Potter, David M. *People of Plenty: Economic Abundance and the American Character.* Chicago: University of Chicago Press, 1954.

Principles and Acts of the Revolution in America. Edited by Hezekiah Niles. New York: A. S. Barnes, 1876.

Ramsay, David. *The History of the American Revolution.* 2 vol. London: John Stockdale, 1793.

Riemer, Neal. "The Republicanism of James Madison." *Political Science Quarterly,* 69, 1 (March 1954): 45–64.

Risjord, Norman K. *The Old Republicans: Southern Conservatism in the Age of Jefferson.* New York: Columbia University Press, 1965.

Robbins, Caroline A. *The Eighteenth-Century Commonwealthman: Studies in the Transmission, Development and Circumstance of English Liberal Thought from the Restoration of Charles II until the War with the Thirteen Colonies.* Cambridge, Mass.: Harvard University Press, 1959.

Robertson, William, D.D, *The History of America.* London: W. Strahan, T. Cadell, and J. Balfour, 1777.

Roche, John. "The Founding Fathers: A Reform Caucus in Action." *American Political Science Review,* 55, 4 (December 1961): 799–816.

Rogin, Michael Paul. *Fathers and Children: Andrew Jackson and the Subjugation of the American Indian.* New York: Alfred A. Knopf, 1975.

Rossiter, Clinton. *1787: The Grand Convention.* New York: Macmillan, 1966.

———. *Seedtime of the Republic: The Origins of the American Tradition of Political Liberty.* New York: Harcourt, Brace, 1953.

Rudolph, Lloyd I. "The Eighteenth-Century Mob in America and Europe." *American Quarterly,* 11, 4 (Winter 1959): 447–69.

Rush, Benjamin. *Essays, Literary, Moral and Philosophical.* Philadelphia: Thomas and Samuel F. Bradford, 1798.

———. *Letters of Benjamin Rush.* 2 vol. Edited by L. H. Butterfield. Princeton, N.J.: Princeton University Press, 1951.

———. *The Selected Writings of Benjamin Rush.* Edited by Dagobert D. Runes. New York: Philosophical Library, 1947.

Rutland, Robert Allen. *The Ordeal of the Constitution.* Norman, Okla.: University of Oklahoma Press, 1966.

Sampson, R. V. *Progress in the Age of Reason.* Cambridge, Mass.: Harvard University Press, 1956.

Sanford, Charles L. *The Quest for Paradise: Europe and the American Moral Imagination.* Urbana, Ill.: University of Illinois Press, 1961.

Schechter, Frank I. "The Early History of the Tradition of the Constitution." *American Political Science Review,* 9, 4 (November, 1915): 707–34.

Schmitt, Gary J., and Robert H. Webking. "Revolutionaries, Antifederalists, and Federalists: Comments on Gordon Wood's Understanding of the American Founding." *The Political Science Reviewer,* 9 (Fall 1979): 195–229.

Schwartz, Hillel. "The End of the Beginning: Millenarian Studies, 1969–1975." *Religious Studies Review*, 2, 2 (July 1976): 1–15.

Shaffer, Arthur H. *The Politics of History: Writing the History of the American Revolution, 1783–1815*. Chicago: Precedent Publishing, 1975.

Shalhope, Robert E. "Republicanism and Early American Historiography." *The William and Mary Quarterly*, 3rd ser., 39, 2 (April 1982): 334–56.

———. "Toward a Republican Synthesis: The Emergence of an Understanding of Republicanism in American Historiography." *The William and Mary Quarterly*, 3rd ser., 29, 1 (January 1972): 49–80.

Slotkin, Richard. "Nostalgia and Progress: Theodore Roosevelt's Myth of the Frontier." *American Quarterly*, 33, 5 (Winter 1981): 608–37.

Smelser, Marshall. "The Federalist Period as an Age of Passion." *American Quarterly*, 10, 4 (Winter 1958): 391–419.

———. "The Jacobin Phrenzy: Federalism and the Menace of Liberty, Equality, and Fraternity." *The Review of Politics*, 13, 4 (October 1951): 457–82.

———. "The Jacobin Phrenzy: The Menace of Monarchy, Plutocracy, and Anglophilia, 1789–1798." *The Review of Politics*, 21, 1 (January 1959): 239–58.

Smith, Adam. *An Inquiry Into the Nature and Causes of the Wealth of Nations* [1776]. Edited by Edwin Cannan. New York: Modern Library, 1937.

Smith, David E. "Millenarian Scholarship in America." *American Quarterly*, 17, 3 (Fall 1965): 534–49.

Smith, Henry Nash. *Virgin Land: The American West as Symbol and Myth*. New York: Vintage Books, 1957. Reprint. 1970.

Smith, Timothy L. "Righteousness and Hope: Christian Holiness and the Millennial Vision in America, 1800–1900." *American Quarterly*, 31, 1 (Spring 1979): 21–45.

Smith, William Raymond. *History as Argument: Three Patriot Historians of the American Revolution*. The Hague: Mouton, 1966.

Starn, Randolph. "Meaning-Levels in the Theme of Historical Decline." *History and Theory*, 14 (1975): 1–31.

Stourzh, Gerald. *Alexander Hamilton and the Idea of Republican Government*. Stanford, Calif.: Stanford University Press, 1970.

Stromberg, R. N. "History in the Eighteenth Century." *Journal of the History of Ideas*, 12, 2 (April 1951): 295–304.

Sundquist, James L. *Dynamics of the Party System: Alignment and Realignment of Political Parties in the United States*. Rev. ed. Washington, D.C.: The Brookings Institution, 1983.

Toon, Peter. "The Latter-Day Glory." In *Puritans, the Millennium, and the Future of Israel: Puritan Eschatology 1600–1660*, edited by Peter Toon. Cambridge: James Clark, 1970.

Toulmin, Stephen, and June Goodfield. *The Discovery of Time*. London: Hutchinson of London, 1965.

Tuveson, Ernest Lee. *Millennium and Utopia: A Study in the Background of the Idea of Progress*. 1949. Reprint. Berkeley, Calif.: University of California Press, 1964.

————. *Redeemer Nation: The Idea of America's Millennial Role*. Chicago: University of Chicago Press, 1968.

Walzer, Michael. *Exodus and Revolution*. New York: Basic Books, 1985.

Warren, James, Mercy Otis Warren, and Elbridge Gerry. *A Study in Dissent: The Warren–Gerry Corrspondence, 1776–1792*. Edited by C. Harvey Gardiner. Carbondale, Ill.: Southern Illinois University Press, 1968.

Warville, J. P. de. *New Travels in the United Staes of America. Performed in 1788*. New York: T. & J. Swords, 1792.

Washington, George. *The Writings of George Washington*. 14 vol. Edited by Worthington Chauncey Ford. New York: G. P. Putnam's Sons, 1889–93.

Weinberg, Albert. *Manifest Destiny: A Study of Nationalist Expansionism in American History*. Baltimore: Johns Hopkins Press, 1935.

Welter, Rush. "The Idea of Progress in America: An Essay on Ideas and Method." *Journal of the History of Ideas*, 16, 3 (June 1955): 401–15.

Whitney, Lois. *Primitivism and the Idea of Progress in English Popular Literature of the Eighteenth Century*. Baltimore: Johns Hopkins Press, 1934.

Wiebe, Robert H. *The Search for Order, 1877–1920*. New York: Hill and Wang, 1967.

Wilson, James. *The Works of James Wilson*. Edited by Robert Green McCloskey. Cambridge, Mass.: Harvard University Press, 1967.

Wilson, Major L. "The Concept of Time and the Political Dialogue in the United States, 1828–48." *American Quarterly*, 19, 4 (Winter 1967): 619–44.

————. *Space, Time, and Freedom: The Quest for Nationalism and the Irrepressible Conflict, 1815–1861*. Westport, Conn.: Greenwood Press, 1974.

Winch, Donald. *Adam Smith's Politics: An Essay in Historiographic Revision*. Cambridge: Cambridge University Press, 1978.

Wolin, Sheldon. "Reagan's Country." *The New York Review of Books*, 27, 20 (18 December 1981): 9–12.

Wood, Gordon S. "Conspiracy and the Paranoid Style: Causality and Deceit in the Eighteenth Century." *The William and Mary Quarterly*, 3rd ser., 39, 3 (July 1982): 401–41.

————. *The Creation of the American Republic, 1776–1787*. Chapel Hill, N.C.: University of North Carolina Press, 1969.

————. "A Note on Mobs in the American Revolution." *The William and Mary Quarterly*, 3rd ser., 23, 4 (October 1966): 635–42.

Yarbrough, Jean. "Federalism in the Foundation and Preservation of the Republic." *Publius*, 6, 3 (Summer 1976): 43–60.

————. "Republicanism Reconsidered: Some Thoughts on the Foundation and Preservation of the American Republic." *The Review of Politics*, 41, 1 (January 1979): 61–95.

Young, Alfred F. *The Democratic Republicans of New York: The Origins, 1763–1797*. Chapel Hill: University of North Carolina Press, 1967.

Young, James Sterling. *The Washington Community, 1800–1828*. New York: Columbia University Press, 1966.

INDEX

Adair, Douglass, 68, 79, 120, 150
Adams, John, 23, 195; on class conflict, 77;
  on concept of constitutional balance, 70–
  71, 73; on education, 173; on endurance of
  Constitution, 161–63; on mixed government, 134; on psychology of control, 177–
  78, 180–81; on the use of history, 124
Adams, John Quincy, 179, 180–81, 182,
  203
Adams, Samuel, 65, 74; on citizenship, 171;
  on corruption, 50; as proponent of classical
  republicanism, 13; as traditionalist, 52
agrarianism: and Antifederalists, 113; and
  expansionism, 104–6; as initial developmental stage, 83–89; and republicanism,
  87–88
agricultural market: and commerce and industry, 97–98; and expansionism, 106–9;
  as intermediate developmental stage, 89–
  96; and republicanism, 93
agriculture, and manufacturing, 92, 94–95,
  102
Agrippa (pseudonym). *See* Winthrop, James
An American (pseudonym). *See* Barton,
  William
Americans: as chosen people, 19, 24, 26, 49,
  207–8; as model for rest of world, 23, 35–
  36, 207–8
Ames, Fisher, 168
Amicus Republicae (possible pseudonym for
  Benjamin Thurston), 72, 73
Antifederalists, 12–13; and agrarianism,
  113; and expansionism, 114–15; and role
  in founding, 139, 141–45, 146–50, 151–
  56; and use of history, 121–23; and use of
  philosophical precepts, 126–27; and use of
  political theory, 131–32, 137
Appleby, Joyce, 6, 7, 38, 83, 104
Aristotle, 5, 7, 45, 87, 105, 123, 131; on
  constitutions, 68, 70, 71–72

Arnold, Benedict, 31
Articles of Confederation, 142, 146
Austin, Benjamin. *See* Candidus
Austin, David, 190–91, 198–99, 202
Austin, Samuel, 201

Bacchus, 21
Backus, Charles, 181–82
Bacon, Sir Francis, 45, 123
Bailyn, Bernard, 4–6, 40, 65, 73, 153, 205
Baldwin, Thomas, 194
Bangs, Edward, 202
Banning, Lance, 6, 12, 39, 40, 159
Barlow, Joel, 109–10, 135, 166, 167, 175
Barnard, Thomas, 195
Barrell, Nathaniel, 144
Barton, William, 83, 97–98, 101–2
Beard, Charles, 205
Belknap, Reverend Jeremy, 47, 56, 74–75,
  95, 202
Bellah, Robert, 207
Bercovitch, Sacvan, 27, 30, 49, 185
Berens, John, 18
Berger, Peter, 14
Berkhofer, Robert, 105
Berthoff, Richard, 6, 205–6, 209
Biblical interpretation: combination with
  secular events, 21; by evangelicals, 18–19,
  31, 41–42; and millennialism, 185–86
Bingham, William, 51
Bloodworth, Timothy, 149
Bolingbroke, Lord, 65
Bonaparte, Napoleon, 199
Boorstin, Daniel, 119, 139, 150
Bridge, Josiah, 161
Britain, 111
Brockaway, Reverend Thomas, 22, 23, 28
Brown, William, 200
Buckminster, Reverend Joseph, 24–25, 29,
  30, 35, 65, 66, 81

229